Dress Cultures in Zambia

Drawing on half a century of research in Zambia and regional scholarship, Karen Tranberg Hansen offers a vibrant history of changing dress practices from the late colonial period to the present day. Exploring how the dressed body serves as the point of contact between personal, local, and global experiences, she argues that dress is just as central to political power as it is to personal style. Questioning the idea that the West led fashion trends elsewhere, Hansen demonstrates how local dress conventions appropriated Western dress influences as Zambian and shows how Zambia contributed to global fashions, such as the colourful *chitenge* fabric that spread across colonial trading networks. Brought to life with colour illustrations and personal anecdotes, this book spotlights dress not only as an important medium through which Zambian identities are negotiated but also as a key reflector and driver of history.

Karen Tranberg Hansen is Professor Emerita at Northwestern University. Her research focuses on the informal economy, clothing, and consumption. Her previous publications include *Distant Companions: Servants and Employers in Zambia, 1900–1985* (1989), *African Encounters with Domesticity* (1992), *Keeping House in Lusaka* (1997), and *Salaula: The World of Secondhand Clothing and Zambia* (2000), which was awarded the Anthony Leeds Prize in Urban Anthropology in 2001, and the Society of Economic Anthropology Book Award in 2003. She is the recipient of several book prizes and awards including the Conrad M. Arensberg Award from the Society for the Anthropology of Work in 1997.

THE INTERNATIONAL AFRICAN LIBRARY

General Editors

The International African Library is a major monograph series from the International African Institute. Theoretically informed ethnographies, and studies of social relations 'on the ground' which are sensitive to local cultural forms, have long been central to the Institute's publications programme. The IAL maintains this strength and extends it into new areas of contemporary concern, both practical and intellectual. It includes works focused on the linkages between local, national and global levels of society; writings on political economy and power; studies at the interface of the socio-cultural and the environmental; analyses of the roles of religion, cosmology and ritual in social organisation; and historical studies, especially those of a social, cultural or interdisciplinary character.

For a list of titles published in the series, please see the end of the book.

Dress Cultures in Zambia

Interwoven Histories, Global Exchanges, and Everyday Life

Karen Tranberg Hansen

Northwestern University

International African Institute, London

and

CAMBRIDGE
UNIVERSITY PRESS

Shaftesbury Road, Cambridge CB2 8EA, United Kingdom

One Liberty Plaza, 20th Floor, New York, NY 10006, USA

477 Williamstown Road, Port Melbourne, VIC 3207, Australia

314–321, 3rd Floor, Plot 3, Splendor Forum, Jasola District Centre, New Delhi – 110025, India

103 Penang Road, #05–06/07, Visioncrest Commercial, Singapore 238467

Cambridge University Press is part of Cambridge University Press & Assessment, a department of the University of Cambridge.

We share the University's mission to contribute to society through the pursuit of education, learning and research at the highest international levels of excellence.

www.cambridge.org
Information on this title: www.cambridge.org/9781009350365

DOI: 10.1017/9781009350310

First published 2023

A catalogue record for this publication is available from the British Library.

Library of Congress Cataloging-in-Publication Data
Names: Hansen, Karen Tranberg, author.
Title: Dress cultures in Zambia : interwoven histories, global exchanges, and everyday life / Karen Tranberg Hansen, Northwestern University, Illinois.
Description: First Edition. | New York : Cambridge University Press, 2023. | Series: The international African library | Includes bibliographical references and index.
Identifiers: LCCN 2022050942 (print) | LCCN 2022050943 (ebook) | ISBN 9781009350365 (Hardback) | ISBN 9781009350341 (Paperback) | ISBN 9781009350310 (epub)
Subjects: LCSH: Clothing and dress—Cultural aspects—Zambia/Clothing and dress–Historical aspects—Zambia.
Classification: LCC GT1589.Z33 H357 2023 (print) | LCC GT1589.Z33 (ebook) | DDC 391.0096894–dc23/eng/20221201
LC record available at https://lccn.loc.gov/2022050942
LC ebook record available at https://lccn.loc.gov/2022050943

ISBN 978-1-009-35036-5 Hardback

Contents

Figures

Acknowledgements

The idea of this book formed slowly during the last two decades as my work increasingly turned towards the cultural aspect of clothing consumption, an issue that had been central to my research on secondhand clothing in Zambia and on which I worked during the 1990s. As an anthropologist following clothes beyond the point of purchase, I have grappled for years with two questions. One was how clothes were used, the meanings that were attached to them, and the dress practices in which they and their wearers were involved. The second question concerned Western-styled garments, worn in Zambia since the early colonial period and widely incorporated as local dress. I wondered why attitudes to Africans wearing Western-styled clothing were so overwhelmingly condescending and dismissive, most certainly those of colonial authorities and white settlers in Zambia but also dress scholars from art history and anthropology, among other disciplines. As a matter of fact, there is very little Africanist scholarship on these questions. Until recently, some scholars also dismissed the factory-printed textiles from Europe that since the end of the 1800s especially in West Africa dressed African bodies with style and panache as not being 'African enough' (Gott, Loughran, Quick, and Rabine 2017; Picton 1995: 25).

Why is the West 'out of place' when it dresses African bodies? My work on secondhand clothing consumption in Zambia qualified this question from many angles. But there is much more to say about these matters. Drawing on a lifetime of research in Zambia extending over nearly 50 years, most of it in the capital, Lusaka, beginning in the early 1970s, I reflect here more generally on changes in clothing practice and the place of dress in Zambia's social and cultural history. In the challenge to give agency to dressed bodies, I source my own published and unpublished works for relevant details. I draw as well on a rich body of regional scholarship and other works on dress and consumption. Each chapter comes from a different part of my research, mainly conducted during the 1990s and onwards, but also reaching back to my first work in 1971–72 and to different research projects I undertook during the 1980s. What is more, I also draw on work I have conducted during the last two decades. The research includes archival work I carried out in Zambia during the 1980s and 1990s, Great Britain in the 1980s, and South Africa in 2013, which this book cites occasionally. Some of this research was featured specifically in my work on secondhand clothing, a topic then so unprecedented that the attention it attracted readily overshadowed the book's general clothing account (Hansen 2000a).

While my work on dress practice in Zambia developed its own life, I found much inspiration for observations in this book from *Salaula: The World of Secondhand Clothing and Zambia* (Chicago: University of Chicago Press, © 2000). Some sections of Chapters 2 and 3 are from 'Urban Research in a Hostile Setting: Godfrey Wilson in Broken Hill, Northern Rhodesia, 1938–1940', *Kronos* 2015, 41: 193–214. Additional details in Chapters 2 and 9 derive from 'Fabricating Dreams: Sewing Machines, Tailors, and Urban Entrepreneurship in Zambia', in Robert Ross, Marja Hinfelaar, and Iva Pesa (eds), *The Objects of Life in Central Africa: The Historiography of Consumption and Social Change, 1840–1930* (Leiden: Brill, 2013), 167–85. Some of the discussion in Chapter 5 draws on 'Dressing Dangerously: Miniskirts, Gender Relations, and Sexuality in Zambia', in Jean Allman (ed.), *Fashioning Africa: Power and the Politics of Dress in Africa* (Bloomington: Indiana University Press, 2004), 66–85. Snapshot 2, *Chitenge*, expands an earlier version of a brief essay, 'From Grandmother's Dress to the Fashion Runway: *Chitenge* Styles in Zambia', in Suzanne Gott, Kristyne Loughran, Betsy D. Quick, and Leslie Rabine (eds). *African-Print Fashion Now! A Story of Taste, Globalization, and Style* (Los Angeles, CA: Fowler Museum, 2017), 160–61. Chapter 6 developed in 2009 as a keynote lecture to the Africanist Association of the American Anthropological Association at the annual meeting of the American Anthropological Association and during workshops in 2014 and 2016 at the Institute for Humanities at the University of Cape Town. It was published as 'Chiluba's Trunks: Consumption, Excess and the Body Politic in Zambia', in Deborah Posel and Ilana van Wyk (eds), *Conspicuous Consumption in Africa* (Johannesburg: Wits University Press, 2019), 96–111. Some observations of Chapter 8 were presented in earlier form in 'Fashioning: Zambian Moments', *Journal of Material Culture* 2003, 8(3): 301–10. More recent insights in Chapter 9 are taken from '"Our Dress": *Chitenge* as Zambia's National Fabric', in Heike Jenss and Viola Hofmann (eds), *Fashion and Materiality: Cultural Practices and Global Contexts* (London: Bloomsbury Visual Arts, an imprint of Bloomsbury Publishing Plc, 2020), 140–56, while others come from '"Not African Enough?" Global Dynamics and Local Contestations over Dress Practice and Fashion Design in Zambia', *ZoneModa Journal* 2019, 9(2): 1–15. Chapter 4 revises an unpublished paper I presented in 2008 at the annual meeting of the American Anthropological Association. Aside from the first two Snapshots, I wrote the remaining ones specifically for this book. In addition to these influences, throughout the book I also make use of selected elements from journal articles and book chapters as recognised in citations or footnotes when relevant. I am grateful to many publishers for approving the use of materials here. While owing a great debt to my previously published works, this book extends my long-term research interests in Zambia in many new directions.

During all my stays in Zambia I was affiliated with the Institute for Economic and Social Research (the former Institute for African Studies) of the University of Zambia. Throughout the years I have benefitted from the advice and friendship of numerous Zambian and expatriate colleagues as well as archivists, librarians, and other resource persons, far too many to recognise individually except for two recently deceased senior scholars and special friends. Elizabeth Colson, renowned senior anthropologist of Zambia, took a keen interest in my work, even in her retirement to a small farm-house in the Southern Province. In her last communication before she passed away in 2016, she commented on the Chinese influences on the women's dress styles she noticed in the provincial towns of Monze and Mazabuka. She kept urging me to accompany one of my suitcase-trader friends on a clothing trip to China.[1] And senior historian Mwelwa Musambachime died in 2017. Brimming with insights and advice, he was helpful beyond expectations, including during the period he served as Zambia's Ambassador to the United Nations (2000–05). He was also jolly, a quality in short supply among academics. I miss them both. In addition, I wish to acknowledge the very special hospitality of Dr Jacob Mwanza and his wife Ilse Mwanza, who facilitated my work in innumerable ways, offering extraordinary friendship. What is more, I have especially enjoyed the collaboration of many Zambian research assistants, first and foremost my chief assistant Norah Chitengu Rice from 1971 to her death in 1999, who taught me much about life in Zambia, including basic sartorial rules. She features in this book, whose message she shaped considerably. She, her family, and the hundreds of Zambians from many walks of life with whom I have interacted during research over the years have played incredibly important roles in my Zambian socialisation for which they hold my fondest gratitude.

[1] Personal communication, 12 June 2016.

My field research and archival work have been generously supported, beginning with a graduate scholarship from Rotary International, which took me to Zambia in 1971–72, subsequently by frequent faculty support from the University of Minnesota (1979–82) and Northwestern University (1982–2012) as by well as by research grants from the National Science Foundation, the Social Science Foundation (United States), and the Wenner-Gren Foundation for Anthropological Research. Residential fellowships at the National Humanities Center, the Rockefeller Foundation's study centre at Bellagio, Italy, and the Woodrow Wilson Center enabled me to concentrate on my writing in conducive settings of intellectual interchange that inspired my work. Several observations in this book were presented at conferences, workshops, and as invited lectures in the United States, Europe, southern Africa, and, in 2013, in Japan. Attentive participants everywhere offered useful criticism and constructive feedback.

I am grateful to editors from Cambridge University Press and the International African Institute, Stephanie Kitchen and Harri Englund, for supporting this book from the proposal stage through external reviews and production. I could not have wished for more supportive intermediaries. Any errors are of course my full responsibility.

Beyond these very identifiable acknowledgements, the concerns of this book have developed against an intellectual backdrop in which interdisciplinary dress scholarship has flourished. Indeed, dress matters and is no longer considered a frivolous concern neither by its users nor by scholars. My own role as an anthropologist in this (Hansen 2004b) has expanded my professional exposure to include among my interlocutors design scholars concerned with sustainability and economic historians focusing on the histories of material objects, their roles in and effects on our changing lives globally. Andrew Bank, South African historian of regional anthropology and more, read several versions of the manuscript with such generous enthusiasm that I felt encouraged to continue developing it. Most specifically and above all, my long-term colleague and friend, the eminent dress scholar Joanne B. Eicher, has nudged me several times into writing an anthropological dress book. Reluctant to take on a cross-cultural challenge, I kept insisting that I wanted to work with what I know best, Zambia, and to engage local dress practice as a lead actor in that country's history. In this way, the concerns of this book arise from my previous work, extending them in new directions. I hope that my book will engage established scholars of Africa and elsewhere and attract a new generation of students who are eager to carry out research on global dress fashions of the future.

Prologue
The Global World of Dress in Zambia

By the late 1990s when I had completed the research and writing for my book, *Salaula: The World of Secondhand Clothing and Zambia* (2000a), several processes with global scope overlapped to change the global clothing landscape in previously unimaginable ways, including in Zambia. The digital age had brought Internet access and new inspirations from transnational images, products, and styles. It also facilitated Internet commerce and innovations in both new and secondhand markets. Generally regarded as a phenomenon stemming from the beginning of the twenty-first century, fast fashion affected clothing markets everywhere. The expiration in 2005 of the World Trade Organization's Multi-Fibre Arrangement enabled tariff-free entry for clothing and textiles manufactured in China into previously restricted markets on an unprecedented scale. Concerns about the growing import from China into Zambia soon eclipsed the public criticism of imported secondhand clothing, which continued to fill its own popular market niche.

During the first two decades of the twenty-first century, the growing global climate crisis raised major environmental issues, revealing among them significant challenges facing the textile sector (clothing, footwear, and household textiles) of the global economy. Increasingly, these issues are linked to concerns with ethics and sustainability. With its complex value chains involving production and consumption, textiles touch the lives of everyone worldwide. The fashion segment leads the textile market, in 2020 accounting for a major part of global revenue, and demand is estimated to grow over the next 15 years. As one of the world's largest users of basic resources such as water, the polluting effects from the sector are huge.[1] Against this backdrop, secondhand clothing

---

[1] Popular media, using piecemeal sources, have described recent pollution from the textile sector as second to that of the oil industry or as worse than that of the aviation and shipping sector combined. This chapter's general observations draw on Innovation Fund Denmark (2021: 4). In 2020 according to this report, the fashion sector accounted for more than 74 per cent of global textile revenue.

acquired a new cachet for its sustainability and its role in circular economies. In effect, the increasing use of secondhand clothing found a new place in the changing relationship between production and consumption. In the West, secondhand clothing consumption is projected to grow more than that of new clothing, and its online shopping is increasing. Some well-known brands are developing in-house clothing resale and establishing partnerships with digital secondhand clothing platforms, finding new users for preloved fashions, especially luxury brands (Bloomberg Quicktakes 2021).

The global COVID-19 pandemic during 2020 and 2021 significantly reduced or closed production of clothing and apparel almost everywhere. Problems at many points of the global commodity circuits and their upstream and downstream supply chains came into glaring view along with widespread retail closures and the piling up of excess inventory. At one end, in South and Southeast Asia, poorly remunerated garment workers were not paid, while at another, in France and elsewhere, some luxury brands incinerated unsold goods to prevent devaluing the brand name on resale markets; brand retailers in the United States and Europe sold deadstock to upcyclers to use in their design rather than ending as waste in landfills. In the process, several secondhand clothing export markets ceased importing for a while for fear that the coronavirus might contaminate clothing. At the time of writing, many markets, including in Africa, have reopened, yet textile recyclers and secondhand clothing graders from the United States to Europe continue experiencing problems because of collection restrictions and space and social distancing measures on their sorting floors. Meanwhile, since I completed my *Salaula* book at the end of the 1990s, new actors have entered the global export of secondhand clothing, among them India and China (Brooks 2015; Ma 2020; Minter 2019: 141, 166–67; Norris 2010).

Taken together, these processes constitute a turning point in the world's clothing economies that is blurring boundaries between producers, sellers, and consumers everywhere and shifting the conventional centre of gravity of fashion away from the West, as I discuss in this book's last chapters. The sartorial landscapes are changing. In Zambia the result is not a break with the past but rather a re-working of the cultural dimensions of the clothing economy in conflict with or accommodation to changing times. During all of this, the significance of a well-dressed appearance continues to cut across the country's history. To be sure as I emphasise throughout, dressed bodies are the point of contact between local knowledge and the broader global context. For dressed bodies have agency and the potential to remake social worlds and challenge constraining norms of valuation. In this way, dress helps make history. Right from my first field research during the early 1970s, Zambian women's changing dress practice left a lasting impression on me. While dress style and performance might not have seemed out of the ordinary at the time, their significance in everyday life for women in Zambia was both personal and political, and they inspired this book.

Plan of this Book

Fashioned by three bodies of scholarship – the anthropology and history of African Studies and dress scholarship – this book focuses on dress practice and changing livelihoods in Zambia, exploring their mutual interactions and shifts. It is an account in which dress is both an actor shaping events and a practice influenced by the course of events. In it, I bring together local histories of consumption with their actors, performances, and spaces to explore how the dressed body serves as the point of contact between personal, very local experiences and the broader global context.

If the power of the dressed body derives in part from the special nature of clothing as a commodity, its significance in specific cases has to do with the circumstances that made it appear special. Since the early days of the colonial encounter in what today is Zambia, Western-styled clothing became and has remained a centrepiece of consumption, a focal point of everyday life, in effect constituting a key token of modernity. But we cannot explain the social and cultural significance of dress practice and its changes unless we examine how this commodity has been delivered and how it has entered people's lives, as I do here.

I organise the book thematically and chronologically with some overlaps. Each chapter has a distinctive focus, yet all chapters build on one another, introducing new actors and processes as the account unfolds. The book's three parts pertain broadly to the late colonial period and the early independence years, followed by postcolonial developments, and ending with more recent global perspectives. Six brief 'Snapshots' expand my main line of inquiry. They serve as indulgences, enlivening the account by providing details about specific issues that appear in passing in the main narrative yet invite additional attention.

Following this Prologue, Chapter 1 sketches the backdrop for my focus on dress practice as history, formed by my long-term research in Zambia and the Africanist and dress scholarship that frames it. Turning specifically to Zambia, Part I, 'Dressing Well', engages with general questions about clothing access and dress practice during the late colonial period and the early post-independence years. Its two chapters, with the end of World War II as a rough turning point, explore the acquisition of clothing consumption skills, clothing availability, and the localisation of Western-styled dress. Chapter 2 focuses on labour migration with cities and towns as central spaces of work and consumption, enabling the development of both new clothing practices and the tailor's craft. Men's suits and women's dresses are actively featured in these processes. Chapter 3 examines how in the context of the late colonial period's nationalism and politics Africans made Western dress conventions their own. In recreation and leisure activities their dress performance developed new local appeals, dressing for freedom in the immediate pre-independence period and after.

Part II, 'Dress and Undress', broadens the clothing discussion to specific considerations of sexuality, gender, and power. Chapter 4 examines questions about the sexualisation of distinct parts of women's bodies and the change of shame frontiers as demonstrated in several body-baring events since the late colonial period. Although the shifting meanings and different contexts of such events resonate with overall societal changes, questions about dress and undress remain charged issues in Zambia. Chapter 5 discusses the construction of decency and proper dress that keeps provoking moral panic when women wear miniskirts and tight clothing in public. Although they continue to take place, public stripping events unfold against the backdrop of changing circumstances. Chapter 6 turns the focus to the ostentatious dress practice of one person, former president Frederick Chiluba, for a discussion of dress as a screen for corruption and deceit. When, I explore in this chapter, is excess considered to be 'too much' and why?

Part III, 'Fashionable Transformations', demonstrates how Lusaka's rapid postcolonial growth, along with the huge expansion of the informal economy, opened diverse developments in clothing practices and cultures of consumption. It explores how people in Zambia creatively make fashion their own in an increasingly globalised world where dress influences flow in multiple directions and the West no longer is the final arbiter of style. Focusing on young women and men, Chapter 7 introduces the secondhand clothing market as a popular source for the fulfilment of clothing desires, while discussing the cultivation of appearances along with some of the dress dilemmas that arise from youth, gender, and location. Chapter 8 turns to dress performance and the discerning skills applied when acquiring clothing in order to produce dressed body displays with demonstrative effects, while Chapter 9 explores knotty questions about the construction of 'African' in dress and fashion practice and the local meaning of the types of dress practices this book has showcased, especially in the case of *chitenge* fashions. Focusing on clothing consumption issues in the present and immediate future, the Conclusion briefly reviews the main argument of the book while exploring possible futures for local fashion in a global world of clothing production and consumption that is thoroughly challenged on several fronts.

1   Dress Practice as History

Past and present across most of Africa, people have been and remain passionate about how they appear in public, and Zambia is no exception. When Zambian women today talk about 'our dress', they are referring to clothes that are tailored from brightly coloured printed cotton fabric referred to as *chitenge* in the Chinyanja language. My research assistant Norah Rice presented me with my first *chitenge* outfit in 1972 prior to my departure from Lusaka, where we had been exploring married women's work opportunities in the low-income township on the outskirts of the capital where she lived with her family (Hansen 1975). The fabric was produced by Kafue Textiles of Zambia, a fully integrated textile mill owned jointly by the state and private enterprise, which had opened for business in 1969, five years after independence (*New York Times*, 26 November 1989) (see Figure 1.1). We had bought the fabric with an abstract pattern in wine-red and dark blue colours at a factory outlet in the centre of Lusaka, one of several such outlets across the country. Seated on the living room floor in her home, she had sewn the two-piece garment herself. Unlike today's ornately decorated outfits, this dress was plain, with a straight skirt reaching well below the knee, a top with a V-neck bordered by ties to fold into a bow, and three-quarter-length straight sleeves. I do not recall the brand of her hand-operated sewing machine; it might have been an old Singer model as one of today's most popular machines, the Shanghai-produced Butterfly brand, may not have been available at that time because of import restrictions.

Then and later – for we continued to work together until she passed away at the end of the 1990s – my research assistant taught me how to dress in public. I still recall her consternation when, also in 1972, an American girlfriend and I took her to a steak lunch at Lusaka's Intercontinental Hotel wearing bell-bottom jeans while she had dressed up in *chitenge* wear. I was in my mid-twenties then and she, 13 years my senior, sought to teach me proper dress decorum. In 1981, when I commuted to the township on a bike, she instructed me not to wear jeans on a bicycle. Her advice drew on a variety of norms that converged

Figure 1.1 Billboard advertising fabrics manufactured by Kafue Textiles of Zambia, Ltd., near the factory at Chilanga, 1992. Author's photo.

on the dressed body, including mission-inspired notions of decency, cultural ideas about the privacy of specific body parts, and Western-inspired dress practice. Although the weight of some of these norms has shifted since the colonial period, they continue to affect women's dressed bodies through to the present.

In fact, while dress practice was not central to my research when I first began my work in Zambia in 1971, during subsequent years I could not help noticing that dress was an important part of everyday life and that it figured actively in shaping people's lives. I learned that changes in clothing practice were written into Zambian history, which it helped to enact. Bringing the dressed body to the fore in my account of changing engagements with clothing not only adds an unusual angle to our understanding of late colonial and postcolonial Zambian society; it also offers new ways of exploring dress as a scholarly activity. Inspired by my years of accumulated knowledge about Zambia, this book unfolds clothing histories from my published and unpublished works where most of them, except the secondhand clothing story, have played accessory roles. Here, I examine all of this evidence alongside a rich body of historical and interdisciplinary scholarship on dress. Inviting attention in its own right, clothing, I argue, helps people make history and create sociocultural change just as much as history helps drive their new dress practice and fashion cultures. Altogether, exploring the dress and fashion scene in relation to changes in the political and social setting opens up a surprising range of issues that have endured across history in Zambia. They converge on the dressed body and make the significance of a well-dressed appearance the heart of that story.

Changing dress practice opens windows into the social, economic, and political developments that over the course of the twentieth century and into the present have shaped how people in the region of central and southern Africa that today is Zambia experienced and acted upon their world. Such interwoven histories bring into sharp focus several potentially culturally charged issues during the colonial period in terms of race, and between generations, classes, and urban and rural dwellers. Dress is as central to changing notions of status, identity, and personal style as it is to political power. As historian Phyllis Martin has pointed out, the association of dress with the physical body and the body politic is a particularly potent combination (2004: 229). Mediating between self and society, the dressed body provokes supportive as well as contentious reactions, giving rise to enjoyment and admiration as well as to tensions, anxieties, and debates.

Because they pay considerable attention to appearance, people in Zambia eagerly discuss the clothes of others, and they comment at length and in detail about the dress of people in power. Such lively preoccupations with bodies and dress involve women as well as men, although news media and scholarship have showcased women much more frequently than men when accounting, for example, for bare-breasted women demonstrators or describing the stripping of young women wearing miniskirts in public. Challenging deep-seated moral and cultural dress norms, such events have provoked reactions of indignation, shame, and even violence. Sadly, they continue to take place. But when African men's attire makes the headlines, the news-breaking commentaries tend to revolve around excessive consumption as a screen for corruption and deceit. To be sure, dress norms weigh down unevenly on women's and men's bodies. As I demonstrate, dress readily becomes a flash point of conflicting values that fuel contests in colonial encounters, across class, between gender and generation, across the rural-urban divide, and in recent global cultural and economic exchanges.

Global Interchanges

As driving forces in the industrial revolution, cloth and textiles played major roles in mediating historical encounters in Africa prior to the onset of colonial rule and subsequently, deeply intertwining dress practice with major transformations of people's livelihoods locally and globally (DuPlessis 2016). To be sure, textiles and clothing are weighty subjects in African history in economic and cultural terms and they continue to be so today. For decades prior to the arrival of Europeans during the fifteenth century and during the slave trade across both the Atlantic and the Indian oceans well into the nineteenth century, the cloth and clothing trade was big business (Kriger 2006; Machado 2009; Machado, Fee, and Campbell 2018; Presholdt 2008). Along with the trade spread new dress conventions. Islamic-inspired dress had already, from around 1000 and onward, spread in the Sahel/Sudanic region and along the East African coast. Although European-style clothing had been known and worn by local elites in coastal areas since the late fifteenth century, it did not become part of ordinary people's dress practice until the late nineteenth century (Cameron 2010: 371–72). Exposure to Christian missions introduced new styles of garments (Comaroff and Comaroff 1997). Talking about the backdrop for this transition with reference to southern and eastern Africa, historian Robert Ross identifies a major shift in the material culture of consumption 'between the 1880s – earlier in some parts of South Africa – and the 1950s, though in most parts of the continent it had been completed before then'. According to him, this 'entailed the virtually complete reclothing of half a continent, and also the remaking of a whole variety of other articles of consumption' (2008: 121). Changes in styles and dress practice and the widespread adoption of Western-styled wear also entailed different valuations, as African consumers modified such garments to suit their own purposes. New forms of social differentiation arose at times, full of contradictions, as we shall see in this book in controversies over women's dress practice.

Briefly, through all of this, African and Western notions of dress practice interacted, drawing on each other for sources of inspiration, 'although at times with conflicted and compromised outcomes' (Martin 2004: 228). Marked colonial disdain for Africans wearing Western-styled dress tended to mistake African dress practice for imitation rather than recognising the desire to be part of a changing modern world. Today, especially in the former white settler colonies in southern and eastern Africa, we must reckon seriously with the centuries-long wearing of Western-styled garments. Here, as I have argued for the case of Zambia, people have dressed in Western-styled clothing for so long that the garments have been incorporated into everyday dress practice to become local. Yet until recently the West has tended to see only imitations of itself in the global circulation of its garments. As a result, an overdrawn   distinction   lingers   between   Western-style   clothing conventions, on the one hand, and local or traditional ways of dress, on the other. Seeking to unsettle this stubborn Western-centric fashion vision in scholarly accounts, dress scholars Joanne Eicher and Barbara Sumberg proposed the term 'world fashion' as more appropriate to capture the effects of increasing globalisation on contemporary dress practice (1995: 296). Both dress historian Margaret Maynard and I have suggested the term 'global fashion' for this process (Hansen 2004c; Maynard 2004).

At issue in these works is the search for an explanatory framework that encompasses all of these influences, not in opposition to but alongside each other, and to focus, as I do here, on their creative tensions. In today's increasingly globalised world with its rapid exchange circuits between local and global actors, the privileged position of the West in influencing dress in Africa has given way to new interchanges spanning the globe and to many diverse, and constantly changing, sources and inspirations that are at play in shaping dress practice from within and beyond the African continent (Cheang, de Graaf, and Takagi 2021; Jansen and Craik 2016: 1–22).

Bodies, Dress, and Materiality

Such a focus acknowledges the active roles of dressed bodies in how clothing put to use during social interaction is shaping and transforming history. There are several additional arguments for this focus, some of which I spell out below, while I discuss others in subsequent chapters when they become particularly relevant. More generally, when exploring how dressed bodies 'work', anthropologists and dress scholars continue to draw inspiring insights from the work Terence Turner conducted several decades ago in Brazil's Amazon rainforest. Because it both touches the body and faces outward to others, the body surface has a dual quality, which Turner characterised as a 'social skin' ([1980] 1993). Extending these insights to analysis of dress practice in Africa, anthropologist Hildi Hendrickson explained their value: 'Being personal, [the body surface] is susceptible to individual manipulation. Being public, it has social import' (Hendrickson 1996: 2).

This dual quality of the body surface makes dress a very special thing, unlike most other things. What is more, we do not wear our clothes passively but are actively involved with them. As embodied practice, dress and the body are intimately entangled with the particularities of time, location, and context (Entwistle 2000). The agency dress possesses does not stem from it as a thing in itself, although its materiality matters by affecting how we experience what we wear and makes our clothes interact with our bodies. Its agency arises in practices of use and consumption, through performances in everyday life, and during special events and occasions. In short, dress is a fundamental aspect of social interaction, involving both wearers and viewers.

While much of the appeal of dress is visual, the sensuous experience of fabric on the body that helps bring dress to life makes materiality matter importantly both in the selection of dress and its wearing as well as in how we take care of it. The sensual and aesthetic – what clothes feel and look like – is, according to British social anthropologist Daniel Miller, 'the source of its capacity to objectify ... morality, power and values' (2005: 1). In effect, this view attributes material agency to the wearer's dress practice. Nina Sylvanus' anthropological work on wax cloth and dress in Togo has shown this aspect with great insight, demonstrating how the rich material and semiotic quality of the cloth helps dress come alive, bringing joy, creating a story, generating desire – in short, having agency (Sylvanus 2016: 11–16). Wax cloth may be special in this respect because of its layered history, yet as I discuss later, such animation also pertains to other printed textiles like *chitenge* in Zambia. It too has sensuous qualities that draw the attention of both wearers and viewers. When shopping for textiles and dressing, women test the touch of a textile and its quality. Enhancing their dressed body presentation, they make considerable efforts to care for their garments when it comes to laundry, drying, and ironing as well as in the accessories they select to match their outfits. All these efforts contribute to the 'clothing competence' (Hansen 2013b) they demonstrate by being well turned out. And the quality, style, and taste of their dressed bodies are both 'seen' and 'read' by a discerning public who understands how to interpret them (Haynes 2019: 38; Sylvanus 2016: 44–48).

Africa in Dress Scholarship

Anthropology has a proud tradition of studying material culture, including body adornment, cloth, and textiles (Luvaas and Eicher 2019; Weiner and Schneider 1989), a tradition that extends to Africa where art historians have added rich details about aesthetics, forms, and fabrics (Picton and Mack 1989; Picton et al. 1995). Turning to history, textiles and clothing are substantial subjects in Africa and beyond (DuPlessis 2016; Kriger 2006; Presholdt 2008). When the reigning anthropological focus shifted from evolution to function during the 1920s and then to structure during the 1940s, material culture studies fell out of favour only to blossom in recent years (Küchler and Miller 2005). For quite a while, dress scholarship prominently featured the rich cloth traditions of West

African societies (Byfield 2002; Perani and Wolff 1999; Renne 1995; Ross 1998; Rovine 2001), while paying limited attention to the diverse clothing repertoires of the late colonial and postcolonial periods that go beyond Western and 'traditional' African dress options. Today this is all changing (Akou 2011; Brown 2017; Nwafor 2021; Rabine 2002; Richards 2022; Sylvanus 2016). Outside Africa, anthropologists Daniel Miller and Emma Tarlo played major roles in re-establishing dress practice as an important topic of inquiry that includes a focus on historical changes and mass consumption (Miller 1987; 1998; Tarlo 1996). The clothing engagements and dilemmas they describe from India and the Caribbean concern larger debates involving individuals and groups in specific historical circumstances. Rather than viewing culture as the product of a specifically place-bounded society, today we view it processually as created through agency, practice, and performance, approaching it as cultures 'in motion' (Rodgers 2013: 1–19). This shift helps reorient the way we understand 'traditional' not as a temporal status of a textile, garment, or image but rather as styles or media that make connections with, or evoke, local culture and history (Rovine 2015: 18–19).

In general, over the last couple of decades, dress research has emerged as an interdisciplinary domain of scholarship that includes cultural studies and performance studies, among several disciplines. Dress scholarship has flourished in recent years with new conventional and online publication venues as well as social media. So has research on dress and fashion in Africa, inspired by a rich body of interdisciplinary scholarship that is adding important insights to our understanding of the changing place of clothing and of dress practice in several African countries since the late colonial period. Below, I discuss some works I find notable for situating dress historically in changing socioeconomic and cultural contexts and turn then to some recent works that are helping to place Africa on the global fashion map, thus challenging previous images of the continent's role as marginal, on the fringe of the established fashion scene.

I begin during the colonial period in Zambia where in fact African dress was written into pioneering anthropological research conducted in several rapidly growing mining towns by scholars associated with the Rhodes-Livingstone Institute. They include in the late 1930s to early 1940s Godfrey Wilson in Broken Hill (today Kabwe), and in the 1950s, J. Clyde Mitchell, Arnold Epstein, and Hortense Powdermaker in towns on the Copperbelt, as I discuss in some detail in Part I of this book. The significance of this work has been elusive in recent scholarship for two reasons. One reason has to do with the overall lack of recognition of research on dress, the status of which for a long time was not considered legitimate but viewed as a rather frivolous focus for anthropological research. The second reason concerns specifically the lack of appreciation for the published works by these anthropologists in scholarship condemning its colonial underpinnings.[1] Rereading these works carefully and with close attention to context has given me rich observations from that period about the dressed body as a battlefield involving race, gender, and generation in everyday lives in towns during the late colonial situation. As historian Megan Vaughan has argued, these works 'actually leave open greater possibilities of multiple interpretations and meanings' than critics have attributed to them (1994: 15). Although Wilson's statement about African clothing desires probably is one of the most memorable quotes from his work, it invites repetition as it goes to the heart of my concerns: 'The Africans of Broken Hill are not a cattle people, nor a goat people, nor a forest people, nor a tree cutting people, they are a dressed people' (1942: 18).

Perhaps it is not surprising that I am drawn for inspiration to historical works that bring urban leisure activities during the late colonial period into sharp focus. In fact, scholarly interest in exploring leisure in relation to the changing political and social scene has helped reveal a wide range of positions expressed by the changing fashion scene. For example, Laura Fair's work on post-abolition urban Zanzibar details how women used dress practice to demonstrate their freedom from slavery and articulate Zanzibari identities (2001; 2004). Discarding their required dress practice as slaves, in fora such as dance groupings and initiation rites women developed new dress practices, communicating their independent self-making ambitions. On the other side of the continent, in colonial Brazzaville, Phyllis Martin describes how African male workers from several regions used their newly earned cash to purchase clothing, experimenting with imported European-style fashions, while some young women and women holding jobs alternated between wearing European-styled dresses with short skirts and *pagne*, wrapped-around printed cloth (1994; 1995).

The capital of colonial French West Africa, Dakar in Senegal, the 'Paris of Africa', has a long reputation for elegance and fashion.[2] Historian Dior Konaté explains how women used fashion to show their

---

[1] For a groundbreaking study of work conducted from the Rhodes-Livingstone Institute, see Lyn Schumaker, *Africanizing Anthropology* (2001). Bernhard Magubane's critique of the use in these works of clothing as an index of social change explained it as an imposition of the values of the white colonizers (1971). Vaughan argued that his critique was misdirected (1994: 15–16).

[2] I discuss the examples from Senegal and Angola in Hansen (2023).

support to the Bloc Africain, a political movement that mobilised colonised people across French West Africa, in a campaign for the vote of African women in 1945 (Konaté 2009: 244).[3] Expressing their growing political involvement, women adopted a dress they called the *robe bloc*, wearing it at political meetings from the 1940s into the 1950s. When demonstrating and engaging in political activity, women would wear the dress, which was long and red, the colour of the Bloc Africain, and spectacular new coiffures (Konaté 2009: 236).

Konaté and dress and literature scholar Leslie Rabine both describe the change of the *robe bloc* from political dress to a fashion garment among urban women during the late 1940s and 1950s when war-related import restrictions on fabrics and consumer goods were done away with. Rabine explains how dressmakers innovated the style of the colonial missionary–influenced high-waisted loose dress, the *ndoket* (camisole), decorating its surfaces with embellishments and trim, making the bodice more form fitting and using lots of fabric in its construction. One style from 1948 had a dropped waist, perhaps, speculates Rabine, inspired by Dior's 'New Look' of 1947. 'European in its design, yet local in conceptualization', the *robe bloc* reflected a new political consciousness and self-confidence (Rabine 2010: 308).

Describing how young Angolans strategically employed dress to carve out space for participation, historian Marissa Moorman casts revealing light on the complicated relationship between local and imported dress styles. Angola remained a 'Portuguese territory' until 1975 when a protracted guerrilla struggle that began in the early 1960s resulted in independence. Even in a context of marked repression of political and cultural activity in late colonial Luanda, the capital, young Angolans used dress, dance, and music to imagine their new nation. While colonial policy promoted Portuguese dress and denigrated African clothing as quaint or folkloric, older women from the urban elite, *bessanganas*, dressed quite distinctly in several layers of *panos* (wrappers) on top of a long-sleeved blouse along with a smaller *pano* headwrap. Younger women wore European-style dress, often with a *pano* wrapper around the waist, and a headscarf. 'Young women who used *panos* with miniskirts or European dress in the 1970s nodded to the *bessanganas'* style as uniquely Angolan while also adopting it. By neither dismissing it as archaic nor reproducing it layer by layer, these young women

---

[3] Leslie Rabine names the dress for the Bloc Africain in one publication (1997a: 103), while in another publication (2010: 308–9), she attributes the emergence of the *robe bloc* to the mobilization for Senghor's party.

demonstrated a new posture of Angolan womanhood that was both local and worldly' (Moorman 2004: 88).

Young Angolans reached beyond the colonial horizon with local fashions and cultural activities that expressed both their difference and cosmopolitan outlook. Using local instruments and dress they performed American-style tap dancing and songs of Carmen Miranda in the dance halls of Luanda during the 1940s and 1950s. This local scene included fashions associated with rock 'n' roll in the United States and Europe as well as bell-bottom trousers, shirts with huge collars, big sunglasses, and 'Afro' hair (Moorman 2004: 84–85, 94–95). They 'dressed and coifed themselves', Moorman explains, 'in the image of film heroes both white and African-American in order to more clearly express who they were and how they were Angolan. They embraced their education, their European-style dress, and their grandparents' *panos* in the same gesture' (Moorman 2004: 98). When political and cultural activities were banned during the early 1960s, young women as described above adopted *panos* on top of their European-style dress, proclaiming their sense of an urban Angolanness. Their quotidian self-styling 'gave them a lived experience of independence which made political sovereignty both imaginable and desirable' (Moorman 2004: 98).

As these examples clearly demonstrate, local engagements with Western-styled clothing varied by place and time across Africa, reflecting diverse dress traditions and norms as well as changing cultural and economic politics. Still, it is remarkable how scholarship on textiles and dress in Africa has been tardy, if not reluctant, to reckon with the importance of Western-styled clothing, noticing it mainly in passing rather than taking it seriously as a regular part of local dress practice. Historian Robert Ross' global historical overview is a recent important exception (Ross 2008). For a long time secondhand clothing was not considered to be a worthwhile research topic, thus foreclosing substantive investigation and the provision of new insights. Yet imported secondhand clothing is a commodity with a long history of use in Africa and widespread consumption today. The West and Africa, as I have argued in my previous work (Hansen 2000a), exist in each other's space, which today is thoroughly globalised with interchanges of people, ideas, and commodities between the local and the global that would have been hard to imagine in most of Africa towards the end of colonialism in the 1960s.

Several recent scholarly publications and lively social media discussions are placing Africa on the global fashion map, thus changing tired images of the continent's role as marginal, on the fringe of the established fashion scene (Gott and Loughran 2010; Gott, Loughran, Quick, and Rabine 2017; Hansen and Madison 2013; Jennings 2010; Rabine 2002;

Rovine 2015; Shaw [2011] 2014). Among the chief movers of African dress from a marginal to a central position in fashion scholarship, art historian Victoria Rovine provides a panoramic synthesis of African design in the global fashion market (Rovine 2015). She is well known for her work on *bogolan*, a cloth from Mali, on African designers in Paris, and on African design as an artistic medium (2001). Focusing on professional designers, both women and men, in several countries in West Africa, South Africa, and Paris, her more recent work explores a creative fashion market that is exclusive. South Africa, for example, has a well-developed fashion industry, unlike most of the rest of the continent where a formal fashion infrastructure is not well developed. 'Fashion matters', as Rovine demonstrates (2015: 30), and art historian Christopher Richards focuses on the fashion scene developed by women in Ghana from the mid-twentieth century and on. Examining fashion as art he reveals a cosmopolitan fusion of styles (Richards 2022). A wide-ranging anthology on 'African' print fabrics adds a vivid dimension to Rovine's high-fashion panorama that nearly hides from view the enormous popularity of this important design element (Gott, Loughran, Quick, and Rabine 2017). The Africanisation of printed fabrics, developed in colonial interchanges between Europe and Southeast Asia, continues to unfold, as I discuss in Part III of this book. Across most of the continent, such printed fabrics have widespread and enduring appeal to huge populations of fashion-savvy consumers who dress in 'the latest' produced by tailors, dress makers, and designers; engage in self-fashioning from the 'China shop' (a shop selling Chinese imports); and pursue the extraordinary dress possibilities provided by the secondhand clothing market.

Exploring Dress Practice in Zambia

Although I never really planned it, clothing and dress practice have come to play inspiring roles in my research in Zambia ever since my first study of women's work in the informal economy in Lusaka in the early 1970s. Trained as an economic and urban anthropologist, in all my works I have examined different ways of making urban livelihoods. Yet throughout my many research projects in Zambia dress practice continued to grow with me not only because of its visibility but also, and more important perhaps, because of issues arising around dress practice. As I noted at the outset, throughout the years of my coming and going to Lusaka, it was impossible to ignore people's lively engagements with dress and the importance of dressed bodies in everyday life. A few examples suffice to illustrate.

During my research on domestic employment, I was struck by colonial employers' frequent disapproving reactions to the dress practice of their mostly male household workers and their concern that Africans were stepping out of place when wearing Western-styled clothing (Hansen 1989: 42–43, 68–69). When conducting research on women's work in the informal economy in a low-income township in Lusaka in the early 1970s and 1980s, I realised that women's clothing, or lack of it, indexed the quality of conjugality and gender relations because of the cultural expectation that husbands were to provide their wives with clothes. Even when urban women earned money in their own right, newly acquired clothes easily provoked husbands' suspicion, sometimes leading to domestic trouble and court cases (Hansen 1997: 118–40). Then during the 1990s my chief research focus turned directly on dress and consumption as I followed the flow of secondhand clothing from closets in the West to markets and wardrobes in Zambia, wondering what people made with and of other people's clothes (Hansen 2000a). What had been conceived largely as a study in economic terms developed as a cultural agenda to examine dress practice. In fact, my anthropological focus increasingly turned to what people were wearing, the meanings they attributed to dress, and how to interpret such meanings. Subsequently, the rapidly growing local design and fashion scene attracted my attention in explorations of this creative frontier of economic engagement and its involvement with global style trends.

As a field of research in its own right, changing clothing practice provides a meeting place where anthropology straddles history with fine-grained, long-term ethnographic research. Spanning nearly half a century of my work in Zambia, my book draws on a wide range of methodologies and sources, ranging from the anthropologist's stock in trade, participant observation, to archival research. Discussing some of my methodological choices in more detail as they become relevant to specific chapters, at this point I merely list some of my main approaches. The diverse subjects I examined over the years invited the use of a wide range of methods, both conventional and innovative. They include conducting household surveys, studying consumption practices, recording budget expenditure, carrying out all sorts of interviews, participating in kitchen parties (bridal showers), and spending weeks in outdoor markets observing sales and shopping practices involving secondhand clothing, as well as analysing essays written by secondary school students, and memoirs of former colonial household employers I interviewed in Great Britain, among many others. Spending time with tailors and their clients, I explored how style matters were negotiated. I also consulted government archives in Zambia and Great Britain, newspapers and magazines, and letters to the editor as well as, in more recent years, Internet-based sources. Even in the time of Internet-based news, printed newspapers and magazines in Zambia continue to be read by many more than the person purchasing them, and they circulate widely. In the 1980s, when scarcity of all kinds of goods was a daily experience in Lusaka, a common joke had it that Zambia never would experience a political coup until the day when both newspaper and beer delivery ceased. And while letters to the editor may not be representative, their commentaries connecting letter writers to newspaper readers help us catch the tenor of their time.[4]

---

[4] For a discussion of the critical use of the press as a source, see Ivaska (2011: 28–34).

Part I

Dressing Well

2   The Migration Nexus

Once he retired from his job as a security guard in one of the international hotels in Lusaka, Zambia's capital, in the late 1970s, Isaac Chitengu Rice always dressed in a suit when out and about in the peri-urban township where he lived with his five children and his wife Norah, my long-term research assistant. Like generations of men before him, he had left his village in Zambia's Southern Province sometime in the mid-1950s as a labour migrant and found work in Johannesburg. In 1959, he married his wife. They later spent a couple of years in Zimbabwe (then Rhodesia) where he had relatives,[1] and in 1969 they moved on to Zambia, settling in Lusaka. Although age and a life of work were taking their toll on him, he had obviously been a great charmer, sociable and outgoing. Knowing the importance of cutting a good figure, he wore his suit and tie or a bow tie with panache.

The significance of a well-dressed appearance cuts across history in Zambia, connecting decades of long-distance trading on both coasts: the Indian Ocean and the Atlantic with today's global circulation of goods and ideas. From the mid-nineteenth century onward, accelerating imports of industrially produced textiles extended consumption and new dress practices beyond the elite to ordinary people. In particular, the colonial period left long-lasting marks as imported textiles and cut-and-sewn clothing became accepted standard wear, replacing garments made from bark, skin, and hides or woven cloth from a very limited local cotton production. In fact, imported textiles and clothing became far more than quotidian wear. They became objects of desire. In this changing regional socioeconomic context, new ideas about wealth, social status, and authority came together in clothing, and for a long time, labour migration was the most important means of acquiring them.

---

[1] In 1965 the country name of Southern Rhodesia changed to Rhodesia, when the white minority government declared its unilateral independence from Great Britain (UDI, unilateral declaration of independence).

Clothing loomed large in the experiences of migrant workers in the deeply racialised colonial situation that organised their livelihoods. From the last decades of the nineteenth century and on, thousands of Zambian men migrated far and wide throughout the region to work on mines, on farms, and in towns across southern Africa, on mines in the Belgian Congo, and in the gold fields and sisal plantations of Tanganyika (today Tanzania). From the late 1920s once the copper mining industry was established, they worked within Zambia as well. By the mid-1930s more than half of the able-bodied male population was working for wages away from home, as many outside the territory as within it (Roberts 1976: 171).

By the 1940s, most of the destinations in accounts of colonial labour migrants were mining areas within Northern Rhodesia and the wider region. Lusaka, the capital since 1935, was the country's administrative headquarters and grew only slowly. The economic focus during the post–World War II period was largely on the Copperbelt, while Elisabethville in the Belgian Congo (today Lubumbashi) was the cultural hub of the region. It is perhaps not surprising that the historiography and urban anthropological research of this period tend to be biased towards the lives and experiences of male mine workers, as I noted in my study of domestic workers in Lusaka (Hansen 1989: 31).[2]

Working during the first half of the 1930s, men spent most of their hard-earned cash on purchasing factory-produced commodities that were replacing handmade tools and household goods. The 'desire for trinkets and the White Man's castoff finery', according to one European observer of the effects of labour migration, was replaced by 'a conscious desire for blankets, showy clothes, the European knife and axe, the mirror, mouth-organ, gramophone, sewing-machine and bicycle' (Davis [1933] 1968: 54).[3] Above all, miners bought clothes for themselves and their dependents. Because colonial authorities until the World War II years insisted on women and children remaining in the villages, any historical clothing account is a deeply gendered one. In this account, possessing an agency nearly their own, suits became men's most coveted garment. And in fact, suits continue to play this cherished role today in Zambia.

During the first decades of the twentieth century, clothing access depended on location in relationship to the changing centres of economic activity, and on the building of roads and railways.

---

[2] See Duncan Money (2021) for an account of the bias towards male mine workers on the Copperbelt in Zambia's historiography.
[3] This inquiry was made on behalf of the International Missionary Council.

Early migrants experienced many trials and tribulations. In their first jobs, they were paid in yards of cloth. Hut taxes were imposed around this time, when remuneration for work gradually changed from cloth to food rations and cash. After several work stints in Southern Rhodesia and service during World War I, Malekenya, a Ngoni man from Fort Jameson (today Chipata), reached Broken Hill (today Kabwe) in 1919. The zinc and lead mine in Broken Hill started production in 1906, the same year the northbound railway reached the town. 'In those days', he explained when interviewed in the late 1930s, 'there were no motor cars.... We spent three and a half weeks [to walk to Broken Hill], the place [was] not built yet, [there were] only camps there'. Chingongolingo Ngoma, a 'very old man' working as a tailor at an Indian store in Broken Hill, had his first job with early white settlers at Fort Jameson. 'Everybody was being paid ... cloths of white calicoes', he recalled. Magula Ngoma received two yards of cloth per month in his first job as a domestic worker in Fort Jameson. After serving in World War I, in 1920 he left with friends, 'walking on foot that time', to Kafue, just south of Lusaka, where a European hired him to purchase maize in the villages in exchange for salt and beads. After various jobs in Bulawayo in Southern Rhodesia, he came to Broken Hill in 1923, finding work on the mine (Hansen 2015: 206).[4]

As rail and motorised transport made movement easier, many men were hired by labour recruiters to work in the mines in South Africa and Southern Rhodesia. One of them, Livingstone-based labour recruiter Jehiel Jacobs, outfitted men before they left for Southern Rhodesia. On their return, part of their deferred pay from completed work contracts was available for purchases at Jacobs' stores. The articles of clothing he supplied to new recruits consisted of a blanket, a sweater, and a pair of shorts. In a letter of complaint Jacobs sent to the district commissioner concerning the portion of wages for new recruits he was allowed to spend on outfitting them, he explained: '[T]hese recruits come into Livingstone in a semi-nude state and in practically all cases do not want to go on their journey in that condition. In the interests of my recruiting business I do not overcharge these boys and sell goods to them at a very small profit to myself' (Hansen 2015: 211–12).

While furnishing near-naked migrants with such rudimentary garments might have ensured them some decency and warmth, it did not

---

[4] Hansen (2015) references an article in which I draw on observations from the Wilson Collection in the Archives and Manuscript Division of the University of Cape Town Libraries. The quotes are drawn from interviews conducted by Godfrey Wilson's research assistant in Broken Hill, Zacharia Mawere.

promote dignity.[5] Considering the types of garments that made up the standard outfit of a newly recruited migrant worker, the attraction of suits is hardly surprising. After a period of work in Bulawayo in Southern Rhodesia sometime in the 1920s, Herbert Zilole Mawere re-joined a former employer in Livingstone, travelling with him to Fort Jameson in his home area. 'Everybody was happy', reported his younger brother Zacharia. 'But some difficulties arose then they came to Fort Jameson.... [T]he trouble did not come from his master but from some other Europeans. They hated him because he did not wear the cloth[e]s which Europeans used to offer their boys, but he himself used to put on a suit, and he wished always to put on a suit in the Southern Rhodesia style' (Hansen 2015: 211).[6] Settling in Fort Jameson, he opened a bakery where, according to his brother, he employed most of his relatives (2015: 203). There is no doubt that experiences acquired during years of migrant labour helped create new opportunities.[7]

The suit persists in migration accounts of a later generation of men who, like Isaac Rice, returned to Zambia after working in South Africa and Southern Rhodesia during the 1950s. From the North-Western Province Makajina Kahilu, born around 1930, made the long trip overland to Johannesburg, nearly 1,800 kilometres away, largely on foot, in pursuit of a nice suit. Along the way, he made several stops on the Zambian Copperbelt, in Livingstone and Southern Rhodesia, before proceeding to Johannesburg where the 'latest fashion' was to be found. He only returned to settle in Mwinilungu, he explained, 'once he had obtained two black suits and other consumer goods, such as a saucepan radio' (Pesa 2019: 234, 294). His contemporary, Isha-Kasheweka from Barotseland (today Western Province), born in the early 1930s, was one of many local men who were recruited in the 1950s to work on the gold mines of Johannesburg, from where he returned a total of four times. When interviewed in 2009, he still had fond memories of his time in Johannesburg. He also had a suit, which he wore proudly on special occasions. Although he bought it several years after his return to Zambia from South Africa, the suit 'may still be regarded as a remaining

---

[5] Charles van Onselen comments on the rudimentary outfitting in his stirring account of the night trains that between 1902 and 1955 moved migrants from Mozambique to and from mines in South Africa (2019: 75–76).

[6] The 'Southern Rhodesia style' is likely to be a gloss for the suits worn by white male settlers.

[7] In his study of entrepreneurship during the colonial period, historian Yona Ngalaba Seleti includes 'Zilole Mawere of Chipata' among the African men who were successful in the transport business in the 1950s (Seleti 1992: 168). I believe that he might be the person described by his younger brother Zacharia in this narrative.

material artefact of his youth, a reminder of a time when he was a young, smart and very popular returning migrant, who had his bright future as an adult set out before him' (Barrett 2013: 93).

The avid desire for clothing by migrant workers is richly supported in observations that take us farther north in Zambia to the Luapula Province on the border with the Belgian Congo. During the opening decades of the twentieth century before the establishment of the Zambian copper mines, many men from Luapula migrated to Katanga in the Congo, where they acquired not only skills as workers but also experience as consumers. As hub of the Congolese mining industry, Katanga Province hosted a large European population, and it attracted African migrant workers from a wide region. In the late 1920s and early 1930s Elisabethville (today Lubumbashi) had several stores operated by Jewish and Greek traders, some of them dealing in clothing with the city's growing African population (Fabian 1990: 99–101). Large volumes of textiles and clothing were imported to satisfy the demands of both the European and African populations.

When men from Luapula described their migration experiences in Katanga, it was the availability of attractive clothing that made a difference to what through the 1920s were rough and dangerous years of mine work (Higginson 1989). While many young men were recruited to perform contract labour on the mines, some went on the long journey on their own. Others worked as domestic servants and still others learned how to tailor. Many workers spent the cash part of their wages on material goods, especially on clothing. Lasaila Nkandu remembered: 'These labourers also came back fairly well off, especially as regarded clothes. They spent all the francs that they were paid on clothes' (Musambachime 1996: 71).

In accounts by elderly residents of Luapula Province, the provincial headquarters of Mansa and tailors come together in a striking way.[8] When the town slowly grew during the first quarter of the twentieth century, its limited African employment scene included building construction and lowly jobs related to the administration such as messengers and office orderlies. In addition, according to R. Chungu Kanswe, 'In Mansa a common job was that of house-boy ... [and] some people were employed as tailors in the stores' (Musambachime 1996: 52).

---

[8] This oral history project was conducted by the Department of History at the University of Zambia by second-year students Raben Chanda and Daniel Yambayamba in Mansa District in Luapula province in 1974. This chapter refers to the published version (Musambachime 1996).

As a young man, Sebio Mulenga had come to Mansa from Mporokoso in the Northern Province to join a 'brother'. 'We hoped to get some employment at the boma [administrative headquarters] and learn various trades or skills.... It was common for young men to go on long journeys in search of jobs and wealth' (Musambachime 1996: 21). Working initially as a kitchen helper, he learned tailoring from a well-known tailor from Nyasaland (Malawi) who took him on as an apprentice. Between 1918 and the early 1920s, young Mulenga travelled widely in search of jobs, working briefly in Ndola on the Copperbelt and in Broken Hill before finally returning to Mansa. But tailoring jobs did not last long, because he did not have his own machine. 'I worked as a tailor in Ndola but did not stay long on the first job because my white employer did not provide me with a sewing machine.... There was nobody I knew who could lend me a sewing machine' (Musambachime 1996: 21). Then he heard that Mandala Stores in Broken Hill needed a tailor.[9] He was interviewed but did not get the job because he did not own a sewing machine (Musambachime 1996: 22). When a white man lent him a machine, he got the job in Broken Hill, only to leave it almost immediately to take up employment with Thom's Stores in Ndola, who required a qualified tailor. Thom's Stores soon sent him to Mansa, along with two men to carry the sewing machine and his personal belongings. They walked the approximately 250 kilometres. In 1923, when he was 23 years old, he was employed at Boot's Store in Mansa. 'There were few tailors then', Sebio Mulenga recalled. He was paid by the number of shorts he sewed on a daily or a monthly basis. When working fast, he recalled, he earned 'too much for a black man during the colonial days' (Musambachime 1996: 23).

J. B. Mwansabombwe also worked 'for Mandala', beginning in 1934. 'Because I was too young, I was assigned the duty of fixing buttons on garments. When I became a little older, I became a tailor. From tailoring, I was placed behind the counter to help sell items in the store. Later I was promoted.... I supervised the twenty-two tailors that Mandala employed in the store. I was given yards of cloth, which I cut into pieces and distributed among the tailors' (Musambachime 1996: 23). Among the many tailors Wilson found in Broken Hill during the late 1930s, it was 'very difficult for any but a highly skilled tailor to secure ... employment unless he brings his own machine' (1942: 36). Some tailors in

---

[9] Mandala Stores were established by the African Lakes Corporation, a trading company based in Malawi that also had stores in Northern and Luapula Provinces in Northern Rhodesia. The Mandala Store in Mansa was established in 1909 (Musambachime 1996: 26).

commercial employment, he noted, used their own machines on Sundays in order to make an extra income (1942: 36). To be sure, growing towns like Mansa and Broken Hill were crucial settings for jobs, trades, skills acquisition, and consumption. In such towns, stores and tailors found eager customers in the returned migrant workers for whom clothing was a high-priority consumer item, both for their personal use and as a desirable commodity to be taken to the rural areas.

Clothing Consumption and Availability

One afternoon in 1995 during my research in Luapula Province, my local research assistant Damiano Chonganya and I made a courtesy call on Damiano's grandfather. After serving in the Congolese army on the Belgian side of the border during World War I, Chonganya senior had married a woman from Luapula, and together they returned to Mansa, where he set himself up as a building contractor. Recalling his youth, he told us that guns, bicycles, and sewing machines were the imported industrial products that African men had to have if they were to achieve economic success in the changing context of everyday life in colonial Northern Rhodesia during the first half of the twentieth century (Hansen 2013a: 167). Damiano's father, in turn, born around the time of World War I, learned to tailor from a 'brother' in the Congo. He returned to Luapula, went to mission school, and later found work at the Mandala Stores in Mansa, where he advanced from tailor to office orderly (Hansen 2013a: 171).

From the point of view of labour outfitters and many European employers, shorts were 'the clothes boys used to wear'. But African men preferred wearing long trousers and suits and they went to great lengths to obtain them. The tailor enters our account here as does the technology of imported sewing machines. In the late nineteenth century and first quarter of the twentieth century some sewing machines made the long overland journey from ports in South Africa, where Singer had a subsidiary, to Northern Rhodesia. Other machines would have arrived from Elisabethville in Katanga, the cultural and economic hub of the region until well after the opening of the Copperbelt mines in the late 1920s (Hansen 2013a: 169–70). Translating clothing needs and desires into desirable garments, tailors contributed importantly to the process of making Africans knowledgeable and discriminating consumers of clothing.[10] In the early years, Sebio Mulenga recalled, tailors sewed

---

[10] Elizabeth Fretwell (2018) offers rich observations about the history and development of the tailor's craft and tailored clothing in Benin from the pre-colonial kingdom of

men's everyday wear such as khaki shorts, shirts, and uniforms, and women's plain dresses. But for strolling around the town, men did not want to wear shorts but 'a new pair of trousers of distinguished appearance' (Wilson 1942: 18). Tailors made a wide range of Western-styled garments. As a result of new dress sensibilities, the repertoire of tailors expanded to include garments that required more skill and attention to individual client desire in the design of suits and elaborately styled dresses.

During the colonial period when most wage labour was performed by men, the tailor's work was constructed as a man's job in cultural terms that reflected the gender division in the migrant labour system in the wider region. As we just saw, young men learned to tailor from senior tailors, some of them migrants from neighbouring Malawi, and some from India. Many were employed by storekeepers and could be seen working on porches outside the stores. Some were hired, others worked on commission, and still others set themselves up in the African residential areas or walked around with their machines, offering their services. In effect, the tailor's craft was an important activity that enabled men to find urban employment almost anywhere.

Labour migration and urban living turned Africans into active consumers. In the growing cities and towns they acquired not only knowledge about consumption practices but also insights into how and where to pursue them (see Figure 2.1). Racially segregated consumption spaces and shopping venues had markets and stores where African urban residents could purchase clothing and apparel. In fact, they spent a good portion of their cash earnings on clothing, as Wilson reported from Broken Hill in the late 1930s when mine workers spent more than half of the cash portion of their wages on clothes (Wilson 1942: 80). He also noted that nearly every African worker pooled his wages with a partner, alternately, each month. 'Giving chance', as his research assistant Zacharia Mawere described this rotating credit arrangement, compels a person to go into debt by lending to another during one month while getting more money in the month when it is due to himself (Hansen 2015: 208). A worker might spend a single wage packet far too easily, whereas a pooled sum enabled him to purchase larger items 'like a suit, which he really needs badly' (Wilson 1942: 77).

The bulk of the clothes were sold in European and Indian-owned stores and sourced 'on the world market from Japan, America and

Dahomey through the mid-twentieth century. She describes apprenticeship, interaction with imported secondhand clothing, and the growing entry of women in the occupation, as well as changes in men's and women's dress practice.

Figure 2.1 Men in suits. Employees of a dry-cleaning establishment in Lusaka in the 1950s. Photo by Peter Fraenkel, reproduced with permission.

Europe' (Wilson 1942: 20). The local African markets also featured clothes sellers, most likely of secondhand garments referred to then as *kombo*, perhaps named after Mokambo, a border town between the Copperbelt and Belgian Congo (Hansen 2000a: 60–76). Unlike Northern Rhodesia, where the import of secondhand clothing was prohibited, the Congo allowed it, and used clothing appears to have been readily available from at least the 1920s in the Congo. A growing informal trade to Northern Rhodesia developed in the 1930s, if not earlier, and onwards (Davis [1933] 1968: 42).[11] The heyday of the secondhand clothing trade from the Congo into Luapula and the Copperbelt was during World War II and immediately thereafter, especially from the

[11] This was part of a two-way trade in fish from Luapula to the Katanga mines in the Congo and secondhand clothes, imported from North America and Europe into the Congo and taken across the border into Northern Rhodesia. For details, see Hansen (2000a: 60–70).

1940s through the early 1950s, when war-related import quotas made new clothing and textiles both scarce and expensive. During those years African men from Northern Rhodesia and beyond travelled to Mokambo, other border-crossing points, and all the way to Elisabethville in Katanga to purchase *kombo* to resell back home.

The most famous of the many people who explored the Congo connection is undoubtedly Kenneth Kaunda, Zambia's first president. In his autobiography, Kaunda explained how he and his wife 'determined to work together to improve our standard of living' when they both worked at a boarding school in Mufulira on the Copperbelt in 1948. 'We decided to buy second-hand clothes from Mokambo ... and send them up to my home [Chinsali in the Northern Province] to be sold for a small profit.... Each person [at that time] was only allowed to bring back one jacket and one dress or shirt.... I would organise a group of schoolboys and on a Saturday afternoon we would cross the border at Mokambo and come back wearing the strangest assortment of clothes' (Kaunda 1962: 30). In 1949 the Kaundas moved back to Chinsali, where Kaunda became active in political mass mobilisation. His savings enabled him to obtain the three things he needed most urgently in this transition: a bicycle to move about and attend meetings, a watch to be on time for meetings, and a sewing machine to repair whatever secondhand goods needed mending (1962: 36).

Because of the limited scale of the colony's domestic textile and garment manufacture, African consumers turned to other sources to obtain clothing. Mail-order firms in Britain were a very popular source for new and stylish clothing. During the late 1930s, some miners in Broken Hill placed orders with well-established mail-order firms, for example, John Noble, Lennards, and Oxendale. Showing Wilson an invoice, Wilson Mundulu, a member of the African Welfare Association, told him: 'My average is four times a year. Just now another parcel is coming.' In the home of William Busuka, a miner and tribal elder, Wilson saw several mail-order receipts from Oxendale for purchases between 1936 and 1939, one of them for an alarm clock.[12] The orders included more men's garments than women's, for items such as suits, shirts, trousers, hats and caps, and shoes. Among women's garments were requests for blouses, petticoats, and cardigans. Some orders included blankets (Hansen 2015: 211).

---

[12] With their associations, these two men held positions of authority in the developing African community in the mining settlement. Tribal elders advised white managers of mining compounds about disputes and customary practices. See Epstein (1992a: 42–48).

African miners on the Copperbelt also were keen customers of mail-order firms in Britain. J. M. Davis described how in 1932 several workers would pool their orders to avoid paying individual processing fees. He explained mail-order purchases as a defensive strategy 'as throughout Northern Rhodesia the prices charged Natives by White and Indian store-keepers are ethically unjustifiable … It is short-sighted mercantile policy and will act as a boomerang on the [Northern] Rhodesian trader' (Davis [1933] 1968: 73–74). During World War II, when import quotas and currency restrictions reduced the volume and variety of clothing locally available, Africans eagerly turned to mail-order firms abroad. R. B. J. Moore, a missionary from the London Missionary Society, observed in the early 1940s that a 'man in town becomes a catalogue fiend. Overseas mails are loaded with catalogues from Oxendales and other mail order firms. Almost any evening a group of men may be seen in a compound or location sitting on dirty boxes poring over a catalogue for clothes, while one who can write makes out the order' (1948: 57–58).[13]

During her field research among the rural Bemba in the early 1930s, British social anthropologist Audrey Richards was struck by the constant talking about clothes ([1939] 1969: 16–18). A clay figure of a smartly dressed 'young man in European clothes with a hat on' even featured in a song accompanying a performance of a girls' initiation ceremony she observed in 1931 ([1956] 2021: 103, 210). Wilson highlighted the attraction of clothing at the urban end, pointing out that Africans in Broken Hill discussed clothes 'unceasingly, in much the same way that … villagers discuss their cattle' (1942: 18). And during her research in Luanshya on the Copperbelt in 1953 and 1954, American cultural anthropologist Hortense Powdermaker found clothing to be 'a perennial subject of conversation and for boasting'. Her paraphrase of a conversation between two miners in 1954 provides an example of the type of garments Africans purchased from mail-order catalogues as well as of local reactions to their acquisition. The focus of attention was an overcoat from Oxendale. One of the men described three other overcoats featured in the catalogue, adding, '[T]hey are not good. The one this man ordered is beautiful. In June [the winter in this part of Africa] he will be wearing it to the beer hall, since he is a strong drinker, and people will all be looking at him. The coat is brown in color and has very long hair. If he wears it in town, policemen can be asking where he got it [theft suspected].

---

[13] Critical of and outspoken against colonial and mine policies towards African urban workers and education, Moore was transferred to a rural area in 1941. By the time of his early death in 1943, Moore was preparing a doctoral thesis in social anthropology at London University. See Morrow (1989).

The other day when he put it on, three Europeans asked him where he got it. Ah, it is wonderful.' Both men wanted such a coat, one of them wishing to order it before his next visit to his village: 'People at home will just fall off the chair when they see that coat' (1962: 94–95).

Migrants spent a good part of their cloth-related cash expenditure on purchasing clothing for relatives and dependents. In fact, migrants brought, or sent, a profusion of clothes to their relatives, judging from detailed accounts of the contents of travel kits belonging to African workers returning from migrant labour on the Copperbelt to villages in the early 1930s (Davis [1933] 1968: 401–2). The amount and variety of clothing in the travel kits illustrate the high value attached to clothes by both migrants and people in their home villages. When he was around 16 years old in 1949, Sindikani Phiri left home in the Eastern Province to seek work in Southern Rhodesia. He first worked on a dairy farm, then in a shoe factory. 'When I was in Southern Rhodesia', he explained, 'I was earning good money and on returning [in 1951] I had thirteen pounds, a bicycle and other things, such as shorts, [long] trousers, six shirts and a jacket' (Marwick 1974: 145). In Broken Hill in the late 1930s Duncan C[h]anda showed Wilson a list of goods, including their costs, he had taken with him on a visit to his home village, including one blanket, one cloth, four dresses, and two cloths for his mother.[14] On another visit, he brought along several dresses and lots of cloths. In 1936 William Busuka sent his young brother home with money and clothes for his parents, including cloth for his mother and mother-in-law (Hansen 2015: 41).[15]

In a situation where access to a wider world of manufactured goods was restrained, clothing remained an important source of wealth and served as a means of exchange. Taken together, low wages, the rising cost of living, and wartime restrictions on many types of manufactured goods made accumulations of clothing the one sure saving option. 'If they [miners] have clothes saved up', Wilson noted, 'they can convert a dismissal into an honourable journey home'. He estimated that at any moment, there was 'about £6,000 worth of unused clothes, or of cash saved up for buying clothes'. 'These clothes are kept', he elaborated, sometimes in boxes in their own homes, sometimes in the stores where they were purchased (Wilson 1942: 18). A legal ordinance from 1915 regulated the box system that enabled workers to accumulate clothing in stores either for safekeeping or as a security against payment

[14] Chanda is a common Bemba name as both first name and family name. Wilson writes it as Canda. In Chibemba the 'ch' sound is often written with the letter 'c.'

[15] The references to cloths are likely to mean pieces of fabric, typically two yards long, commonly used as wrappers.

(Hansen 2000a: 35). It also provided a convenient storage arrangement for the many migrants who lived in single quarters, sharing dormitory-style accommodation (so-called bachelor housing) with many other male workers with limited access to private space.

The function of clothing as a store of wealth folded up in boxes in stores, pushed under beds, placed on top of rafters, put in inexpensive suitcases (listed in travel kits), or tied up in bundles of wrapped cloth gradually gave way to a growing concern with the individual in the urban context. Developments in society at large during World War II and after made the box system obsolete, and in 1948 the legal ordinance that had regulated it was repealed (Hansen 2000a: 35). In the meantime, more women had come to town, many of them wanting to be consumers in their own right rather than having husbands purchase clothes for them. They wanted stylish dresses in fashion rather than plain frocks with yokes and puffed sleeves. By the mid-twentieth century when war-time restrictions on imports had been lifted, African urban residents were able to purchase clothing from several sources: imported factory-made, imported secondhand from the Congo, locally produced by small-scale tailors, and, to a very limited extent, manufactured in local factories. Indeed, tailors experienced brisk business, judging from the steep rise in the import of sewing machines (Hansen 2013a: 174). By then, the significance of clothing as wealth had been almost entirely overridden by its role as a commodity with a value determined by the supply and demand of the market.

'What I want is a dress'

Where were African women in discussions of clothing during the late colonial period? Ellie Mukonko had been involved in selling *kombo* from the Congo in Luapula villages during the 1940s. When I interviewed this elderly man in Mansa in 1995, he told me that because women had had more limited access to clothing than men who had been migrant workers, they often pressed special orders on him and his young co-workers. 'What I want is a dress' was a common order with specification of size and style (Hansen 2000a: 36). At least three factors are involved in pushing women onto the side-lines of this era's clothing discussion, helping to hide the story of African women's active engagement with clothing. One is the deeply gendered history of clothing consumption, which through labour migration drew in African men much earlier than African women. Another concerns normative assumptions about gender and authority that constructed men as heads of households and in charge of clothing transfers to wives and dependents. A third issue arises from the available sources that, although they were not all written by men, overwhelmingly report the opinions of men, African as well as European, about African women's clothing needs and desires, as demonstrated with the exceptional example of a woman missionary I briefly describe below.

Mabel Shaw, a missionary from the London Missionary Society, is well known in Zambia for instilling notions of female domesticity in her pupils at Mbereshi, one of the first colonial boarding schools for girls, which she founded in Luapula Province at the beginning of the twentieth century. Her sartorial agenda advanced modest dress such as simple frocks for girls and double wrappers of cotton and calico worn with headscarves for adult women. But when visiting the Copperbelt in 1931 she was appalled that former schoolgirls had stopped wearing mission-prescribed clothes. Seeing their stylish dresses, high-heeled shoes, and cigarette smoking as evidence of the corrupting effects of modern urban life on Christian lives, she did not grasp how former students embraced elegant attire as well as Christian values to claim social respectability and important church positions in the rapidly changing urban areas (Kalusa 2022: 61–75).

Although they were not supposed to, women lived in the mining areas from the earliest years (Chauncey 1981: 142). They certainly spoke by their action, leaving the villages as men had done previously, even though chiefs during the 1930s had the right to deny them permission to travel to towns and some set up road blocks on travel routes to enforce the ruling (Parpart 1994: 247). And urban authorities had the right to 'repatriate' unaccompanied women and children to the villages. During these same years, labour relations were tense, especially on the Copperbelt as Broken Hill did not experience the strikes that unsettled the north in the mid-1930s and again in 1940 (Henderson 1975). Recognising the stabilising influence of the presence of spouses on labour turnover and men's interactions when away from work, mine and township authorities began to provide 'married housing' for their workers, first on the Broken Hill mine and later on the Copperbelt. Plots of land were also made available for women to cultivate as a means to improve men's food rations or to sell produce in the market. We know very little about women who held wage labour jobs except that few worked as domestic servants (Hansen 1989). Conducting informal economic activities such as beer brewing, fish trading, and food preparation, some women reduced their dependence on men, establishing greater authority in their own right (Chauncey 1981: 142–44).

Residing with relatives in municipal townships, some single women moved in with miners for a while, providing domestic and sexual services (Chauncey 1981: 151). Proof of marriage was not required, and with the uneven urban sex ratio, many relationships were temporary. Wilson reported from Broken Hill that women were 'normally ... found to be living with their second or third husbands' (Wilson 1942: 41). As a young woman from the Eastern Province explained to Zacharia Mawere, Wilson's research assistant: 'I like when we come on the line [the north-south railway line] to be married to several husbands ... the reason being to have more cloth[e]s'. 'I feel very much pleased to have money for beer drinking and to buy everything I like. But at home in Fort Jameson I cannot do this.' 'Men and women', Mawere commented, 'always appreciate the building of a person and richness just when he or she is well dressed' (Hansen 2015: 205).

There is one platform where women stepped into fuller view in a discourse that casts some light on the significance of clothing in their everyday lives. That is the native courts in both rural and urban areas, at which some people who brought their domestic troubles spoke about their conjugal relations and problems in the language of clothes. The native courts were the lowest judicial bodies in Zambia's legal hierarchy, with jurisdiction over civil disputes under customary law, involving such issues as marital and property claims (Epstein 1953). British legal anthropologist Arnold Epstein, who pioneered the study of the development of the legal system during the late colonial period, suggested that in many respects 'the urban courts were following, as much as creating, Copperbelt practice' (1981: 279). Supervised by a presiding justice, who at times sat with several court justices, none of whom were trained lawyers but were considered knowledgeable about customary law, the native courts dealt with matters that relatives, church members, and other informal mediation efforts had proved incapable of resolving (Hansen 1997: 118–40).

In court, women's dress, or lack thereof, was a barometer of the quality of conjugality and gender relations that was immediately understandable to the African court councillors and the people attending court. Martha and her husband David, for example, had been quarrelling because Martha had a lover. In the suit he brought against her for desertion in a Plateau Tonga native court in the late 1940s, David explained that Martha had returned her clothes when she refused to have intercourse. When David discovered that she had a lover, he explained that then he knew 'that was what gave her power to refuse the clothes I bought for her'. But Martha, who never had become pregnant during their four years of marriage, argued that it was David who had taken her clothes. 'Why do you take my clothes when we fight?' she asked (Colson 1958: 194). In the court's assessment, David's behaviour demonstrated his lack of authority over Martha. He had not even completed the bride wealth payments for her. In this case the court granted a divorce (Colson 1958: 193–205).

In one of many urban cases from the mid-1950s demonstrating a husband's lack of support, Brenda asked for divorce in the Ndola Urban Court on the grounds that her husband frequently beat her, did not provide her with 'traditional' medicine to facilitate conception, and above all that he 'did not clothe her' (Epstein 1981: 82). Mangaleti went to the same court, also seeking divorce, and her case reveals some of the charged meanings of clothing in the context of urban everyday life. She explained how her husband had supported her when she first came to live with him: 'My husband would give me 20s [shillings] out of his earnings. But after I had taken only a shilling to buy relish [vegetables/meat] he would come and take the rest off me and spend it on beer. One day my mother took the 20s which he had given me, and I used some of it to buy two dresses. I put the dresses away in the hut and then when I came back later, I found that he had burned them' (Epstein 1992b: 26).

It seems from the court record that the husband, Cewe, was playing around. Given the evidence, Mangaleti's father alleged that his son-in-law 'was fornicating with every girl he saw'. Cewe had brought Mangaleti back to her parents when she insisted that she still wanted to remain with him. The father-in-law's version of the clothing purchase referred to a quarrel. Cewe had become furious when Mangaleti returned from the store with two dresses: 'No, you only had £1. There's no one who can buy two dresses for £1.' Mangaleti's father went on to explain how Cewe then 'took the dresses, tore them up and burned them because of his jealousy' (Epstein 1992b: 27).

Two dresses rather than one, purchased for an amount that would not cover their cost, meant to Cewe that someone else, a man, had given them to Mangaleti. But the court showed little sympathy. Wasting his money on beer, Cewe had not kept his wife properly. He had not given her sufficient money for herself, and he had been rude towards her parents. Judging that he had not fulfilled his obligation to care for her, the court ordered Cewe to compensate Mangaleti because he destroyed the dresses and admonished him to honour and respect his in-laws (Epstein 1992b: 31–32).

In another case, also from Ndola, a husband who had taken a third wife was brought to court by his two senior wives for not supporting them properly. As one of them explained, 'we have no dresses, and here on the railway line we have to look smart' (Epstein 1954: 31–34). Indeed, as Wilson noted, some women did 'judge husbands and lovers according to the amounts of money they are given to spend on clothes' (1942: 18). There was the cultural expectation, as Martha's and Brenda's cases illustrate, that husbands provide wives with clothes. The nature of the male–female relationship was both expressed and reconfigured through clothing. The normative expectation that men dress women has a reverse side that provoked David to take back the clothes he had bought for Martha when he realised that she had a lover. It also gave rise to the kind of suspicion Cewe expressed over the question of who pays for women's dresses and particularly if their clothes look expensive or extravagant. Court cases like these capture some of the charged tensions in gender relations on the domestic front and beyond, fuelled among other things by women's growing consumption abilities and the availability of new dress options.

New Look Dresses

The developments I have described here took place against the backdrop of a rapidly changing scene in the post–World War II years. The economy expanded. More family housing was built in towns, and women who migrated to towns alone were no longer sent back to the villages. When women came to towns in larger numbers during and after World War II, they went for the new fashions with abandon (Parpart 1994: 250–54). By that time, wearing modern clothing had become common among girls and women on the Copperbelt (Kalusa 2022: 63). A report on the commercial prospects of Northern Rhodesia in the early 1950s, when African purchasing power had improved somewhat, noted that a man's 'first expenditure is on clothing for himself and his womenfolk and the latter usually see to it that they are not overlooked … [The African] woman … attaches considerable importance to matters of design, style and fashion in her dress goods and she generally knows just what she wants in the way of cloth[ing] when she goes shopping' (Hansen 2013a: 174). Of high priority in women's dress choices, styles and designs resonated with popular culture, as articulated in a song in town English and Chinyanja by Alick Nkhata, the most famous vocal artist of the 1950s, in which a domestic servant sought to entice a woman by promising her plenty of 'New Look' dresses (*ama new look ni plenti*):

> Come live with me in the yards [the white residential areas].
> You're gonna get bread an' butter
> I have everything
> New Look in Plenty.
> You will have so many dresses
> You'll be changing clothes all day.
>
> If we two appear in public,
> young men will be shaking
> because of your beautiful clothes (excerpt from Hansen 1989: 163–64)

Recognizing that African women were in towns to stay, the colonial government began working on two fronts: establishing basic and secondary schools for girls whose education lagged far behind that of boys, and organising domestic science teaching programmes, especially in towns, for adult women in order to make them into better wives and mothers (Hansen 1992). The sewing machine enters here as a technology to enable women's home craft (see Figure 2.2).

The colonial welfare department, established during the 1950s, introduced domestic science classes in urban townships as the mining companies had already done on the Copperbelt. With the 'winds of change' now blowing across this part of Africa, a variety of training centres were established to hone the domestic skills of women who were, or might become, wives of 'advanced' Africans and the new men in power.

A result of these new developments is captured beautifully in a framed photograph I saw in 1995 on the wall of a small restaurant in Kashikishi, the lakeside town in Luapula Province that served as an entrepot for various sorts of commerce between Zambia and the Congo (then Zaire),

Figure 2.2 Bringing the sewing machine home, 1959. Courtesy of Livingstone Museum.

where my research assistant Damiano Chonganya and I were exploring the history of the trade in *kombo* (secondhand clothing) across the border. In a striking composition, the studio photograph, probably taken in the late 1960s or early 1970s, depicts the female owner of the restaurant. Wearing a tailored *chitenge* (colourful printed fabric) dress, she is seated in an upholstered chair adorned with antimacassars (locally referred to as doilies). And there on the table in front of her stands a portable hand-operated sewing machine, a conspicuous visual presence, ready to take pride of place as a domestic appliance, contributing to a new living room aesthetic. With this photographic image, we have come full circle, bringing the sewing machine home, domesticating it. What is more, as we shall see in Part III of this book, by then the sewing machine was no longer an important means only for men to establish themselves. It also had become a strategic technology that women used to move up in society.

3   Dressing for Freedom

The smartly dressed returned migrant unsettled the role of clothing consumption in marking social difference in the racially divided colonial situation. We saw an example in the previous chapter through the hostile reactions of local whites to Herbert Zilole Mawere's clothing on his return from Southern Rhodesia to Fort Jameson sometime in the 1920s. In the late 1930s Godfrey Wilson described how reactions of white residents to the adoption and display of European dress by Africans in Broken Hill 'now angers, now bores and now amuses them' (1942: 19). Although he himself was an astute observer of African preoccupations with clothing, Wilson may not completely have grasped the sensibilities behind the appeal of Western clothes.

One day in 1940 during his field research in Broken Hill, a slight tiff developed between Wilson and his personal servant when he declined the servant's request for a pay advance. The servant wanted to purchase formal evening wear in order to attend a ballroom dance competition between the local dance club and visiting dance clubs from the Copperbelt. Distraught, he lamented: 'These people are coming here from the copper belt and we don't know *what* [italics in the original] they will ... be wearing; I simply must have some proper clothes' (Wilson 1942: 19). Wilson's reaction is surprising as it was a common practice in domestic employment to advance a portion of a worker's wage for specific purposes (Hansen 1989: 269–73). More important for my purpose here, the African dress sensibilities in play in this request were not immediately apparent to Wilson. Nor did the panel that in the early 1940s discussed a report on African urban costs of living understand how clothing mattered. The preliminary report on a minimum standard of living suggesting that African women should have several dresses did not sit well with the colonial authorities (Hansen 2000a: 43–44). A. L. Saffrey, who had conducted the research and authored the report, explained: 'The house to house investigation showed that most women have at least five or six dresses. These dresses are constantly worn, usually in rotation, and cannot be regarded as capital goods accumulated for presents when visiting the villages. An old dress is occasionally given away to a relative, but nowhere did one find stocks of new clothes such as were found by Godfrey Wilson at Broken Hill' in the late 1930s (Hansen 2000a: 36).

By this time, as Saffrey had noted, clothing no longer served as a store of wealth. But the demand and supply forces of the market did not entirely drive clothing consumption, as I suggested in the previous chapter. Far from it. From being a rare thing, clothing had become a necessity that people craved. And a well-dressed appearance was about much more than dollars and cents. The post–World War II years were a turning point for access and urban African women commonly had more than one dress, just as the khaki suit no longer satisfied wage-employed men. Women and men eagerly put themselves together with clothing they appropriated from a wide range of domestic and foreign sources: shops, stores, and hawkers; tailors; mail-order firms; locally obtained second-hand clothing; and imported *kombo*. In Alick Nkhata's song about New Look dresses, young onlookers shook with delight and women changed clothing all day. And Powdermaker's visiting miner had villagers fall off their chairs when looking at a well-dressed person who, in Wilson's words, astonished the world with 'clothing of distinguished appearance' (1942: 18).

Dress Performance

In the late 1940s the copper mining industry prospered. Strikes in 1935 and during the 1940s and early 1950s had led to the formation of African trade unions and, in the late 1940s, to wage increases. The change in the mid-1950s to a cash-only wage instead of a combination of cash and food rations affected purchasing power by giving people more money to handle (Hansen 2000a: 46). The slow development of African education expanded beyond the mission to include government- and mining company-supported schools, and between 1948 and 1958 the number of secondary schools increased (Powdermaker 1962: 277). Girls' education continued to lag behind that of boys. While few African women were wage employed, many carried out small-scale trade activities in and around homes, streets, and markets. Husbands did not always approve of such activities, and domestic relationships, judging from colonial scholarship of the period, were often fraught as I described in the previous chapter when conflict over men's normative control reached court because of women's desire for dresses (Epstein 1981; Kalusa 2013: 160–62; Powdermaker 1962). Urban African housing construction, including houses for families, expanded rapidly in both mine and municipal townships where most recreation activities were organised by the welfare centres. A range of sports clubs, especially football, the cinema, and women's clubs promoting housekeeping and tailoring, provided spaces for social mixing as did the mining and municipal beer halls that generated revenue for welfare activities oriented towards Africans (Ambler 1990: 296–97). Although women's brewing and selling of traditional beer had been illegal since the 1930s, all townships had *shebeens* where different types of beer and distilled alcohol were available.[1] Some urban residents attended church service every Sunday, dressing in their 'Sunday best' (Epstein 1981: 106). The radio was popular with many programs in local languages (Fraenkel 1959; Powdermaker 1962). And there was dance: traditional, ballroom, and jive.

Contemporary and more recent scholarship has explored several dimensions of the rich popular culture of leisure that developed around such activities, casting light, for example, on how football and films enabled players and audiences to question the racial divide that structured many aspects of their daily lives and helped inspire visions of a different world (Ambler 2001; Chipande 2016; Powdermaker 1962).[2] These same years witnessed a hardening of political attitudes, influenced greatly by the opposition of Africans in Northern Rhodesia to the Central African Federation, which the colonial office made their country part of from 1953 to 1963, together with Southern Rhodesia (today Zimbabwe) and Nyasaland (today Malawi).

Clearly, in their active engagement with a changing social and political world in which Europeans were no longer the chief arbiters of style, Africans had made European dress conventions their own. In effect, clothing mediated new aspirations about finding one's place and respect in the changing society through display and eye-catching styling that made its European origin merely one of many inspirations. Knowledge about clothing consumption was above all practical knowledge, acquired from participation in group activities and individual networks in urban life both at work and at home, in recreation and entertainment, and at markets and in streets. The effects of dress were produced in performance, by people presenting themselves for display and knowing that they looked good, for example, when strolling around town, in markets and beer halls, at dances, and during country visits. In such interactions the visual impact of being noticed was always in focus, involving a sharp eye

---

[1] *Shebeens* are places where alcohol is sold without a licence. The term was widely used across southern Africa and is suggested to derive from *sibín* in Irish, referring to illegal whiskey.
[2] For an overview of popular culture, see Becker (2012).

for detail, active recall of bodies in dress, and constant and detailed talk about clothing matters. We may catch glimpses of how this worked in some of the urban studies undertaken during the late colonial period and in more recent works on leisure.

We begin in the early 1950s, right at the outset of the federation, when Arnold Epstein conducted research in the copper mining town Luanshya. Here, Epstein realised that leisure-time activities perhaps gave the clearest indication of how the changing African urban communities were coming to terms with the new sets of relations and changes in their own culture (Epstein 1958: 9).[3] The beer hall, he noted, was an important setting and with repeated visits

> a pattern begins to emerge. Young men, dressed in gaily-coloured open-necked shirts, and wearing cowboy hats, squat on the ground or move around strumming a guitar and singing the latest Copperbelt 'hit-numbers' or otherwise seek to gain the attention of the *bakapenta* [from the English word 'to paint,' often used for prostitute], the 'young ladies of the town'.... In another group, some of the town's leading personalities, all smartly dressed in lounge suits are engaged in quiet conversation in English with a well-known African visitor from Kitwe or Lusaka. They gossip about personalities and discuss the political news from other towns, and they make arrangements for later meetings in their private homes. (1958: 10)[4]

A footnote explaining 'hit-numbers' invites explanation as it opens a window onto the world beyond the colony towards which Africans were orienting themselves. Epstein explains: 'Many of the songs derive from the "hill-billy" type of cowboy song but re-interpreted in terms of African musical idiom. Gramophone records of these songs have a very wide sale' (1958: 10). There is no doubt that the 'hill-billy' type of music Epstein referred to is that of American singer-songwriter Jimmie Rodgers (1897–1933), the biggest star on the American popular music scene between 1927 and 1933, the father of country music.[5] Anthropologist John Barnes used a photograph from his research among the Ngoni in the Eastern Province during the mid-1940s to depict young men dressed in collared shirts and T-shirts, dancing. The caption reads: 'A Jimi Roja dance at an installation ceremony. This dance, named after an American dance leader, is allowed only on important occasions' (Barnes 1959, plate 15; Hansen 2000a: 54).[6]

---

[3] See Phyllis Martin's magisterial study of leisure during the colonial period in Congo Brazzaville (1995).
[4] Kalusa discusses some elements in this scene (2013: 147).
[5] According to one source who describes its appropriation by the Kipsigis in Kenya, missionaries brought records with Jimmie Rodgers' music to East Africa (Petrusich 2017).
[6] Thanks to Roger Sanjek for pointing this photograph out to me.

Young men wearing cowboy hats, listening to hillbilly-style cowboy songs in Epstein's beer hall scene, demonstrate how influences from American Westerns had spilled into popular culture in colonial Northern Rhodesia, 'following filmgoers into the streets and houses and eventually back to their rural home villages' (Ambler 2001: 99) as in the Jimi Roja dance performed in a Ngoni village in the 1940s. The cinema, locally referred to as the bioscope, offered Africans in Northern Rhodesia a medium that reached beyond their colonial horizon with images of cultural styles and influences from a much wider world. By the late 1930s, outdoor film shows were an established feature in mining and municipal townships, mixing entertainment and current events. A mobile film unit began touring the countryside in 1942. The films were heavily cut to avoid images or story lines censors imagined might challenge the race-based colonial order (Ambler 2001: 82, 88).

Of all film genres, American cowboy movies were the most popular. Drawing on observations made by Harry Franklin, the Director of Information Services, historian Charles Ambler describes a common sight in streets and alleys on the Copperbelt of groups of young Africans 'dressed in home-made paper "chaps" and cowboy hats, and carrying crudely carved wooden pistols' playing cowboys and Indians.[7] They shouted 'Jeke, Jeke', the local expression for 'Jack', the term audiences gave to all heroes in cowboy films, and a tribute to actor Jack Holt. The influence of Westerns and gangster films was also evident, according to Franklin, on young men wearing 'ten-gallon hats, kerchiefs, and so forth' (Ambler 2001: 81; Powdermaker 1962: 261–62).

Hortense Powdermaker, who explored African reactions to films in Luanshya in the early 1950s, suggested that the 'cowboy has become part of the African world and has even taken on African characteristics. He is supposed to have witchcraft, to be the son of a "big" man, and to show traditional respect toward elders' (Powdermaker 1962: 263). Popular in many cities across Africa during the 1940s, the appeal of Hollywood Westerns to urban youth had to do in part with the films' ritualization of violence as well as with their performance of a type of masculinity that was neither traditional nor colonial (Burton 2001; Gondola 2016).[8]

Radio listening was popular, available in the town welfare centres and at home on an inexpensive battery-operated set known as the Saucepan

---

[7] Chaps are leather trousers without a seat, worn by cowboys over ordinary trousers to protect the legs.

[8] In Leopoldville in the Congo during the 1940s, they called themselves Bills, in a take on Buffalo Bill. Celebrating fighting and body building, they wore cowboy hats and other elements of cowboy dress in their critique of the colonial system (Gondola 2016).

Special, introduced during the late 1940s, and on electric radios once houses were wired. Among the transmissions were programmes in several local languages, local and foreign news, message requests, educational talks, sport reports, stories and plays, and the most popular of all, music and songs. One of the African radio announcers, Alick Nkhata, had experience with music. Demobilising from World War II after serving as a sergeant in Burma, he had worked with renowned ethnomusicologist Hugh Tracey, touring the region and recording local music (Fraenkel 1959: 51). Joining the Central African Broadcasting Service in the 1950s, Nkhata composed and performed songs on the radio alone or with his quartet and presented live shows in town welfare halls, singing of the new Africa. Extraordinarily gifted in capturing the town life spirit of the time, he translated traditional music idioms into accessible Western styles, composing music and songs in Chinyanja or Chibemba, sometimes adding town slang and colloquial English (Fraenkel 1959: 51). Strumming his guitar, he sang with humour and verve about town wives who painted their lips, the *bakapentas* in Epstein's beer hall scene, as well as about the ignorance of wives from the rural areas and the loneliness men might experience in town when away from their homes. Prominent among his themes were the excitements of town life, drinking, dancing the jive, and having sex (Powdermaker 1962: 233–34). As we saw in the previous chapter, in his songs there were plenty of dresses and New Looks.

Many ethnic groups had distinctive dances, and weekly competitions by dance teams had become an organised activity every Sunday afternoon and on public holidays. According to anthropologist J. Clyde Mitchell, a dance called *kalela* was the most popular of all these dances, with African spectators thronging the dance pitch, obviously and loudly enjoying themselves (1956: 5). In 1951, he watched several *kalela* dance performances by a team of young Bisa migrant workers from the Northern Province in the municipal township in Luanshya on the Copperbelt. Similar type dances between teams of military rank had been performed widely across the region in the past (1956: 9–11).[9] The team Mitchell watched was made up of dancers and drummers consisting of 19 young men, headed by a leader and assisted by a woman. Rather than using military uniforms, *kalela* dancers wore 'the smart clothes of the European business or professional men' (1956: 14). 'The costume of the rank-and-file dancers', Mitchell noted, 'was well-pressed grey slacks, neat singlets, and well-polished shoes. Some carried white

---

[9] Mitchell suggested that the roots of such dances might be traced back to shortly after World War I (1956: 11).

handkerchiefs in their right hands. Their hair was carefully combed with a well-defined parting.... The sound of drumming could be heard for miles round.... The dance was made up of short shuffling steps accompanied by a slight swaying of the body' (1956: 2). Dressed in sharp contrast to the dancers, the team leader wore a dark suit, shirt with collar and tie, hat, and a pair of white-rimmed sunglasses. The team leader invented the steps and composed the lyrics. The team included a 'doctor', dressed in a white hospital gown with a red cross in front, and the only woman in the team, a 'nursing sister' dressed in white, walking around with a mirror and a handkerchief to enable dancers to check if they were neat and tidy, and wiping sweat from their faces (1956: 3).

Kalela was popular for several reasons. The drumming was spectacular and the dancers well dressed. Yet it was the songs, Mitchell suggested, that were the main attraction. Performed in the Chibemba of the Copperbelt with many anglicisms and town pidgin thrown in, the songs focused on the urban situation and the changing sociopolitical environment. Some songs lampooned the smart modern miss using face powder and paint, others were about football, and above all, the songs recognised the ethnic diversity of the urban population (1956: 5–8). All the dancers were single young men who had paid a good deal of attention to their personal appearance.

Mitchell's engagement with the smart European-style dress worn during dance performances lends itself easily to misreading as emulation and imitation.[10] But when interpreting such dress practices as imitation, only the 'European-ness' is brought into view while the local references drop out of sight. Mitchell clearly recognised this when he remarked that the 'European way-of-life has now become so much a part and parcel of life in the urban areas that the Europeans themselves have faded into the background' (1956: 16). While they dressed smartly in the European style, none of the young dancers had white-collar or lower professional jobs (1956: 2–3). Indeed, Mitchell's observations capture the local significance of the strikingly dressed dancers in *kalela* enacting their ambiguous role in a colonial occupational system still underpinned by race.

Ballroom dancing clubs had sprung up in most of the towns in the early 1930s and 1940s, holding practice sessions several times a week and competition dances in the welfare halls almost monthly. From the fees members paid to dance associations they could expect support at

[10] For such misreadings, see Magubane (1971: 425) and Matongo (1992).

funerals, when going on home visits, or when moving to another town. But they were first and foremost dance clubs in which dress took pride of place, as we saw at the outset of this chapter in the exchange in 1940 between Wilson and his personal servant over the matter of the servant's intense desire to obtain a formal suit in order to be dressed properly for a ballroom dance competition with a visiting team in Broken Hill. White residents were sometimes invited to 'come and see how well the Africans dance' and to judge, both the dancing and the dress (Wilson 1942: 18). In his notes from one such event Wilson described half of the men wearing evening dress but only one with a real stiff shirt. Others, like a houseboy and waiter in uniforms, wore work clothes. At another event he reported men dressed in ordinary jackets, trousers, and ties, and a store *capitao* wearing a black serge suit and a white bow tie.[11] Most of the women were in evening dress. 'I enquired its origin from Mwamba [who explained that] sometimes Europeans sell them second-hand, and the tailors also make them' (Hansen 2015: 209–10).

On 2 March 1940, a 'Grand Big Show Competition Dance', featuring ballroom dance champions from clubs in several Copperbelt towns, was held in the railway compound in Broken Hill.[12] Wilson had invited along his wife, South African–born anthropologist Monica Wilson, asking her to 'cover the frocks', as she noted in a letter to her father in South Africa. As a matter of fact, Monica Wilson's coverage of 'the frocks' offers rare and detailed information.[13] Consider the following from her characterization of women's dresses: 'Winner. White satin, very well cut. Cape edged with expensive fur. High heeled evening shoes. Small pale blue felt cap on the back of her head (very becoming). Red glass earrings. Partner in tails.' Or this one: 'Silk, trimmed with large black clubs, [a]round hem and on bodice – obviously an expensive model. Worn with black glasses, straightened hair. Almost all wore bandeaux [head-bands] of some sort.' Turning to the men's wear, she notes: 'A number (both the winners among them) in ordinary tails – quite becoming. One wore a white scarf all evening hanging down under his jacket in front. Another wore dark glasses (these two in tails). One in white cotton trousers, tail coat (much too large), green pork pie hat, in dark glasses.' Attentive to hairstyle, she noted that Santana, the secretary of the African Dance Club visiting from Ndola, wore an 'ordinary tweed jacket, but had his hair crushed

---

[11] The *capitao* supervised a group of workers.
[12] Flyer inserted in archival file BC880, E9.9, Dancing. I also describe the dress at this dance competition in Hansen (2023).
[13] M. Wilson (1940). I came across Monica Wilson's typed notes in 2013 when I did research into the Monica and Godfrey Wilson Papers at the Archives and Manuscript Division of the University of Cape Town Libraries.

up – Partly straightened' and that some performers, both women and men, wore a 'whiteish brown face powder'. Much like a specialist, Monica Wilson approached the materiality of dress and accessories as contributing to embody the entire fashionable gestalt of the dancers (Eicher and Roach-Higgins 1992: 13).

Style elements from many directions converge in these descriptions, including conventional European formal evening wear but also several striking garment combinations and accessories such as dark glasses worn during a night-time event, the long white scarf, and the green pork-pie hat. Would intercontinental inspirations from the 1940s be at work here, when in the United States the pork-pie hat was popular among zoot-suiters and jazz musicians?[14] We may not know, but what is readily apparent is a joyous scene of dressing well, entertainment, and pleasure that is nearly erased when such dress practice is explained merely as imitation of European dress.[15]

At another dance competition in 1949, almost ten years later, held in the Maramba compound in Livingstone, a then 23-year-old unmarried colonial civil servant was invited by Friday, the head waiter at the Fairmount Hotel in Livingstone where he messed, to serve as a judge. Six white judges were present: two married couples, a woman post office clerk, and the young civil servant. They awarded prizes donated by local businessmen, judging the performers on their dancing of waltz, quick step, and fox trot, and selecting the best-dressed man and woman. The standard of dancing was exceedingly high and the effect of the range of dress startling. Most of the men wore full evening dress, a lot of it many years out of date but very well taken care of. The women dressed in a variety of styles 'almost to a woman in the hand-me-downs from the husband's or partner's bwana's dona'.[16] The head

---

[14] The pork pie hat, flashy and colour-coordinated, became associated with African American culture and zoot suits during the 1940s. Lester Young, jazz saxophonist from the mid-1920s to the late 1950s, regularly wore a pork-pie hat when performing. After his death the composer Charles Mingus wrote an elegy for him, 'Goodbye Pork Pie Hat'. See Laws n.d. https://culturedarm.com/behind-the-story-charles-mingus-goodbye-pork-pie-hat.

[15] African American–influenced jazz music was popular in South Africa and would have been listened to at the mines and in towns by migrants from Northern Rhodesia. African American minstrel music and gospel introduced in the beginning of the twentieth century shaped the sounds of South African jazz that developed through the 1930s and on. See Ansell (2004) and Vinson (2012).

[16] *Bwana* is a Swahili term for boss or important person, used widely in East and southern Africa for a white person. *Dona* derives from donna for woman in several Latin languages (Italian, Spanish, Portuguese). In domestic service employment in Zambia it referred to the white woman of the household and was often explained as stemming from the Portuguese.

waiter Friday, who wore his 'Soup and Fish', won the best-dressed male category and, recalled the observer, 'service at my table improved accordingly' (Hansen 1989: 162–63). The source of music at this event was a gramophone. In his notes from dance performances in Broken Hill during 1940, Wilson remarked on the excellent skills of the Africans who played, for example, a two-person band consisting of a concertina and percussion (drums and cymbals). The concertina player, a Bemba domestic servant, noted Wilson, 'was highly skilled. During one of the intervals in the dancing he played "Reveille" absolutely faultlessly and got clapped for doing so' (G. Wilson 1940). At a competition in the Kitwe African dance club in October 1950, a six-piece African band played, and tango was included among the dance styles (Hansen 1989: 163).

The male dancers in Broken Hill, Wilson reported, were mostly 'drawn from the clerks, the personal servants and the commercial workers, whose knowledge of European ways [was] greater than [that of] their fellows' (1942: 18). Lifetime servants explained to me in 1984 how they would stand on the veranda watching their white employers dance and then go practice in their quarters. Long-time professional servants who had been dance champions in Lusaka in the 1940s and early 1950s told me that dance club participants included workers from several walks of life. Their performances in Lusaka's old welfare hall drew crowds who enjoyed the fancy display. But in 1952 a senior welfare officer commented from Lusaka: 'Dances and concerts are popular, though [there has been] little improvement in either.... Partner dances were tried to encourage married couples to dance but they were not successful. European dancing continues to be patronised by men from broken homes, unmarried men and prostitutes[;] decent married folks are seldom seen dancing' (Hansen 1989: 164). Domestic servants were often consulted by workers in other jobs because of their knowledge of European ways including dress etiquette, style, and care. But their knowledge of the dress domain remained far from a monopoly, especially after some job mobility and purchasing power came within reach for African men during the late colonial period (Hansen 1989: 164–65). In the mid-1950s from Ndola on the Copperbelt, Epstein reported that African white-collar workers regarded ballroom dancing as *fya bukaboi*, the quintessence of the *kaboi* (servant) way of life. Illustrating this notion, he described 'a young government clerk who had received a bursary to attend university in South Africa. There he had to learn European-style ballroom dancing to avoid taunts by his new friends. Back home on the Copperbelt he had never learnt to dance' because of the negative association of ballroom dancing with servant culture (Epstein 1992c: 117).[17]

Closing his observations on the dance scene in Lusaka in 1952, you can almost hear the welfare officer sighing: 'Every effort is made in clubs to keep African dancing in force but jiving is a keen competitor' (cited in Hansen 1989: 164). Jive, at this point in time, and other dance styles were becoming more popular in urban African life than both traditional and ballroom dance. On a radio recording visit to the welfare centre in Kitwe on the Copperbelt in the first half of the 1950s, exploring what types of programs people liked to listen to, Peter Fraenkel, then an officer at the Central African Broadcasting Services, talked to a young man wearing 'a loud-check shirt and a cowboy hat'. 'Jus' gimme jive!' the young man responded making his way through the bevy of children crowding around Fraenkel while holding on to his silver-studded belt. 'I'm the best jiver on the whole Copperbelt.' Flinging out his arms, doing lithe and liquid dance steps, he chanted a Southern Rhodesian tune:

> Wa, wa baby,
> Oh, baby.
> I wanna jive.
> I wanna jive.
> I wanna jive
> day and night
> with you. (Fraenkel 1959: 80)

Suit and Dress Sensibilities

The post–World War II years were a turning point for access as I noted previously, when urban African women commonly had more than one dress and the khaki suit no longer satisfied wage-employed men. No doubt as Saffrey had noted, women in towns usually had several dresses. Style was an issue as well. R. J. B. Moore was particularly impressed by African women's sense of style: 'There are many dazzling frocks ... [and] evening dresses bought from ladies in the European town, coloured handkerchiefs on heads, crocheted caps or stylish hats worn on one side' (1948: 57). Some women found inspiration from the monthly radio magazine the *African Listener*, published by the colonial information service, in features about how to dress well, with matching handbag,

---

[17] These observations differ considerably from the characterisation by Miles Larmer, who describes that period's attention in scholarship to Western-styled clothing and leisure activities such as ballroom dancing as a 'disproportionate focus on the African Elite' (2021: 170), citing Ferguson in footnote 27 (1999: 175).

shoes, and hat (*African Listener* 1957a: 12; 1957b: 9).[18] Agnes Mwalimu, a 65-year-old storekeeper when I interviewed her in 1995 at a market in Mansa in Luapula Province, and some of the men I talked with there, commented on women's display of changing fashions. The flared skirts and dresses with gathered sleeves that were common in the 1950s gave way to sleeveless dresses in the 1960s. High heels were worn on special occasions. Women who were less outgoing would wear headscarves rather than hats. During our conversation, Mrs Mwalimu took pains to point out that a *chitenge* (colourful printed fabric) in the 1950s mainly was worn as a wrap-around and not, as later, tailored into a stylish outfit.

African men were also fashion conscious. A report from 1950 on the colony's commercial prospects noted:

the men, especially those who work in towns and earn higher wages are keen observers and imitators of European fashions and can be found animatedly discussing shop window displays of European garments. Khaki drill is still one of the staple classes of cloth on sale for native wear throughout the area, as nearly all working natives possess one or more of such suits (open-necked shirts either with 'shorts' or 'slacks') but their taste, especially in the towns, is definitely for the flamboyant, and the more recent North American styles in shirts, ties, slacks, jackets and hats accordingly have great popularity. (Hansen 2000a: 38–39)

The elderly men I interviewed in Luapula described men's fashions and their changing clothing preferences. The tight trousers that were all the rage in the 1940s, for example, gave way to very wide trousers in the 1950s. Hats were an important part of a well-dressed man's appearance, according to Mr Kamuti, who smiled when describing how during weekends in the early 1960s men wore fashions from across the region in the welfare hall in Mansa. His upbeat remarks make clear that people took extreme pride in dressing well and boldly displaying themselves with an air of style about them. Here you would really see people dressed up, he told me, including a man in a blazer and waistcoat, his shirt sleeves rolled up with an armband, wearing a busby hat and a walking stick, and smoking a pipe; this was a person who had been to South Africa. Those who had been to the Congo had their own way of showing clothing off; men would wear collarless shirts, and some even put on striped trousers. This 'craze for foreign', which continues to resonate in postcolonial Zambia, was captured then, according to Mr Kamuti, in a song by Alick Nkhata about how people went abroad to seek wealth and brought back goods from the Congo and South Africa (Hansen 2000a: 38).

---

[18] The information service launched the *African Listener* soon after the saucepan radio became widespread in the late 1940s. In 1958 it was followed by and renamed the semi-monthly *Nshila*, which was published well into the 1960s, also in Malawi.

What to wear became increasingly a pressing issue as independence approached. When in the mid-1950s Kenneth Kaunda was the second in command to Harry Nkumbula, the president general of the African National Congress, he once wore a loincloth at a demonstration (Fraenkel 1959: 181). He did not continue to use it, unlike Gandhi, who during the years of Indian cultural nationalism always wore a *khadi* (homespun) loincloth. Nkumbula, by contrast, at public events often wore his London School of Economics blazer (Fraenkel 1959: 173), a garment that expressed local African men's ideas of good dress practice much better than did loincloths.

'Because we did not have a national dress as such in Zambia', recalled long-time politician Vernon Mwanga in his biography, on the occasion of his appointment as deputy high commissioner in the United Kingdom prior to independence in 1964, 'the High Commissioner's wife improvised togas of African print.... It turned out to be a very ordinary piece of red and white stripe[d] cloth ... available from the shops [in London]' (1982: 95). During Zambia's independence celebration, Kenneth Kaunda and some of his colleagues wore similar attire. The style was modelled on Ghanaian wraps. Sources within the National Assembly in the Parliament of Zambia hold that President Kaunda at the annual opening of the assembly always wore a cloth from Ghana gifted by President Kwame Nkrumah, who is reported to have presented *kente* cloth to other African leaders in the early 1960s (Osseo-Asare 2021). Parliamentarians refer to this cloth as a *kanga*, a popular East African rectangular printed textile with borders on all sides (Hansen 2000a: 81). Although he is famous for wearing *kente* cloths draped like togas, Nkrumah also dressed in custom-made British suits and Chinese-styled jackets referred to in Ghana as Zhou Enlai.[19] As president Nkrumah's fashion legacy demonstrates, a business suit 'can be much more than a Western-style garment' (Osseo-Asare 2021: 598).

The dress practice of men wearing cloth draped around the body as a toga or a sarong never took hold as 'national dress' in Zambia. Zambian historian Walimu Kalusa describes how during the height of the struggle for political freedom in the 1950s and 1960s leading African politicians who attended constitutional talks with British officials were 'unfailingly clad in immaculate business suits complete with neckties and well-polished shoes'. Wearing such attire, he suggests, the nationalists

---

[19] Known for his participation in the cultural revolution, Zhou Enlai (who died in 1976) played major political roles in China. He also helped popularise the utilitarian Mao suit (called *zhoungshan* suit in China) as an alternative to the Western business suit and the decorated Manchu robes of the last emperor of China.

demanded respect and recognition from the British officials and 'engaged them on equal terms' (2013: 163). In local hands, he suggests, 'imported goods became a means by which Africans (re)negotiated their history in ways which European rulers, mining companies, advertisers and missionaries neither fully understood, nor effectively controlled' (2013: 165). As we have seen, wearing European-styled suits did not in and of itself constitute imitation but rather embraced notions of freedom and selfhood in the anticipation of independence.

In newly independent Zambia, President Kaunda was instrumental in turning 'the clothes boys used to wear', which we recall from the previous chapter, into a new tradition by designating the bush suit of colonial vintage as 'national dress', with the important addition of long trousers rather than shorts. In this way a slightly revised version of the dress of the human bearers on Zambia's coat of arms has become an example of a created tradition sometimes called 'traditional' or 'national'. President Kaunda popularised this dress practice that became known locally as the 'safari suit'. Vice President Simon Kapwepwe was the only politician in the First Republic (1972–91) to staunchly advocate a cultural national-ism in the arts that also referred to dress. While most of his colleagues donned safari suits, which became almost de rigueur in government and parastatal offices, Kapwepwe often sported loose short-sleeved shirts made of colourful printed fabrics such as *chitenge* or *kanga*.

An entire generation of anti-colonial activists from Zambia and else-where wore suits and ties as adult men still do today across most of the southern African region. But unlike men's dress, which never turned into a public issue, women's dress practice and their dressing 'properly' provoked intermittent public reactions and they continue to do today. As I explore in Chapter 5, recurring debates from the 1970s and beyond revolved largely around miniskirts and tight clothing, with trousers and jeans playing subordinate roles. Railing at miniskirts and advocating 'traditional dress' for women, the House of Chiefs and the Women's Brigade of the ruling party constructed women's dress as respectable when it reached below the knees and did not reveal 'private parts', which in this part of Africa include thighs and buttocks. Several years later, when miniskirts had long ago passed out of fashion, the president's wife, Betty Kaunda, who often wore *chitenge* suits, advised women to dress decently, and 'discard all foreign modes of dressing which [are] not compatible with local taste' (Hansen 2000a: 82) (see Figure 3.1). The construction of decency in women's dress, and its changes, is my focus in the next two chapters, which explore how changing gendered and sexu-alised meanings have been attached to clothing and women's bodies from before independence and beyond in Zambia.

Figure 3.1 *Chitenge* dress, early 1980s. Mrs Betty Kaunda (centre) in Maputo Airport, Mozambique, with female entourage and Mrs Chisano (right), wife of the minister of foreign affairs in Mozambique. Courtesy of Zambia Information Service.

Snapshot 1: The National Fabric

The colonial dress styles exemplified by the clothes 'boys used to wear' and the women's *chitenge* wrapper that I introduced in this book's first chapter now re-enter our account with renewed significance. In 1964, when Zambia became independent from British colonial rule, the country presented itself symbolically to the world of nations with a newly designed coat of arms. The new republic's heraldic imagery features a shield with black and white wavy lines, representing white water cascading over black rock in the Victoria Falls, with a fish eagle on top and a crossed hoe and pick underneath. The eagle stands for freedom, the hoe and pick for farming and mining. To the left and right of the shield are a man and a woman, the man dressed in a bush jacket and shorts, and the

Figure 3.2 Coat of Arms of the Republic of Zambia. Zambia
Information Service.

woman in a piece of cloth tied at the waist and a square-necked top with a
yoke and gathered sleeves. She is adorned with beads and an ivory
bracelet. They both wear sandals. At their feet are symbols of some of
the country's natural resources: an ear of maize, a mine head-frame, and
a zebra. At the bottom is a banner with the political motto: One Zambia,
One Nation. With a vision promising development, the many ethnic
groups of the new nation were to be melded into one unitary polity,
Zambia (see Figure 3.2).

When the ministerial consultative committee for the independence
celebration asked Zambian artist Gabriel Ellison to design the new coat
of arms, it insisted on human figures as bearers. Considering several
suggestions for the dress of the bearers, the consultative committee

members settled on dress styles that were common during the last two decades before independence in spite of their ambiguous colonial inspiration. When I interviewed the designer, she told me that the all-male committee members agreed much more easily on the male bearer's clothing than on that of the female bearer. In her role as designer, she had unsuccessfully proposed birds or wild game as bearers, arguing that the image of people as bearers was unlikely to withstand the effects of time (Hansen 2000a: 78).[20]

Subsequent developments indicate that Gabriel Ellison was partly right in her argument. The coat of arms has indeed been subject to criticism for its colonial associations, particularly with the male bearer's bush suit. Adult African men who worked in menial jobs for the colonial administration commonly tended to wear shorts, as did the many grown-up men who served in the private households of white employers. Even then, the bush suit of colonial vintage took off as required wear for men in official jobs in the new nation but with an important twist: rather than wearing shorts, men now wore long trousers. Called a safari suit in Zambia, this plain clothing style became the standard wear of the country's first president, Kenneth Kaunda, during his long-term presidency (1964–91). Like several other leaders in newly independent African nations, Kaunda used dress to express his personal and political identity (Osseo-Asare 2021). In Zambia the safari suit was widely adopted by men employed in government and civil service positions as well as in private sector jobs and it was worn at state functions. In the neighbouring countries it was often referred to as 'a Kaunda suit'.[21] Kaunda's wardrobe of safari suits often included short-sleeved jackets with lapels, yet during his many years in office, perhaps as his socialist leanings became more marked, he was also seen wearing Mao-inspired jackets with banded collars (Mandarin collars).

The safari suit features in a fashion scholar's discussion about globalisation and colonialism. Adding to the wider circulation of this colonially inspired dress style, a reproduction of Zambia's coat of arms is included.

---

[20] Gabriel Ellison interview, 12 September 1997, Lusaka. Cited in Hansen (2000a: 78).

[21] Burgess adds an interesting twist from Zanzibar to the provenance of the safari suit. Drawing on photographs appearing during 1966 in the government newspaper *Kweupe*, he describes the dress styles of Sheik Karume, the first president of Zanzibar after the 1964 revolution, who most often wore Western-styled clothing, including long trousers with either a coat and tie, or a simple open-collared shirt. Karume appeared only twice during 1966 in a Muslim long white shirt, once in a military uniform, and three times in a Nyerere-style 'Kaunda' suit (Burgess 2002: 308). The jacket of the Nyerere suit, sometimes referred to as a Tanzania suit but more frequently as a Mao-style suit, was without any conventional collar. The collarless jacket is sometimes referred to as a Nehru jacket with reference to Jawaharlal Nehru, India's first prime minister (1947–64).

In this account, the original bush suit on the image is described as a safari suit and serves as a case study of 'the only national coat of arms that features a recognizable fashion garment'. The 'fashion garment' referred to is the safari jacket designed by Yves Saint Laurent for casual luxury wear (Barnard 2014: 169–71). When in the late 1960s the designer developed a ready-to-wear approach to clothing at the fashion house of Dior, he, perhaps inspired by his Algerian roots, introduced the safari jacket into the sphere of high fashion. The utilitarian style featured oversized military notions and large pockets. As one of Yves Saint Laurent's signature styles, the safari jacket continues to be reinterpreted by subsequent Dior directors in innovative silhouettes and cuts (Velasco 2021). Not well-versed in history, local and otherwise, the author does

Figure 3.3 Zambian women in *chitenge* outfits. Postage stamp drawn by Zambian artist Gabriel Ellison in 1972. Author's photo.

not get the timing right. The fashionable Dior safari jacket appeared several years after Zambia's independence in 1964. But he is correct in recognizing that some Zambians attach mixed opinions to this particular image of men's dress on the national coat of arms.

Aside from the missionary-inspired top with gathered sleeves and yoked neck, the woman's dress style on the coat of arms is charged with fewer colonial associations than the man's wear. In fact, it showcases a clothing practice that has come to be interpreted as 'traditional'. When Zambia became a one-party state in 1972, a commemorative stamp was issued, also drawn by Gabriel Ellison, featuring three women in wrappers of colourful printed fabric that is called *chitenge* in Zambia (*vitenge* in some regions) (see Figure 3.3). This factory-produced textile is one of several printed cotton fabrics, including wax prints and *kanga* (East Africa), which are worn widely across the African continent (Gott, Loughran, Quick, and Rabine 2017). They are often called African prints. Originally produced in Europe, these fabrics have become Africanised, imbued with meanings whose significance arises from the particularities of time, location, and context (Sylvanus 2016) as I discuss in more detail with focus on Zambia in Part III of this book.

Part II

Dress and Undress

4   Dress, Undress, Body, and Nation

Since the 1990s when boundary-pushing designers began showing varying degrees of undress and exposure on the fashion runway, a display of nudity has been a common feature of metropolitan fashion weeks. But if nudity in fashion has lost much of its power to shock in the West today, degrees of undress are hot button issues in many other parts of our contemporary world where the public display of specific parts of the body does not go unnoticed. In 2008 in KwaZulu-Natal in South Africa, for example, King Goodwill Zwelithini announced that the Zulu maidens should cover their bare buttocks during the annual Reed Dance.[1] This ritual has been performed for generations, and some commentators described the king's order to cover up as 'an infringement on Zulu culture' (Ndlovu 2008: 13). To be sure, when away from the fashion runway, bare body displays may have complicated implications. Always and everywhere situated (Entwistle 2000: 80), notions and practices of dress and undress are bound up with the body politic in complicated ways.

When Julia Mulenga and other African women bared their upper bodies in Lusaka's City Airport in Northern Rhodesia in March 1960 on the arrival of British colonial secretary Iain Macleod, the local and international press picked up the encounter with the 'Mad African Girl' (Nyaywa 1998: 26). Many other events involving women displaying

---

[1] The annual Zulu Reed Dance and the *umhlanga*, the annual Reed Dance of the Swazi (two Nguni-speaking groups), have attracted male voyeuristic attention from local and international tourists who approach them as occasions to watch bare-breasted women rather than as cultural performance events. A news feature described how these events attracted international sex tourists (*Saturday Argus* 2006). Turning beyond southern African cultural performances to more general observations, Catherine A. Lutz and Jane L. Collins in their study of *National Geographic* magazine note that the 'nude woman sits, stands, or lounges at the salient center ... of photography of the non-Western world' (1993: 172). In the United States until the 1960s, before pornography was easily available, 'the magazine was known as the only mass culture venue where Americans could see women's breasts' (1993: 172). Photographs of 'topless' African women attracted eager male readers.

parts of their bodies in public have taken place in Zambia. The occasions and contexts of their performance differ, as do their interpretation. In short, the meanings of nudity and degrees of dress are never static. While men in Zambia have bared their upper bodies in public occasionally, the record overwhelmingly depicts the baring of bodies in public as a female practice. In short, the politics of dress and undress is deeply gendered.

In Zambia, nudity and degrees of undress are contentious issues when 'out of place', that is, when performed in public rather than when subject to the private gaze.[2] Because body politics are sartorial, the body surface is a highly charged site that makes dress and undress powerful matters with bearing on grand questions such as the constitution of society and women's and men's places in it. Demeanour, movement, and gesture are all in play here in techniques of the self and displays of social bodies (Mauss [1935] 1973). The body surface with all its adornments and extensions constitutes a major stage for the enactment of social reproduction. It plays this role because of its unique ability to mediate between self and society. And because the way it does so changes through time and place, there are 'no bodies in a general sense but rather specific bodies, marked by gender, sexuality, class and ethnicity, for instance'. That is, the body is a performance site that is used in different ways to contest or legitimate the power of the state and the position of its citizens (Parkins 2002: 5).

Examining several incidents involving partially dressed women in Zambia, this chapter approaches such events as a part of a changing political scene. My focus on reactions to changing forms of undress in public opens an exceptional window onto late colonial history and post-colonial changes in Zambia. Some of the displays I discuss were protest-oriented, while others were celebratory. Some involved spontaneous action by individuals, whereas others were staged by organised groups. And some were tragically accidental. Although the events I discuss differ widely in scope and exposure, they all engage an issue that continues to resonate strongly locally, namely, the powerful, and changing, sexualisation of specific parts of women's bodies. In the pages that follow, I examine how dress and undress construct the body at two levels, as discourse and practice, and how the textual body relates to everyday life through dress practice (Entwistle 2000: 238–39).

The chapter begins with the 'Mad African Girl' event prior to independence. I next discuss some events that took place in the wake of Zambia's change to a one-party political system in 1972 and go on to

---

[2] For the hyper-sexualization of African women's bodies in the white gaze, see Anne McClintock (1995).

explore episodes just before and after the return to multi-party politics in 1991. A breast-bearing performance in 2007 included a new twist: the addition of bras. My account stops with a body-baring event from 2009 that became the centre of a storm of controversy involving the president's office and the courts. But this is not the end to varied body-baring events in public in Zambia, which invite continued attention to their shifting meanings and changing contexts.[3]

Dress and Undress

Because dress and undress are both intimately and publicly invested with political significance, the dressed body is part of a performance economy whose practices contribute to reconstitute or reconfigure the social and political world. Standard Africanist scholarship has a long but scattered record by anthropologists and others of such practices, the most frequently cited examples including Shirley Ardener's description of Kom women in colonial Cameroon expressing their dissatisfaction with men's actions by singing obscene songs and exhibiting 'vulgar parts' of the body (1973), Judith van Allen's account of the bare breast demonstrations that were part of the Aba women's war against colonial authorities in south-eastern Nigeria (1973; see also Ifeka-Moller 1973), political scientist Ali Mazrui's observations about the relationship of dress and nakedness to assertiveness and rebellion (1969), and Audrey Wipper's discussion of criticism of urban women's dress practice as a flashpoint for their changing roles in postcolonial East Africa (1972). More recent scholarship has renewed the interest in the body surface by approaching dress and undress as highly salient political matters rather than, as was the case for a long time, dismissing them as frivolous (Allman 2004; Masquelier 2005; Parkins 2002; Roces and Edwards 2007).

Because modesty is culturally constructed, it is subject to change. The 'shame frontier' attached to the dressed body changes as new notions of propriety become acceptable and reactions to the sight of the naked body shift (Elias [1937] 1978: 163–68). When describing changing meanings of undress among Igbo women in south-eastern Nigeria during the colonial period, anthropologist Misty Bastian reminds us that 'who is naked and who is nude depends on who is looking' (2005: 35). In Northern Rhodesia, traders, prospectors, missionaries, and early colonial settlers met local people in various types of dress, including skins, hides,

---

[3] I have limited evidence of audience reactions and responses as my chief sources are media reports and my own observations. I also lack detailed information about the performance and staging of some of these events.

and raffia cloth, as well as body scarifications and adornments. Local people eagerly took to imported cloth and cut-and-sewn garments, yet the incorporation of the new commodities into dress practice was uneven, depending on people's involvement in labour migration and exposure to trading posts. As I noted in Chapters 1 and 2, access to clothing was deeply gendered because of restrictions on women's migration until the post–World War II years. Anthropologist Elizabeth Colson told me that when she studied the Plateau Tonga in the 1940s and the Gwembe Tonga in the 1950s, she quite often saw women working bare to the breast.[4]

Across most of this region of Africa, it was buttocks and thighs rather than breasts that had sexual allusions. New ideas about nudity came along with missionaries, as did dress practices that continually have changed in part in response to style and fashion influences from a larger world. As I demonstrated in the previous chapter, more than a century of interaction with others turned suits and long trousers and dresses and skirts into men's and women's standard wear. Even then, degrees of dress and undress remain important issues depending on gender and generation as well as the particularities of specific locations and time. In spite of the rapid flow of style influences from an increasingly globalised world, as I show in the next chapter, young women who wear miniskirts and tight trousers in public space continue to be stripped in Zambia's urban areas in acts that visibly demonstrate men's outrage and may be traced back to the immediate post-independence period. But stripping by individual women, and groups of women deliberately removing parts of their clothing, are two different things (Bastian 2005: 55). As I explore here, the created 'tradition' of women baring specific body parts in public, by design but also by accident, continues to provoke ire in Zambia.

A Political Tradition?

When British secretary of state for the colonies Iain Macleod paid his first visit to Northern Rhodesia to discuss a constitution that involved power sharing across racial groups in late March of 1960, he was met by a 'demonstration of African nationalism, the magnitude of which rarely had been seen before in the Federation … A crowd estimated at more than 3,000 gathered at the airport, broke a police cordon to swarm

---

[4] Personal communication, 6 March 2008.

Mr Macleod's car and several of them thrust their fists through the open window' (*Central African Post* 1960, 28 March). Previous anti-Federation demonstrations had been less rowdy. For example, on the arrival of the Monckton Commission that was tasked to investigate local discontent with the Federation (of Rhodesia and Nyasaland [1953–63]) and opposition to the constitutional proposals, '[w]omen of the African National Congress stood outside the hotel grounds and the airport holding banners. Many of the women had babies on their backs' (*Central African Post* 1960, 11 March). The commission's members were to travel across the country to collect evidence of African reactions to Northern Rhodesia's inclusion in the Federation.

When Julia Mulenga bared her breasts in the airport in Lusaka in 1960 on the arrival of Iain Macleod, she demonstrated against the power-sharing constitutional proposal of the Colonial Office, and speaking in Chibemba, she demanded one person one vote, majority rule, and immediate independence. According to a news report, she was not alone: many of the African men and some of the women, including leaders of an action group, were bare to the waist (*Central African Post* 1960, 28 March). A subsequent letter to the editor written by an African man, perhaps selected by white news editors for its critical stance, lamented that 'the action taken ... at the airport was and is disgraceful and shameful ... The thing which has disgraced me very much is ... women of the U.N.I.P. [United National Independence Party] naked who had no clothes on their bodies. This is satanic action. Women are not respected and this proves that we are not grown up, we are still primitive' (*Central African Post* 1960, 1 April).

Judging from recollections and interviews undertaken several years after these events, although Julia Mulenga did not hold a formal position in UNIP's Women's Brigade that was established during the early days of independence (Geisler 1987: 43), she played an active role in organising women to provide support and supplies. She had been exposed to politics in Lusaka at the Kabwata beer hall where she had a food stall and attended political meetings along with other women. Her house in Matero, an African township, became a meeting place for freedom fighters (Nyaywa 1998: 24). It is not clear from the available information whether the baring of breasts in front of Macleod was a planned strategy or a spontaneous expression of civil disobedience. In subsequent incidents, Julia Mulenga and the UNIP Women's Brigade went on a 'half-naked' protest march along Lusaka's main thoroughfare, Cairo Road, to protest to the Monckton Commission against racial partnership proposals and argue for Africans to be in charge of building the new nation (Nyaywa 1998: 27).

Locally, Julia Mulenga became known as Chikamoneka, a Chibemba term meaning 'it will be seen' or 'victory will be seen' (Nyaywa 1998: 22). By the time of her death in 1984, Julia Mulenga, now Chikamoneka, was fondly remembered as Mama UNIP and viewed as a heroine of the struggle for independence. Since this 1960 event that often, but perhaps not correctly, is mentioned as the first of its kind in Zambia, many other events involving women baring part of the body in public have taken place. It seems in retrospect that within a rather short time a tradition of women bearing their breasts in public had been created as a vehicle of political protest. Even with babies on their backs, women turned into political actors, whose roles were not those of 'Mad African Girls' but of mature political actors.

Were there cultural precedents among Zambia's many ethnic groups for such actions? In an interview in the late 1990s Chibesa Kankasa, whose political career in UNIP encompassed this entire period, had this to say about women taking off their clothes in public:

[I]n traditional Zambia, [this] is one of the strongest ways of expressing anger … during tribal wars, women from the royal family used to strip in order to encourage their warriors not to give up, or to show their anger. Having come from a royal [Bemba] family, it was normal for Mama Chikamoneka and her friends to walk bare breasted in front of the British colonial secretary.… Women who are not from the royal family would not have done it.[5] (Nyaywa 1998: 26)

Bemba women of royal background were entitled to bare their breasts in public, as Audrey Richards noted during her observation of a girls' initiation rite in the early 1930s. At one stage of the ceremony the two initiates enter, wearing pieces of cloth folded on top of their breasts. Spotting them, the mistress of ceremonies shouted: 'Pull your clothes off your breasts' … 'Who do you think you are? People of status?' (1956: 92).[6]

A close reading of the rich anthropological works on the societies within this region will reveal quite a variety of observations about degrees of women's undress in daily activities as well as their observations of modesty in dress and demeanour when interacting with senior men and in-laws. In the past, there were rituals and ceremonial occasions along the lines of the Zulu Reed Dance I mentioned at the outset in which both

---

[5] I have not been able to verify whether Julia Chikamoneka had royal Bemba ancestry.

[6] In the 2021 edition of *Chisungu*, the term 'clothes' used in the original 1956 version has been changed to 'cloths' and a footnote added: 'Women wear their cloths round their waists when working but above their breasts when at leisure. Princesses always wear them in the latter way.' The 2021 edition does not explain the reason for these changes of the original text. Andrew Bank drew my attention to this incident.

women and men danced bare-breasted. But even with precedents, it is incorrect to assume that there are straightforward continuities between such performances. In the initiation ceremony among the Soli, one of Zambia's many ethnic groups, for example, young girls coming of age once wore only strings of beads across their breasts. In recent years some girls have begun wearing bras (Simbao 2010: 67–69).[7] In short, women baring their bodies in colonial and postcolonial Zambia plays out in radically changed contexts. Such performances are created traditions, the tenor of which continually shifts, as we see below (Hobsbawm and Ranger 1983).

Mothers of the Nation

The optimism surrounding the coming of Zambia's political independence in 1964 was shared across the nation. Rising export earnings from copper production throughout the late 1960s supported the expansion of education and urban infrastructure. Nationalisation of the mining companies in the late 1960s turned the majority party UNIP into a managerial bureaucracy. In part because of differences over economic policy, President Kaunda towards the end of 1971 banned other parties and in 1972 declared a one-party participatory democracy to be led by UNIP. Those years saw considerable political protest at different levels of society. The UNIP Women's Brigade became an agent of the party, as did the UNIP Youth Wing whose vigilante groups intervened, often violently, in oppositional activities in streets and markets.

Beginning in the early days of the independence movement, the Women's Brigade was subsumed under the UNIP constitution. In 1975, it was renamed the Women's League. It attracted largely older urban women with little or no formal education. The League was critical of the new fashions, hairstyles, and cosmetics, as I discuss in the next chapter (Geisler 1987: 45–49). In the public setting, it emphasised the importance of motherhood. Two events during my first research period in Lusaka and just prior to the declaration of the one-party state illustrate this.[8] On 14 July 1971, university students demonstrated in front of the French Embassy, requesting President Kaunda to oust French embassy officials from Zambia because of a project involving the production of French Mirage aircrafts on license in apartheid South Africa. A large

---

[7] Simbao attributes the selective wearing of bras to the advanced age of some girls, breast size, and their very energetic dancing (personal communication, 2 February 2020).
[8] This section draws on Hansen 1980: 846–47.

demonstration of women Kaunda supporters walked from downtown Lusaka towards the university campus, 'many of them with babies strapped to their back' (*Times of Zambia* 1971, 14 July). In this instance, as in the case referred to earlier from the colonial period, the media were quick to imply a connection between babies, motherhood, and the nation. Likewise in August the same year, when member of parliament Simon Kapwepwe, a former associate of Kaunda from the independence struggle, had formed a splinter party, a group of UNIP women demonstrated, baring their upper bodies. The newspapers carried large photographs of these bare-breasted women (*Zambia Daily Mail* 1971, 30 August).

Both these demonstrations may illustrate what Max Gluckman had in mind with his theme of custom and conflict: how conflict in one set of relationships, over a wider range of society or through a longer period, leads to the re-establishment of social cohesion (1955: 2). These women's demonstrations were indeed 'rituals of rebellion' of sorts. In this case, the UNIP women exhibited themselves as mothers of the nation and rebelled when their offspring and politicians criticised the existing order. That order was re-established. The university was closed before the end of the term, the most vocal students were dismissed, while the rest were sent home. And the new political party was banned and its leader and associates imprisoned (Hansen 1980: 847).

On several occasions during the years of the Second Republic (1972–91), the UNIP Women's League staged bare-breasted demonstrations in support of the ruling party and President Kaunda. The League discredited itself, according to one observer, their crying and ululating was called embarrassing, and they were told to 'leave politics to (male) politicians and go home to look after their children' (Geisler 1987: 47-48, quoting Schuster 1979: 160). During the years of one-party rule, Zambia experienced rapid economic decline during which relative prosperity gave way to widespread poverty. General dissatisfaction began to express itself also in new movements that demanded a change to multiparty politics. Throughout this period, the role of the UNIP Women's League as mothers of the nation supporting the ruling president was evident until the very end. When Kaunda finally conceded to multiparty elections, he was challenged at the party congress in August 1991 for the UNIP presidency by former MP Enock Kavindele. Offended, Kaunda told the congress participants that Kavindele's challenge was 'the biggest joke of the year' (*News from Zambia* 1991, 23 July–6 August). And UNIP women marched bare-breasted, incensed at Kavindele's challenge of Kaunda as 'father of the nation'.

Striptease in Public?

In 1991, Kaunda was succeeded as president by Frederick Chiluba from the Movement for Multiparty Democracy (MMD). Organised demonstrations featuring women in degrees of undress continued to take place in Zambia's Third Republic. While the former ruling party's Women's League was no longer much in evidence, the field of play had come to include a variety of special interest groups airing their grievances in public and groups of women described as cadres. The term 'cadre' harks back to the socialist-inspired organised support groups of the previous political regime during the one-party state. Today's cadres appear to be recruited for specific purposes. They tend to be young men who are charged to unsettle a public function of an opposing political party, that is, to disturb the peace. They are often paid, in cash or in kind, to carry out the task at hand. There are women cadres as well. One of their regular roles is to go to the international airport on the outskirts of Lusaka wearing *chitenge* wrappers with party logos and the image of the president to dance and sing the praises of the president and visiting heads of state.

Parading bare breasted to express their anger, a throng of women supporters of presidential contender Anderson Mazoka of the United Party for National Development (UNDP) took to the streets of Lusaka when the MMD had won the presidential seat in the second multi-party election at the end of 2001. This head-turning event provoked the Lusaka Police to clamp down on women's protest groups with an order that such 'displays of immodesty would result in women being charged with indecent exposure' (*News from Zambia* 2001–2, 12 December–16 January). Regardless of whether or not they are observing this police order or adopting changing dress conventions, women have in fact worn bras in recent public demonstrations. They are also, and increasingly so as I mentioned at the outset, wearing bras in the cultural ceremonies that are performed on an annual basis in many of Zambia's different ethnic groups.

When in July 2007 finance minister Ng'andu Magande was acquitted of winning his election as member of parliament for Chilanga constituency with bribery or corruption, he was met by MMD women Chilanga cadres wearing *chitenge* wrappers and bras, prostrating themselves before him as he exited the High Court. A male spokesperson explained that the MMD Chilanga constituency conducted the mobilisation of the MMD women who exposed their breasts 'for love of the party'.

'I find nothing wrong', he went on, 'in them choosing to support their party leaders in a traditional style. What is the difference between the MMD women who celebrate the Hon. Magande's victory in a Lenje tradition and ... Ngoni women during the N'cwala ceremony? Do our MMD women have no right to celebrate and rejoice in a style of their choice? What is [so] fun about MMD cadres showing love for Magande?' (*Sunday Post* 2007, 7 August)

The Magande affair, as it became known, provoked heated discussion. Gender activist Sarah Longwe noted that all the MMD women wore identical bras.[9] The event was pre-arranged, she said and wondered if the women were paid to demonstrate. Longwe likened the breast exposure to pornography and accused Magande of exploiting women. 'This is different from Julia Chikamoneka. She was doing it for the nation. Magande is exploiting party cadres. This is violence against women. It is also psychological' (*Post* 2007, 2 August).

A flood of letters to the editor touched on several themes. Letter writer Godfrey Mambwe reacted: 'Seeing a parade of half naked "Magande loyalists" on the front page ... gave me a terrible shock and ... reminded me of the Kaunda era when this act of undressing was popular and a way of twisting the government's arm to respond to people's grievances.... Come on our women, spare us of this unnecessary display of nudity.' Sikapale Chinzewe asked, '[W]hen will Zambian women stop displaying their sacred bodies to all and sundry?' And Jonathan Mumbwa put it very pointedly when adding his bit to the 'strip tease session at the High Court'. He and other writers suggested that Magande should condemn the action of the women and distance himself from it (*Post* 2007, 1, 2, 3, 8, and 17 August).

At the time of the Magande event the Zambian economy had slowly begun to grow as a result of the privatisation of the mining companies and upwards price trends in the global minerals market. But in spite of economic growth during subsequent years, the scale of poverty had not declined. And each new government was saddled with problems that stemmed from the structural adjustment policies of the 1980s and 1990s, including the reduction of employment in both the public and the private sector and huge foreign debts. During those years, displaying breasts in bras was a tactic deployed not only by political cadres, as the following incident illustrates.

Retirees belonging to the Voluntary Separatees Association of Zambia (VSAZ), both women and men, marched to the Cabinet Building in early October 2008 with banners to press the government into paying them

---

[9] Sarah Longwe is a women's rights activist, grassroots organizer, and author of several books about women in Zambia and gender issues.

their terminal benefits. Waving their voters' cards, they warned that they would not vote in the upcoming presidential election at the end of October. Preventing secretary to the cabinet Joshua Kanganja from entering his office, they demanded that he address their problem. The secretary's statement must not have been satisfactory, as the retirees refused to listen to his explanation and demanded that he should go back and meet their representatives. In the process, 'some women started to remove their tops to express their displeasure over the delayed payment'. They were photographed wearing *chitenge* wrappers and bras (*Post* 2008, 2 October). In this event, the women's action appears to have been spontaneous and not pre-arranged. What is more, this breast-baring episode seems not to have prompted commentary in the public. Bras or no bras, this active play between revealing and concealing has added a new angle to the public responses to undress. For a long time associated mainly with breastfeeding, breasts became increasingly sexualised. In these two cases, the Magande event and the retirees' protests, the wearing of bras helped push the shame frontier to also attach sexual meanings to women's breasts. To be sure, clothes, and the lack of them, construct different kinds of bodies.

Traditional Ritual or Pornography?

The breast-baring episodes I have described so far clearly relate to very different and changing circumstances. The Zulu Reed Dance to which I referred at the outset, the Ngoni N'cwala, and other local ceremonies mentioned in commentaries on these episodes, feature the exposure of breasts and other parts of women's bodies. Some cultural advocates in Zambia argue that such performances should be encouraged and preserved 'even though the country is a Christian nation'. But other critics, for example, from the church, consider it wrong to 'parade our young girls and women with hardly anything to cover their essentials' (*Sunday Post* 2008, 5 October). Yet the breast-baring episodes I have discussed are not cultural rituals, and they have few stable symbolic referents. In effect, breast baring is a tactic deployed in a changing political context.

'Tradition' in these commentaries revolves around something very broadly referred to as 'our cultural practices'. Invoking Zambian core values of dignity and respect, Lawrence Temfwe argued in a letter to the editor that 'Magande would be the one to lay prostrate before his "mothers" and plead with them to dress up.' 'Similarly', he went on, 'no respectable "mother" would undress before her "son". Whichever way you look at the action ... it was inconsistent with our cultural practices', he concluded. Letter writer Henry Kasongo reminded readers that 'a woman's body is valueless when it is exposed too much', while Musaiwale Mwewa argued that 'women are only supposed to be in that state with their spouses in a private room or bedroom' (*Post* 2007, 1, 2, 3, 8, and 17 August).

There is more at issue in these episodes than simply the disclosure of a part of women's body. One of the organisers of the MMD women's bra-wearing cadre, Agnes Laima-Ndhlovu, countered the criticism of their scant dress and prostration in front of Magande, arguing that 'Women on the streets of town dress worse than those who were wearing bras.' She explained that the MMD women had bought the bras themselves. Continuing, she explained: 'We were trying to show gratitude because he had won and [we] want him to bring development. There is nothing wrong with wearing bras or removing tops, that is not immoral. There are worse situations. In town, girls are moving [around] naked. Isn't that immoral?' And it was only for a short period, she continued, that the MMD women who celebrated Magande's acquittal did not wear their tops. But 'women in town move with their bellies outside [expose their midriff] for a long time, even the whole day but people don't complain'. She explained that she did not undress 'because she was too fat while the organisers wanted slim women' (*Post* 2007, 3 August).

In the view of Agnes Laima-Ndhlovu, the scant dress of young women who move with fashion in urban space constructs a different kind of body than the bras worn by mature but not 'too fat' women in the Magande episode. The implication is that such young urban women have 'loose' sexual morals. The moral war is fought in words in this case, while in the street the battle is also fought in actual acts of stripping young women wearing miniskirts and tight/transparent clothes, a practice that continues to recur in Lusaka and elsewhere in Zambia, as I discuss in the next chapter. But the comparison is flawed. In the Magande case and the other episodes, the demonstrations were by groups of women, whereas the stripping cases involved individual women.

In sum, Sarah Longwe's comparison of the bra-wearing women's demonstration to honour minister Magande to pornography may have some merit. The point is not the bra and the degree of undress but the prostration of women in front of the minister, subordinating themselves to his power in a highly visual pose. With this supplicating gesture, the women laid themselves open to exploitation and to being used as a tool by a man with much power. As Longwe suggested, the psychological dimension of submission and subordination constitutes a type of pornography.

'Obscenity' on the Sidewalk

All hell broke loose in June 2009 when Chansa Kabwela, a journalist at the opposition newspaper the *Post*, sent photographs of a woman giving birth on the sidewalk in front of the University Teaching Hospital (UTH) in Lusaka to the vice president and some women's rights organizations. The journalist had received the photographs from the woman's husband, who had used a digital camera to capture the situation. Doctors and nurses at the UTH were on strike. Because of the breech position of the infant, two clinics had turned the woman away, and at the country's premier hospital, there was no one to help her. During the birth on the sidewalk, both mother and infant died. The *Post* never published the photographs. Rather, by circulating them, the journalist aimed to draw attention to the consequences of a strike in the health sector.

At a press conference soon after, Zambian president Rupiah Banda, who was in his early seventies when he took office in 2008, condemned the *Post* newspaper for circulating what he referred to as pornography. He demanded a police investigation. As a result, Chansa Kabwela was taken to court on charges of distributing obscene materials with the intent to corrupt public morals. As pornography is illegal in Zambia, she faced five years in jail.

In a court hearing, the arresting officer Sharon Zulu, one of the few persons who in fact had seen the photographs, said that she felt hurt because the images were disturbing; women were not supposed to be exposed to the public in such a manner. 'I felt ashamed and hurt', she said. 'As a woman, [I] felt naked because [my] pride was taken away by exposing another woman's private parts especially during childbirth' (*Times of Zambia* 2009, 9 September). While Kabwela was out of prison on bail, the editor-in-chief of the *Post*, Fred Mbembe, and Cornell University law professor Muna Ndulo were charged with contempt of court because of an article Ndulo had written for the newspaper, describing the obscenity case against Chansa Kabwela as a 'Comedy of Errors' (*Post* 2009, 27 August). In the article, Ndulo observed:

Pictures of a woman giving birth no doubt are inappropriate and the sight should make many cringe but cannot be erotic and do not deal with sex at all. No doubt they are contrary to African tradition but that is not the test for obscenity and that is not what the obscene offences act is designed to deal with. The obscene offences act when it comes to pictures is designed to deal with erotic pictures and their potential to corrupt the morals of those who view them. (*Post* 2009, 27 August)

Above anything else, Ndulo's comments were critical of the way in which Zambian president Rupiah Banda and the director of public prosecution had handled the situation. The case, Ndulo argued, demonstrated poor governance and lack of independence of the institutions involved in it, specifically the police and the prosecution agencies. The case also illustrated 'the dominance of the Presidency over all other institutions. Once the president made the mistake of issuing a directive to the police, the Inspector General of the Police compounded the situation by enthusiastically carrying out the directive' (*Post* 2009, 27 August).

Both court cases were closely watched and reported by international media, and the prosecution was condemned by human rights and media organisations from across the world. On 25 September 2009, a Zambian judge dismissed the contempt charges filed against the *Post* because of Ndulo's controversial article. The High Court judge cited lack of foundation and a procedural error: 'the newspaper article was not committed in the face of the court' (Preminger 2009). And in November 2009, *Post* journalist Chansa Kabwela was acquitted of the charge of 'distributing obscene material' on the grounds that there was no evidence that the photographs would corrupt public morals.

Embarrassing to the head of state because of his non-presidential response to a photo alert about a health crisis, these events may at first sight look like a tempest in a tea cup. Such a view is misleading. Two photographs of childbirth, which hardly anyone in fact had seen, provoked vexing discussions about obscenity. The events are arresting and may be explored from a variety of angles. What we have is a discourse about imaginary bodies because most of the parties involved – commentators, journalists, and writers of letters to the editor – talked about photographs that they had never seen. Had these images circulated on the Internet, they might have been misused by thousands of viewers.[10] In effect, what is an obscene image when no one has seen it, and how can it be considered to circulate? What was at issue, including photographs no one could see, causing uncertainties about how to react, as in the president's gaze, to a sexualised image, or as in Chansa Kabwela's response, to a spectacle of pain? And perhaps above all, there was a shock factor, arising from the death of a mother and her infant during childbirth, in the messy and deeply complicated body-baring event.

---

[10] These letters, published in the main opposition paper, the *Post*, are likely only to represent a selection made by the editorial staff. Remarkably, most, if not all, of the published letters were written by men. It is difficult to know how many readers, women as well as men, were provoked by the event to submit letters to the editor.

Praise Singing and Celebratory Sex

Who does the talking? While the Chansa Kabwela case was still in court, a photograph in the *Sunday Post* (2009, July 26) of a woman MMD cadre singing praises before President Rupiah Banda at Mansa Airport drew critical attention. The photograph depicted a woman wearing a tied headscarf, dressed in a T-shirt and *chitenge* wrapper with the image of the president. The woman was lying down, dancing on the floor, with her legs up, revealing her thighs. The executive director of the Zambia Civic Education Association (ZCEA) commented that the photo of a woman giving birth was a health issue, whereas that of the woman singing praises for the president was a social issue. Disgusted, she went on: 'the first thing that a woman does is to make sure the body is covered before she postulates [*sic*] herself in that manner.[11] She was supposed to make sure her legs are covered' (*Post* 2009, 27 July). And Michael Sata, head of the opposition party the Patriotic Front (PF), entered the fray immediately by recalling president Rupiah Banda's awkward handling of the photographs depicting the sidewalk birth. Sata challenged the president to arrest the MMD cadre in the photo because it was 'a clear case of indecent exposure'. 'He elaborated: 'The president made so much noise on [account of] a picture of a woman in labor, which was never published.... Now, what is he going to say about the MMD cadre who was indecently exposing herself right in front of him?' (*Post* 2009, 27 July).

When he saw the photograph of the MMD praise singer on the front cover in the *Sunday Post*, a letter writer to the editor of the *Post* newspaper noted that he first thought that it was 'one of those [photos] taken from weekend revellers in one of the clubs'. He went on: 'it is a shame to see some women still act in this manner. And how', he ended tongue-in-cheek, 'shall we describe this picture?' Another letter writer commented on the 'very new twist' that praise singing has taken in African politics. Presidential praise singers, this letter writer remarked, 'are mostly women who aim at out-performing each other whenever they see their leaders. They wiggle their waists in such a manner that politicians are so happy to clap for them while these women's husbands remain wondering where their wives learn the dances' (*Post* 2009, 28 and 30 July). All letter writers drew a distinction between the obscene display in the praise singing performance and the labour pain of the woman on the hospital sidewalk. Much like the Magande event, this woman cadre's dance position laid her open to celebratory exploitation by the head of state.

---

[11] The verb 'to postulate' used by the letter writer might be a mistake and should probably have been 'to prostrate'.

To my knowledge, President Banda never reacted to criticisms of the display of private body parts in this praise singing performance.

Body Parts Out of Place

The global fashion runway includes design and style creations with see-through dresses and micro-minis revealing body parts, provoking delight rather than objection, as I noted at the outset. Yet the immediate appeal of these trendy garments entails an aesthetic and, more important, a valuation, that do not translate straightforwardly cross-culturally. Rather, as I have shown for the case of Zambia, the body surface is a battleground on which degrees of undress construct different kinds of bodies, sending mixed messages whose interpretations shift with changing times and shifting dress regimes (see Figure 4.1).

The battles over women's partially dressed bodies that I have described in this chapter invite analysis at several levels. Briefly, we may invoke Roland Barthes' distinction between actual or 'real' garments and the garment of 'representation' (1983). The garment, in this case the body surface/social skin, is not simply an object. Because it undergoes several transformations through an elaborate network of representations, it is always more than the sum of its parts. On the one hand, the episodes revolve around the body in various forms of undress, and, on the other, they are about discourses and representations of the dressed body in Zambia. Ranging widely, these discourses deploy an imagery that shifts between notions of women as mothers and women as prostitutes. There seem to be at least two distinct components to these discourses, one involving the language of nudity and bras in the context of some elusive tradition, while the other invokes a moralising commentary castigating women in the context of the social life of the modern nation.

Because body politics are sartorial, the place of gender and the consti-tution of society are worked out on women's dressed bodies in conflict with or accommodation to prevailing notions of gender and sexuality. The episodes of women revealing and concealing their breasts in public demonstrations in Zambia from the eve of independence until very recently show this dramatically.[12] Public reactions to women's dressed and undressed appearance in these events provide evidence of

---

[12] In her comparative analysis of dozens of protests by bare-breasted African women from 1922 to 2017, literature scholar Naminata Diabate includes only one from Zambia. In 2017, mothers and grandmothers walked topless to express their criticism of the government's detention of their leader, Hakainde Hichilema. He was elected president in 2021 (Diabate 2020).

Figure 4.1 Decent dress. Women wearing (front row from left to right) chitenge wrappers and two-piece 'office wear', popular during the first half of the 1990s. Courtesy of Zambia Information Service.

widespread anxiety about their place in the social and political order of Zambian society, producing a range of constructions varying from mothers to sexualised objects. Age and maturity, including body size, are involved in these processes, as we have seen. Even if the events I have discussed here resonate with practices in other parts of Africa and elsewhere where women have bared parts of their bodies in public, the contexts and timing are specific to Zambia (Diabate 2020; Tamale 2017). Events like these engage the local political economy and issues surrounding women and the particular sexualisation of female body parts when they are out of place.

Such practices of bodily display and performance associated with dress may be understood as political even if they are not always contestatory (Parkins 2002: 2). In effect, women's dress and undress may destabilise, disrupt, or legitimate the power of the state and the meanings of citizenship. Some of the events I have described were protest oriented, others supported the ruling regime, while still others have taken on an aura of cheerleading in celebratory performance for an alpha male. One of the most politically charged observations in the 'Comedy of Errors' article in the *Post* newspaper is likely to have been Ndulo's characterization of the extensive powers attached to presidents in African politics, and the lack of checks and balances on the presidency. When body parts are out of place, as they very clearly were in the events I have discussed here, a senior male may only see sexuality. Considering female bodies in general, as in this instance, matters of dress and undress give rise to grand questions about women's place in male-dominated society. But women also mark out their own very particular bodies in a cultural performance economy of dress and undress through which they situate themselves as modern citizens, as I explore with reference to miniskirts in the next chapter.

5   Miniskirts and Dangerous Dress Practice

Of all objects of everyday life in Zambia, clothes are among the strongest bearers of cultural meaning both for people who wear them and for those who watch their dressed bodies. Widespread cultural sensibilities about gender, sexuality, age, and status converge on the dressed body, weighing down on women's bodies much more heavily than they do on men's. Local reactions to the miniskirt go to the heart of normative cultural assumptions that are deeply embedded in the hierarchical nature of gender relations in most of Zambia's ethnic groups and across the country's class spectrum.

Public debates about African women's dress practice are not confined to Zambia nor do they involve only the length of their skirts. Controversy has arisen over African women's use of cosmetics, especially skin light-eners, as well as on account of their hairstyles and their wearing of swimsuits in beauty contests, for example (Stambach 1999; Thomas 2020). Yet outcries over a variety of African women's dress practices come together, I suggest, in controversies about the length of their skirts.

Miniskirts were banned in several African countries in the region in the late 1960s and early 1970s, including Tanzania, Kenya, Malawi, and Uganda (Ivaska 2011: 86–123; Mazrui 1968; 1969; Wipper 1972). Sociologist Audrey Wipper, for example, examined debates about mini-skirts in Kenya, Tanzania, Uganda, and Malawi from the mid-1960s to 1972, when news reports presented widespread incidents in which women were jeered at and 'physically assaulted, stripped of their clothes in public by youth wingers and college students' (Wipper 1972: 330). Taken together, the miniskirt debates from this period have much to say about the cultural politics of their time, yet they shy away from the most salient question: What is it about miniskirts that continues to provoke public ire about questions concerning culture, gender, and sexuality? Above all, the matter of skirt length becomes contentious in different contexts and for different groups.

When miniskirts first became fashionable in Zambia in the late 1960s and early 1970s, they fuelled discussions about women's proper place in the new nation; 'foreign' influences were blamed for independent women's lack of morality. In the 1990s when the miniskirt returned, the debate developed a sharper and more violent edge, mobilising ideas that associated sexuality with women's dress practice. Incidents involving the stripping of women wearing short skirts and tight clothing occurred in downtown spaces again and again during the 2000s. They have increasingly been followed by protests that are turning violence against women into a general social issue.

Drawing on a range of reactions to women wearing miniskirts in Zambia, this chapter examines some of the entangled issues about gender relations, sexuality, and power that the dressed body both conceals and reveals. The chapter draws on sources from the early 1970s and on, including newsprint media.[1] Inspired by my work on the consumption practices the secondhand clothing trade gave rise to during the 1990s, I explored how meanings became attached to clothing in a variety of different contexts in order to cast light on Zambian understandings and usages of dress. I begin with a discussion of the special significance of the dressed body and cultural notions about gendered bodies and clothing conventions in Zambia. Then follow several distinct sections introduced by brief remarks about the economic, political, and cultural transformations of Zambian society over the intervening years that serve as backdrop for changes in the experiences playing into the construction of women's dressed bodies. The differences and similarities in reactions to miniskirts that cut across the range of sources and time periods ultimately move, I suggest, in a single direction, sharpening the debate to turn the wearing of miniskirts in public into an increasingly dangerous dress practice.

Bodies and Dress

What accounts for the power of the miniskirt to push such sensitive buttons as culture, gender relations, and sexuality? The explanation has in part to do with the way in which the dressed body mediates between self and society. The special power of the miniskirt to provoke debates

---

[1] My principal sources are the two government-controlled dailies, *Times of Zambia* and *Zambia Daily Mail*, and the privately owned *Weekly Post*, which was launched as an opposition paper during the early 1990s when freedom of expression was newly allowed in print prior to multiparty elections at the end of 1991. The paper began appearing daily as the *Post* in 1994. All three papers were published in Lusaka. Freedom of expression began shrinking again when Rupiah Banda became president following the death of Levy Mwanwasa in 2008. The *Post* ceased publication in 2016, while the two government dailies still exist.

about culture, gender, and sexuality has to do with the closeness of this particular garment to the body, and with that body itself and its cultural construction. Clearly, the dressed body is more than a site of representation. Clothing foregrounds the body by revealing or concealing it. Because of the 'frisson' of this interaction, it is difficult to separate a discussion of clothing from the body (Craik 1994: 116). The material specificity of dress practice matters significantly. So do the hierarchical power relations and the institutional structures that sustain gender inequality in Zambia. Feminist scholar Susan Bordo admits that it might be unfashionable to talk about 'the grip of culture on the body', yet this is precisely what I invite us to do in this case (Bordo 1993: 218, 260).

To explain Zambian reactions to miniskirts, we must reckon both with inscription of cultural constructions on bodies and with those bodies themselves. A woman's body partially clothed in a miniskirt in Zambia receives far more critical attention today than her great-grandmother's near-naked body would have provoked during the opening decades of the twentieth century. Culturally and historically changing shame frontiers have helped to redefine the naked body, attaching sexual charge to different parts of the body and prompting the development of notions of acceptable and proper dress and of how and when clothes should be worn (Elias [1937] 1978: 164–66). These notions weigh down on women's and men's dress practices on different terms and are moulded by the unequal power relations through which femininity and masculinity are constructed in society at large. The dress conventions they help to produce constitute a bodily praxis that, as anthropologist Henrietta Moore has observed, 'is not simply about learning cultural rules by rote, it is about coming to an understanding of social distinctions through your body ... and recognizing that your orientation in the world ... will always be based on that incorporated knowledge' (1994: 78).

People in Zambia have been clothing conscious for a long time, as have people elsewhere in the region. European traders, missionaries, and settlers were important actors in introducing both cloth and clothing and, along with them, new notions of morality and dress conventions. While long-held local notions of status and rank informed the ways garments and apparel were put to use, the dress practices that emerged also helped change those notions. Widespread cultural norms attached fewer sexualised allusions to breasts than to buttocks and thighs, although such constructions changed as the shame frontier shifted, as we saw in the wearing of bras in recent body-baring events in the previous chapter. Returning to the question concerning the power of the miniskirt I raised at the outset of this section, above all, the miniskirt touches sensitive buttons about culture, gender, relations, and sexuality because of its proximity to the body, exposing a woman's thighs and buttocks. As members of the House of Chiefs in Zambia argued when calling for its ban in the early 1970s, the miniskirt arouses men's natural desires.

Dressing the New Nation

When miniskirts first appeared on the dress scene in the late 1960s and early 1970s, young women eagerly wore them. Young women's love of miniskirts provoked at least two reactions from within the established polity of the new nation. One was expressed by the House of Chiefs, supposedly the guardians of tradition and authority, whose role was to advise parliament. The other came from the Women's Brigade, an auxiliary body of the ruling United National Independence Party (UNIP) and ostensibly the advocate for women's affairs as wives and mothers. Although the details of the two debates differ, they each encompassed a spirited defence of an imaginary, partial history of tradition that projected backward and forward a remodelled version of women's dress that fitted awkwardly with the changing world of their wearers.

In 1971 the House of Chiefs passed a motion stating that 'Women's dress above the knee should be condemned.' Introducing the motion, Chief Shibwalya-Kapila from Northern Province argued that the House, as the forum of traditional rulers, had the responsibility to stamp out miniskirts. He called on government, parents, and teachers to take action. 'This kind of dressing', he explained, 'is certainly against the tradition ... mini dress above the knee exposes the private parts of a women's body and thus it tempts or attracts man's natural inclination for curiosity and sexual pleasure. So no serious parent would ever like to see his or her child work or sit in her presence in such a costume' (Republic of Zambia 1971: cols. 73–74).

All the other chiefs supported the motion. Chief Mpanda from Eastern Province argued: 'When we men see a woman or girl walking half naked, we are naturally attracted ... it is disgraceful to parents to see the private parts of their daughters.' Chief Mwansakombe from Luapula Province added: 'We are losing our national culture, [yet] some people say we are building national culture, [still] I do not see whether we are building national culture.' And Chief Ingwe from North-Western Province invited the government 'to ban the factories which are tailoring such clothes ... then we shall go back to our customary way of dressing' (Republic of Zambia 1971: cols. 74–77). At the time this debate unfolded, Zambia had one state-supported factory, Kafue Textiles of Zambia, which had opened in 1969, and some small private clothing and textile manufacturers (see Figure 5.1).

Figure 5.1 Miniskirts from the early 1970s. Graduates at Evelyn Hone College, Lusaka. Courtesy of Zambia Information Service.

The miniskirt was not banned. And it was not exactly clear what the chiefs had in mind when calling for a return to 'our customary ways of dressing'. Although the clothing tradition had a shaky foundation, there were other groups within the body politic who, like the House of Chiefs, substituted themselves for parents and guardians in arguments about restoring 'customary' dress. A very vocal voice was that of Chibesa Kankasa, the chairperson of the Women's Brigade in the early 1970s, who added fuel to the debate by conflating dress practice with women's 'proper' roles as wives and mothers.

The Women's Brigade largely attracted urban women who had reached adulthood during the late colonial period. It was primarily concerned with moral and ethical issues (Geisler 1987: 48). The Brigade was hostile towards independent, educated women, blaming them for the moral decay and loss of cultural values in the new nation. Anthropologist Ilsa Schuster's study of Lusaka's first cohort of young single professional women, who were beginning to fill formal positions in the early 1970s, captures Zambian society's ambivalent attitude towards women's new emancipation (Schuster 1979: 163, 167). In the mind of the Women's Brigade, dress functioned as a proxy for women's role in society. Those single professional women purchased their own clothing and did not select proper dress styles. Advising women to wear more respectable attire than miniskirts, Mrs Kankasa played a prominent role in the invention of the 'traditional' *chitenge* suit: a skirt or wrapper with a top, tailored from colourful printed fabric. Her hallmark was a headscarf elaborately folded in 'the West African manner'.

Both strands of the miniskirt debate from the early 1970s shared notions of tradition that made young women's bodies an index of the nation and their place within it. Advocating that women should wear 'traditional dress', the House of Chiefs and the Women's League depicted wearers of miniskirts as women who had been corrupted by non-traditional influences. Such dress practices unsettled authority relations, challenging long-held norms and patterns of behaviour. In many societies in this region, the father–daughter relationship was characterised by avoidance. Women's dress was constructed as 'respectable' when it did not reveal 'private parts', which, as the House of Chiefs debate reveals, includes thighs and buttocks. Taking for granted that men's sexual desire was aroused by the display of women's 'private parts' in miniskirts, this early debate expressed a cultural nationalism with a marked male and generational bias. The debates viewed independent women who wore miniskirts as warped by foreign influences that threatened cultural notions of authority. Considering young independent women's wearing of miniskirts as an indication of their loose morals, both debates turned wearers of miniskirts into a ready shorthand for prostitutes.

Interlude

Zambia's Second Republic (1972–91) was a one-party state with a socialist-inspired command economy in which steady economic decline from 1973 and onwards quashed many expectations of leading better lives. While the miniskirt dropped out of fashion, women's dress practice continued to provoke occasional public commentary (*Times of Zambia* 1981, June–September). Concerns were raised about 'see-throughs' that belittled Zambian culture (*Times of Zambia* 1985, 23 August), and women's wearing of trousers also came in for criticism (*Times of Zambia* 1985, 18 July). The president's wife, Mrs Betty Kaunda, who often wore *chitenge* suits, urged women 'to guard their independence for the benefit of [the] future', adding, 'we should not copy everything that comes from foreign countries, but only good and decent attire' (*Times of Zambia* 1985, 4 February).

As the Zambian economy continued its downward slide during the 1980s, it became more and more difficult to find good attire. The two state-supported textile mills exported most of the cotton cloth and yarn, and import restrictions limited the availability of dress fabric and ready-made garments. It was clothing in general rather than women's dress in particular that drew most attention. How could police work effectively while wearing *pata pata* (plastic sandals), students respect poorly dressed teachers, and newspaper vendors expect to sell the dailies when wearing rags? So scarce was good clothing during the 1980s that some army wives on the Copperbelt were reported to wear their husbands' military attire (*Times of Zambia* 1986, 26 October; 1987, 28 April; 1987, 6 June).

The Second Republic turned the promise of gender equality into an illusion in many fields. Women's presence in formal jobs declined. Instead, they carried out informal economic activities that often provided the margin ensuring survival in the face of men's shrinking wages. But as household heads, Zambian men have conventionally held claims on their wives' incomes, time, and sexual attention. By the end of the 1980s, the discrepancies between those claims and actual economic strategies made the hierarchical nature of gender relations increasingly problematic both on the home front and in society at large (Hansen 1997).

'They call you *hule* [prostitute] and they can rape you'

When the miniskirt reappeared in the early 1990s, the Zambian scene had changed in many respects. Multi-party elections in 1991 ushered in the Third Republic and a policy of rapid liberalisation. The poor economic performance of the two previous decades had turned Zambia, in United Nations categories, into one of the world's least developed countries. In education, health, longevity, child mortality and nutrition, formal employment, and wages, among other indices, Zambians were worse off than they had been in the mid-1970s. The mid-1990s high prevalence of HIV and AIDS did not re-map sexual boundaries but affected the terms of sexual exchange to women's disadvantage. Blaming women for passing on the disease, widespread notions continued to accept men's uncontrollable sexual urges.

Because of its singular significance in mediating notions of both self and society, clothing consumption offers rich insights into how people deal with their place in society. In fact, my exploration of why the miniskirt was constructed as inappropriate was inspired by young women's reactions. Essays on clothing consumption written for me in English composition classes in 1995 by young women and men aged between 17 and 20, in their final year in two urban and two rural secondary schools in Zambia in Lusaka and Luapula Province, offer telling insights into the desires and anxieties of young people at the brink of adulthood in a hierarchically structured and male-dominated society. I constructed this essay-writing exercise in order to invite young adults to describe clothing practices in their homes; how they liked to dress, what they disliked wearing, and why; and where their clothes were bought. The resulting 'clothing autobiographies' are rich in descriptions of clothing practices in the terms used by the young people themselves.

Hortense Powdermaker pioneered the use of the student essay form to collect observations about the self-images of African youth in her research on the Copperbelt during the 1950s (1956).[2] About half a decade after independence in the late 1960s her use of the written essay as a means of exploring the aspirations of young people was extended in social psychological research conducted from the University of Zambia. Leonard Bloom, who had secondary-school and beginning university students write spontaneous autobiographies, noted their desire for independence (1972: 300).

The written essay as a genre of oral narrative adds valuable insights to ethnographic information collected with other methods. A total of 173 students wrote essays for me: 49 at Kabulonga Girls Secondary School and 57 at Kabulonga Boys Secondary School, both in Lusaka, and 38 at St. Mary's Secondary School for Girls in Kawambwa and 29 at St. Clement's Secondary School for Boys, both in Luapula Province. The excerpts from the essays I include here are direct quotations. Aside from adding occasional parenthetical explanations and clarifying spellings, I have not edited the student narratives.[3]

The students who wrote essays for me liked 'to move with fashion'. Unlike their peers a decade earlier, who shopped at state-owned stores with limited choices, this cohort of young people pursued almost unbounded clothing desires. They could shop at Sally's Boutique, a common designation for the shops selling commercially imported secondhand clothing from the West that had proliferated along with the opening up of the economy. Young people from better-off households also bought new clothing in regular stores, boutiques, and outdoor markets, mostly imported from South Africa and Southeast Asia. Some called on tailors as well, mostly for special occasion wear. But regardless

---

[2] For a discussion of the social psychological dimensions of this project, see Vaughan (1994: 17–19).

[3] I received permission to undertake this work from the provincial education secretary in Lusaka and the district education officer in Luapula Province. Secondary school principals or department heads allowed me to contact English teachers, who in turn introduced my interests to the students.

of background, they all frequented Sally's, where they found not only better value for their money in terms of quality but also a diversity of style that allowed them to pursue individuality and uniqueness while looking for 'the latest'.

Young people in Zambia do not put together their clothing universe at random but in ways that implicate cultural presuppositions about gender and authority. These cultural ideals are a product of socialisation and everyday social interaction. Through their early socialisation young girls acquire clothing competence. This competence hinges on what they describe as 'private parts', meaning thighs and buttocks, and 'body structures', which refers to weight and height and also has to do with comportment and presentation. Young girls are taught to wrap a piece of *chitenge* fabric around their waist when working around the home and to wear loose and not revealing dresses and skirts below the knee when in public. They should not wear short skirts when sweeping, for example, because bending over and revealing their thighs is considered to be indecent. In a survey of clothing consumption practice I conducted in one of Lusaka's medium- to high-income areas in 1995, an air-traffic controller had this to say when I asked how he viewed miniskirts for young women: 'I can't allow that', he answered vehemently, 'not even for my own daughters. Young women are not supposed to show their legs in the presence of their father' (Hansen 2000a: 214). In short, young women constrain their bodily praxis through the culturally specific ways in which they have been socialised to dress, carry, move, and position their bodies in space.[4]

Young women of course redefine these ideals within specific contexts. When away from the controlling space of the home, where they are expected to wear *chitenge* wrappers, and outside the regulatory space of school, where they wear uniforms, young women were cautious in their pursuit of 'the latest'. Some young urban women wanting 'to move with fashion' dressed in miniskirts when their parents were out, while others dared to wear miniskirts in public. But many were apprehensive about exposing the body. While this concern arises from the need to show respect to elders, it also pertains to the issue of decency and the mini-skirt's implication of loose morals. When characterising clothes, young women drew connections between sexuality and the construction of femininity and masculinity in society at large. As Abigal, a grade twelve student in Lusaka, explained: 'the clothes I like least are short (mini) and tight clothes; and I like them least because here in Zambia when you

---

[4] The quotes in this section are taken from Hansen (2000a: 214–20).

dress in such kinds of clothes people may start having ideas about you, because some people think that if you dress in miniskirts or dresses, you are a prostitute because they think prostitutes dress like that.... I can give you an example.' She went on: 'Here in Zambia, if you put on a mini [skirt] and tight clothes, men can easily rip your clothes and you might be raped at the same time.'

Abigal's remarks touch on a highly charged issue that preoccupied at least a third of the young women in her class of 49 students who in their essays drew connections between miniskirts and rape. The specific backdrop was the stripping of a woman wearing a miniskirt by street vendors at Kulima Tower, a major bus stop in the centre of Lusaka, on 18 March 1994. The incident was widely discussed in the press and prompted demonstrations by women's groups, addressing two specific issues. One was the growing incidence of sexual violence against women, and the other was women's right to dress the way they want (*Zambia Daily Mail* 1994, 23 March; 1994, 24 March). This particular stripping incident was not the only event of its kind. According to Jessie: 'Here in Zambia when you go to town the street vendors tear your dress ... because it is very short. And they call you all kinds of names, for instance *hule* [prostitute] and they can rape you.' Cleopatra was more explicit: 'In Zambia there is no freedom of dressing. If you wore miniskirts, bicycle shorts or leggings and decided to go shopping in town, you would be stripped naked ... this kind of dressing arouses men's emotions.'

The direct association between miniskirts and rape was informed by several events. Some of them took place in connection with music performances, in particular, the dance routines of the scantily dressed 'dancing queens' who accompany popular performers from the Democratic Republic of Congo (Zaire at that time), including rhumba stars, among them Tshala Muana, Koffi Olomide, and Madilu Systeme Bialu, who performed frequently in Zambia during the 1990s. At one outdoor performance by Olomide in December 1993, five women were raped in the melee that broke out when the delayed concert was called off at sunset, allegedly because men were provoked after watching the 'dancing queens' (*Times of Zambia* 1993, 6 December; 1993, 7 December; 1993, 10 December; *Sunday Times of Zambia* 1993, 12 December). While drunkenness and crowding contribute to the violence that often accompanies such performances (which sometimes escalate to include police fire and tear gas, as in a Tshala Muana event in 1996), it is especially music from the Democratic Republic of Congo and dancing queens that became associated with sexual violence (*Zambia Daily Mail* 1996, 8 November).

Above all, instances of public stripping dramatise the association between women's dressed bodies and sexual violence. The 1994 Kulima Tower incident involved a close encounter with rape when young male street vendors stripped a woman on account of what they claimed to be her indecent dress. The woman, described as 'middle-aged', wore a 'skin-tight skirt just above her knees', according to eyewitnesses. A reporter matter-of-factly described the event: 'a large crowd of onlookers besieged the scene as the vendors pinned the helpless woman to the ground while others held her legs apart ... the youths after satisfying their curiosity grabbed a Chitenge from an old woman, wrapped their victim in it and bundled her into a taxi' (*Weekly Standard* 1994, 21–27 March; *Weekly Post* 1994, 25 March).

With so much public attention focused on the dressed body, it is not surprising that the young women who wrote essays for me were anxious about managing their bodies through dress. Their social and sexual identity is very much lodged in the way in which the body is worn through clothes (Craik 1994: 56). Perhaps this understanding of dress was involved in many young women's liking for jeans; the preferred style in 1995 was a loose cut, giving a slightly baggy silhouette. 'The reason I like jeans', explained Habenzu, 'is that when I wear jeans, I feel comfortable when I am sitting with boys, because I can sit the way I want.' And according to Sameta: 'If I am on a journey or taking a stroll with friends, I walk without being worried. Secondly, when I am in a minibus or where most of these grown-up people are, I don't have to worry about how I am supposed to sit.'

Hlupekile brought home the point about jeans:

The clothes I like best is office wear, that is, skirt and blouse, or suit skirt and jacket.... I like these clothes because in our country Zambia there are lots of rape cases. When you put on a mini skirt, you cannot go around town without being attacked by street boys and even raped. I prefer jeans because when you are surrounded by these kinds of people, it will take time for them to undress you. You can scream and at least people might be able to hear your screaming and come over.

The miniskirt is not the only garment that gave rise to conformity in some areas of life and dissent in others. Trousers did so too, depending on context. The young women at a secondary school in Kawambwa in Luapula Province expressed less concern about the body-exposing issue in relationship to notions of decency, respectability, and sexual violence than their urban peers. Many liked dress and suit combinations and quite a few liked to wear jeans. Yet jeans were not acceptable everywhere. Astridah graphically related the following incident:

When I visited my aunt last month I wore jeans. Immediately she saw me she started shouting. 'Is this the way you dress as a daughter of Lupupa? Our clan or family does not allow a woman to put on male clothing. I am telling you Astridah, in our family with your father, we don't allow such a way of dressing.'

Astridah added: 'I was so shocked. She even complained that we learned this type of dressing from my mother which is not true.'

Compared with many of their age-mates, these young women were relatively privileged because they had made it to the final grade of secondary school. Approximately equal numbers of girls and boys enrol in grade one, but in the mid-1990s the attrition rate of girls was higher than that of boys at all succeeding levels (Duncan 1996: 47). These gender disparities reflect societal norms, discriminatory school allocation ratios, and the fact that many girls drop out of school because of pregnancy. Adolescent women are particularly vulnerable. In the mid-1990s rates of HIV infection among women between 15 and 19 years of age were reported to be seven times higher than for young men of the same age (Webb 1996: 2).

Against this backdrop, the likelihood of violent sex and premarital pregnancy is great. We can almost hear the young women's pained voices when they describe the discomfort they experience as objects of the male gaze and targets of violent male desires. The dress practices they detailed in their essays draw on their understanding of their own gender as very much constructed through sexuality and on the knowledge that their place in society is shaped by that construction.

The National Bedroom

The social and political landscape in which the events I described above took place has changed in complicated ways. In spite of the economic decline during the 1990s, women's lives did not simply change for the worse. Although poverty increased, the opportunity structure changed, and, for instance, more women held political office (Sampa 1996: 214). Women's lobby groups and advocacy organizations began taking issue with inequality on many fronts, including sexual violence in homes, public settings like restaurants, and on streets. Women's dress and miniskirts in particular continued to preoccupy many women who liked to dress in style, and women's dress practice continued to agitate their critics (*Chronicle* 1996, 5–11 July; *Zambia Daily Mail* 1997, 21 August; 1998, 11 April). But whereas in the late 1960s and early 1970s debates over women's dress were largely orchestrated from within the established body politic, the 1990s discussions took place throughout society.

Unlike the young women students whose concerns about miniskirts expressed their anxieties about growing up in a male-dominated society, some adult women in positions of relative power and prestige have dared to wear miniskirts in public. Their dress choice provoked reactions that demonstrate the significance of this particular garment in the problematic mediation of individual desires and group norms in Zambia. Consider the seven-day suspension in 1997 of popular television personality Dora Siliya by the Zambia National Broadcasting Corporation for 'insubordination arising from her wearing miniskirts' that was commented on extensively in the news media. So was the hounding out of the parliament chamber in 1998 of the health minister, professor Nkandu Luo, for wearing a short skirt (*Times of Zambia* 1998, 13 April). Discussions following this and a similar incident, involving the expulsion from parliament of finance minister Edith Nawakwi, turned women's dressed bodies into a battlefront for struggles over their place in contemporary Zambia.

Let me retrace one of these events. Entering the National Assembly on 3 April 1998, MP Nkandu Luo, in her forties, a professor of microbiology and pathology, wore a skirt with a back slit reaching some two inches above her knees, a loose shirt in a colourful floral print, and high-heeled shoes. Seated in the front row with her knees and legs exposed, her troubles began when a male MP raised a point of order, suggesting that Ms Luo's dress provoked male MPs. She instantly became the object of sneers and jeers from male parliamentarians who shouted: 'It is too much.' Ms Luo left the chambers before the deputy speaker described the MPs' comments as 'enough testimony for female MPs to dress properly' (*Times of Zambia* 1998, 4 April; *Zambia Daily Mail* 1998, 4 April). When another woman MP raised a point of order about male parliamentarians harassing their female colleagues, the deputy speaker asked whether she was 'trying to change this chamber into a bedroom? It is a well-known fact', he went on, 'that all men should wear trousers, shirt, tie and jacket and female members should dress in conformity with the dignity of the House. Any normally dressed [female] member should be in an attire [reaching] inches below the knee.' When later that same year MP Edith Nawakwi wore a miniskirt to a session of parliament, she was also pressured to leave the chamber (*Zambia Daily Mail* 1998, 24 September).

Freedom to Dress

Why do miniskirts continue to provoke public reactions that invade women's bodies both literally and figuratively in contemporary Zambia?

One issue has to do with dress codes in institutional settings, which strong-willed women challenge by insisting on their freedom to dress as they please. Another is the impression a woman's body dressed in a miniskirt provokes in the viewer. This impression is context-dependent and shaped by the age, gender, and class difference of the parties involved. And above all, it is informed by what people construe as decent dress, which in Zambia in the incidents I have described here is over-whelmingly determined by men.

Divergent reactions, some supportive, others critical, complicate the issues. The reactions did not follow clear gender lines. What was wrong with Ms Luo wearing a miniskirt in parliament, according to some men, was its arousal of male sexual desires. Albert Ndhlovu from Lusaka thought that it was 'unacceptable for ladies in leadership to dress as if they are going to a disco session or indeed … copying what their own children are doing in the name of fashion'. In his view, leaders were 'duty bound to obey conventional etiquette' (*Post* 1998, 14 April). But some women suggested that dress codes in institutions should be abolished. Esther Mabeya from Lusaka recalled that 'our mothers – some of them nurses and air hostesses – used to wear [miniskirts]. Why should they be an issue today?' Still other women considered miniskirts indecent. One mother from Lusaka, who explained that she had scolded her 17-year-old daughter 'for her skimpy clothes, accusing her of peddling her body', described Ms Luo as a poor role model. She argued: 'Ladies whether we like it or not, men are attracted to naked thighs and there is only one thing that comes in their mind – bedroom' (*Post* 1998, 8 April).

Supporters, both women and men, of women MPs' freedom to dress as they liked viewed the treatment of Ms Luo and Ms Nawakwi as sexual discrimination (*Zambia Daily Mail* 1998, 24 September). Some men saw the events as evidence of sexism rather than an enforcement of dress code. Urging women MPs to work together to change the 'archaic code of dress', Charity Kangwa from Lusaka captured a widely shared impres-sion: 'I see no difference between the *mishanga* street boys, who are in the habit of harassing women in the streets for their dress codes and parlia-mentarians…. [T]he Deputy Speaker, whose role is to ensure that the house maintains its dignity and respect, has defeated this purpose by disrespecting the female members of parliament by his unfortunate "bedroom" remarks' (*Post* 1998, 14 April).[5]

---

[5] *Mishanga* is the Chinyanja word for stick. It was used in the early 1980s to refer to vendors who sold single cigarettes, 'by the stick', and has since come to refer to street vendors in general.

Across these disparate reactions, it is the particular garment, the miniskirt, which is at issue. It exposes the thighs, that culturally constructed part of women's bodies which in Zambia is highly charged with sexual signification. Age and rank intersect with gender in these events, construing the National Assembly as a stage on which mature women MPs 'ought' to dress in a dignified manner. Wearing a miniskirt discredits the integrity of their high office because of its association in the minds of many, both women and men, with sex. When they wear miniskirts, women members of parliament, intentionally or not, unsettle male control of dress, in this way challenging men's hold on the nature and reins of power. In effect, rather than representing cultural backlash, the recurring controversies over miniskirts in Zambia are direct engagements with the changing social world of their wearers.

Dressing Down

Whether they love or hate them, people in Zambia have dealt with miniskirts, and variously so, since the late 1960s and early 1970s. Their debates about miniskirts have diverged in tenor because the socioeconomic and political circumstances against which they have played out are different. The sharper edge of the 1990s miniskirt controversy has to do with the dangers of sexual invasion of young women's bodies and with the accentuated sexualisation of adult women's bodies. On the political scene, it may also reflect men's perceived threat by powerful and up-and-coming women in public office. In many sectors of Zambian society, men continue to objectify women, seeing them as targets for sex and domination. This is why the young women who wrote essays about their dress practice were actively concerned with managing their bodies through dress, in this way seeking to control the sexual construction of their bodies. This is also why some highly profiled women who work in the public view and dress in miniskirts are fighting an uphill battle, challenging their objectification by men.

To be sure, women's dressed bodies receive considerable critical scrutiny in Zambia, as they do in many other countries. But controversies over miniskirts in the West, Africa, and elsewhere cannot be explained away as being 'all the same' (Tamale 2016; Vincent 2008). The circumstances that gave rise to them, the contexts in which they play out, and the weight of their anti-feminism most likely differ as do the cultural politics of their specific generation, time, and place. When the miniskirt first burst onto the Zambian fashion scene, it provoked a debate that centred on women's proper place in the new nation and blamed foreign influences, among them miniskirt fashions, for independent women's lack of morality. The debate that arose in the wake of the miniskirt's return in the 1990s had a much sharper and violent edge. The foreign origin of the miniskirt was no longer an issue. What was at stake now was the garment itself and the local interpretations it gave rise to. The 1990s clothing discourse increasingly associated sexuality with women's dress practice. The accentuated tenor of the debate was underpinned by the sexually repressive handling of young women, on the one hand, and the sexually degrading treatment of adult women in public life, on the other. Indeed, miniskirt incidents such as those I have described here are among the most dramatic invasions of women's freedom as private individuals and public citizens.

In contrast to the situation in the early 1970s, a variety of women's support groups and organizations have been active since the 1990s, lobbying for change in the ways in which Zambian society subordinates women to men. Transformations in gender relations of power require resources of a magnitude that are difficult to imagine. But lessening the danger attached to young women's dressed bodies also depends on altering the organisation of everyday life. Such a process hinges on institutional practices and the importance that changes in schooling, the world of work, and within private households may have on reshaping the opportunities for young people, providing them with ways and means to fashion a differently gendered landscape from the one in which they are growing up. Occasional incidents of the stripping in public of young women wearing short skirts and tight clothing have continued to take place in Zambia's urban areas, especially in such crowded spaces as bus stations, open-air markets, and streets beyond the period during which I have traced such events here. And there is little doubt that some segments of Zambian society will continue to attach highly charged sexual meanings to women's dressed bodies. Indeed, it will take more than public declarations to challenge long-held norms of everyday male/ female interaction. But perhaps these norms may, in their breach, become subject to reinterpretation as women in Zambia work to free their dressed bodies from the control of the male gaze.

Snapshot 2: *Chitenge*

How did women's outfits tailored from *chitenge*, a colourful printed cotton fabric, with a colonial genealogy in imported textiles, become construed as 'good and decent attire' not copied 'from foreign countries', in the words of Betty Kaunda, wife of Zambia's first president, Kenneth Kaunda (*Times of Zambia* 1985, 4 February) as we learned in the previous chapter? Worn and loved as an emblem of tradition, re-styled as fashionable dress, *chitenge* continues to be part of contemporary Zambian women's dress universe, as I explore in more detail in Part III of this book.

Chitenge refers both to a textile and to a dress. Elaborately styled dresses of colourful printed fabrics are referred to in Zambia as *chitenge* (in the Chinyanja language) or *vitenge* (in the Chibemba language). *Chitenge* (*kitenge* in East Africa and parts of the Democratic Republic of Congo; in eastern Congo *liputa* in the Lingala language) is a factory-produced textile, roller printed on one side. During the 1930s, some *kitenge* fabrics imported from Japan reached Zambia from the Belgian Congo, while Europe, India, and America served as other sources (Kitaguwa 2006, 161–62).[6] At that time, the fabrics were worn as wrappers and plain dresses.

As in many other African countries where textile manufacturing factories were established prior to or soon after independence, two integrated spinning and weaving textile plants producing *chitenge* opened in Zambia: Kafue Textiles of Zambia, financed by the state and private industry, which began production in 1969, and the Mulungushi Textile Factory, constructed with financial and technical assistance from China between 1977 and 1981 (Brooks 2010: 114; Guille 1995; Renne and Maiwada 2020). Over the years, both factories experienced frequent closures, changes of ownership and management as a result of new labour regimes, and political and economic upheavals, while occasional rumours of resuscitation hinted at their reopening. Meanwhile, market liberalisation from the early 1990s has vastly expanded the importation of textiles and garments. Although today most *chitenge* fabric is imported from China, it remains the emblem of Zambian women's fashion.

But that was not always the case. In 1989, when Patricia Leigh Brown, a *New York Times* staff writer focusing on design, interviewed the chief designer Francis Chishimba at Kafue Textiles, he told her that when the factory first opened, Zambian women resisted the printed fabrics. 'Part of the population looked down on local culture', he explained. 'Zambia was Westernized. All the girls and women were going for polyester' (*New York Times* 1989, 26 November). As we saw in previous chapters, the president's wife, Betty Kaunda, and the UNIP Women's Brigade chairperson, Chibesa Kankasa, were among the people within public view who wore *chitenge* dresses with pride, inspiring women across the class spectrum to follow suit. Gradually, *chitenge* wear became popular as 'national dress'. Over time, the dresses incorporated style elements from

---

[6] For more on these processes, see the special issue of *Textile History* with a focus on the history of cloth in eastern Africa introduced by Sarah Fee and Pedro Machado (2017).

across Africa and beyond. And they spread regionally in southern Africa, where there is less of a tradition for such dresses. During her field research among Tonga people in the Zambezi valley of northern Zimbabwe in the mid-1980s, anthropologist Pamela Reynolds noted the popularity of imported printed textiles, locally called 'Zambia cloth' and used widely in local gift exchanges (2019: 124, 138, 153). In the mid-1990s women suitcase traders from Zambia commissioned *chitenge* dresses from tailors in Lusaka to resell in South Africa, where at that time they also became known as 'Zambia'.

Changing seasonally, *chitenge* outfits have wide appeal in a dress universe that is strongly inflected by Western-styled wear. 'Traditionally built' full-figured women proudly display their dressed bodies in the latest *chitenge* styles (see Figure 5.2).[7] One event in particular, the all-female kitchen party, which I describe in Chapter 8, is a veritable *chitenge* fashion show where women friends and relatives come together to prepare a bride-to-be for her responsibilities in married life. At such parties participants evaluate and judge both behaviour and dress, collect information, trade, and share insights into sources of clothing design and style, working out the meanings that distinct clothing styles convey (Hansen 2000a: 208–14).

A woman who wishes to commission a *chitenge* outfit can call on local and foreign tailors, many of them men, or designers, most but not all of them women (Hansen 2013a). Much like the dress my research assistant sewed for me in 1972, during the mid- to late 1980s *chitenge* outfits were plain skirts or wrappers and tops, some with decorative details such as ribbons in contrasting colours around necks and sleeves. Tie-dye became common then, made by women from Ghana and Nigeria who taught Zambian women the technique. It was tailored into loose garments, including trouser and top combinations, with a style of embroidery around necks, sleeves, and edges that was referred to in Zambia as 'West African'. During the early 1990s, the trouser and top combination changed to skirts and tops of *chitenge* or tie-dye. These had marked waistlines; peplums; elaborate, built-up sleeves supported by interfacing; and collars, necklines, and fronts embellished with contrasting fabric, buttons, ruffles, or smocking. There were several types of skirts: pencil skirts, plain wrappers, and double wrappers. The mid-1990s rage – tight pencil skirts reaching below the knee with a high slit in front – was called *Tshala Muana*, referring to the popular rhumba singer from Zaire, whom

[7] I take the term 'traditionally built' from the series of novels set in Botswana, *The No. 1 Ladies' Detective Agency*, with which author Alexander McCall Smith describes the proprietor, Mma Precious Ramotswe. Launched in 1998, the popular series continues.

Figure 5.2 Women in *chitenge* outfits at a kitchen party, Lusaka 2007. Author's photo.

we met earlier. The late 1990s style was inspired by the long, loose garments worn by many Muslims in several West African countries and locally referred to as 'Nigerian *boubou'*. It featured flowing gowns of single-coloured dyed fabric, damask or damask imitations, with embroidery in contrasting colours and head-ties (see Figure 5.3). By the turn of the millennium, popular *chitenge* outfits were made up of short-sleeved blouses and skirts. One style, called *donafish*, included a bottom flounce reminiscent of a mermaid's tail.

Exploding onto the fashion stage in recent years, young designers are contributing to a vibrant fashion scene about which I shall have much more to say in Chapter 9. Showing style and creativity, the new designs

Figure 5.3 Four women dressed up for a kitchen party. The one on the left wears a tailor-made office outfit. The second from the left wears a 'Nigerian *boubou*'. The two women on the right wear *chitenge* outfits. Lusaka, 1997. Author's photo.

make their wearers feel part of the world on Zambian terms, which means *chitenge*. '*Chitenge*', said Angela Mulenga in 2009 when I interviewed this 21-year-old designer with a background in business administration, 'will stand the test of time.' And young women, who used to complain that *chitenge* outfits made them look old, are increasingly attracted to the creatively styled *chitenge* fashions, made by young designers who are adding new value to *chitenge* as both everyday and festive wear.

6   The Dramaturgy of Body Politics

By the time of his indictment for corruption, former second republican president Frederick Chiluba of Zambia was already well known for being a great dresser. In one of the first internal criminal trials of an African leader for corrupt activity, the legal prosecution (2003–9) was followed closely both locally and abroad. While the legal proceedings in Zambia dragged on, a special task force was established to investigate the allegations. When in 2005 several metal trunks and suitcases were discovered in a warehouse in Lusaka, revelations about the former president's stunning wardrobe attracted sensationalist attention. Commenting on the revelations of the contents of his stored trunks, Chiluba said: 'Old pictures are there, so you can see how I used to dress.... I was one of the sweetest guys in the street, an entertainer, a politician, a unionist, a man of God. Amen' (*Post* 2005, 15 March, 1, 4).

The revelations proved to be a turning point on which Chiluba's fondness for spectacular dress morphed into his stored wardrobe and in turn became emblematic of corruption. Consider the news-in-brief section in the *New York Times* on 15 March 2005, which, drawing on Reuters, reported the following:

Zambia: Investigators Seize Ex-President's Shoes

Former President Frederick Chiluba reacted angrily to the seizure of his warehoused wardrobe by investigators, including 100 pairs of shoes, 300 shirts, and 150 suits. He said it was meant to embarrass him, but investigators wanted to show how he abused his office during his 10-year rule, which ended in 2002. He was charged with corruption in 2003 but has been free on bail. 'What they have done is to bring my underpants out to the general public', Mr. Chiluba said. 'It is sad that the fight against corruption is being reduced to discussing suits, ties and shoes. Zambians know me and know that I have always dressed very well from the 1960s.' (*New York Times* 2005, 15 March, A8)

Corruption and ostentatious consumption offer juicy news copy and provide dramatic accounts of the lavish lifestyles of former powerful leaders who have fallen from grace. Among the most obvious examples are Mobuto Sese Seko of Zaire (Wrong 2001: 211–31), Jean-Bédel Bokassa of the Central African Republic (Titley 2002), and Omar Bongo of Gabon (Ngolet 2000). Much as in the media, corruption linked with the amassing of vast personal wealth is a standard topic in African Studies (Bayart 1993; Mbembe 2001), as are fraud and widespread misuse of economic resources for personal gain at different levels of society (Olivier de Sardan 1999; Smith 2007). But other than in passing or from a normative perspective, few scholars have engaged seriously with the material culture of consumption and its play in the expression of power.

Former president Chiluba's dressed body invites attention not only because of the flair it added to his corruption trial but also, as I explore in this chapter, because of its connection with the body politic of the nation. Thorstein Veblen's ([1899] 1959) notion of conspicuous consumption may illuminate some aspects of the former president's fondness for bespoke suits and handmade shoes. Coming from a humble background, Chiluba grew into adulthood after Zambia became independent in 1964, advancing through the ranks of the trade union movement. Zambia's copper-based economy boomed during the late 1960s, when the first-class trading areas of towns previously restricted to white customers attracted eager African clients. 'I have always dressed nicely from the 1960s', Chiluba was quoted as saying. 'I have always worn double-breasted nicely tailored suits' (*Post* 2005, 15 March, 4). Indeed, he was very particular about clothes, honing his style, always performing in public.

But in our twenty-first century world, expensive garments and eye-catching accessories do not signal status and honour as straightforwardly as they might have done in industrialising America when Veblen wrote, or even in Zambia in the 1960s when Chiluba began wearing custom-made suits. The better classes, in Veblen's account, abstained from productive work while they emulated one another, impressing their importance on others through conspicuous leisure and consumption. But the moral edge in Veblen's view on conspicuous consumption as the waste of a leisure class that consumed without producing does not translate well across time and space. And dress does not play the unequivocal role in expressing conspicuousness that it might have done in Veblen's time. In today's world of mass consumption and fast fashion, including in highly unequal countries like Zambia, dress is a contested cultural matter that both transcends and blurs the relationship between stratification and consumption. What is more, writing as an economist about a process he viewed largely in negative terms, Veblen was primarily concerned with the conspicuous display of status. As fashion scholar Elizabeth Wilson has pointed out (1987: 50–53, 245), in Veblen's world there is no place for the irrational or the non-utilitarian, for pleasure, or for the use and play with fashion, which is central to Chiluba's crafting of himself as a public persona.

To what extent does a political leader's standing depend on his ability to present himself before the public? Intrigued by excessive ostentation in Nigeria, political scientist Jean-Pascal Daloz (2003) suggested a comparative study of Nigeria, France, and Scandinavia to explore whether power needs to express itself by costly external displays. In a comparison of the conspicuous use of fashion by two outspoken parliamentarians in Nigeria and South Africa, Dino Melaye and Julius Malema, media scholar Garhe Osiebe considers the obsessive use of fashion by members of the political class as a means to draw attention to specific subjects or else a deflection of public attention from the details of governance or the legislative process (Osiebe 2020). Focusing specifically on South Africa, sociologist Deborah Posel (2010) has suggested that consumption practices in the post-apartheid period have been shaped by a peculiar type of capitalism that depended on the racial regulation of consumption. A similar relationship in Zambia might help explain some of the antecedents of Chiluba's love of clothes.

Attempting to explain Chiluba's preoccupation with dress and why his stored wardrobe so vexed local and foreign observers invites a shift of perspective from Veblen's shallow and moralistic emphasis on the relationship between extravagant dress and claims to status and honour. Clothing and dress practice are salient political matters (Allman 2004); so too are the former president's dressed body and the material artefacts at play in crafting his political persona. To be sure, body politics are sartorial, and the body surface is a highly charged site that makes dress and apparel powerful matters affecting grand questions such as the constitution of society and the roles of its citizens. Chiluba's dress practice had bearing on his self-realisation and the consolidation of his presidential power as well as on the social context of persons with whom he was involved (his co-players and minions). Conspicuous consumption, excess, and their shifting evaluations are perhaps best explored as contextual political matters. In this instance, Chiluba's clothing consumption may be viewed in negative terms rather than as a positive display of power.

In the case of Chiluba, I cannot ignore corruption, and therefore I begin with brief background observations about the former president and an overview of the corruption cases against him. Next, I focus on the former president's dressed body, exploring what Chiluba's dress practice made possible. Then I turn to the warehoused trunks that stored his wardrobe, looking at their material contents. And I ask, what are we to make of this kind of consumption?

Background

Frederick Jacob Titus Chiluba, Zambia's first multi-party elected president following former president Kenneth Kaunda's almost 20 years of one-party rule (1972–91), held office for two terms, from 1991 to 2002. He represented the Movement for Multiparty Democracy (MMD), a party that he had helped found. Prior to the 1991 election, Chiluba had held a variety of jobs, some of them menial, before being employed as an assistant accountant at Atlas Copco, a Swedish industrial assembly firm, on the Copperbelt. He rose through the ranks of the trade unions to become, in 1974, the Chairman General of the Zambia Congress of Trade Unions. A northerner from Luapula Province, his origins were humble. Born in 1944 to a Zambian mother at a mission hospital across the Belgian Congo border, it remains uncertain whether his father was Zambian or Congolese.[1] During his first term in office, Chiluba received an honorary doctoral degree from the University of Malawi and a master's degree in political science from Warwick University in the United Kingdom. It is widely believed that his assistant, Richard Sakala, had written the thesis. The former president was always referred to as Dr Chiluba, or colloquially as FJT (the initials of his first three names: Frederick Jacob Titus).

In the early years of his presidency, Frederick Chiluba was the darling of international donor organisations and evangelical Christians. He was a personable man with oratorical gifts, a born-again Christian who brought the passion of the pulpit to his speeches. Soon after taking office, Chiluba declared Zambia a Christian nation. After close to 20 years of Kaunda's command economy, the market was opened, several state-owned firms and companies were privatised, and IMF- and World Bank–supported structural adjustment programmes were implemented. But the donors' initial enthusiasm began declining soon after his election to a second term. The benefits of liberalising Zambia's resource-rich economy had not filtered down to the country's large and very poor population; at that time more than 70 per cent of the population lived on less than one US dollar per day. As Zambia's rating on the Human Development Index of the United Nations Development Programme plummeted, critics talked about the liberalisation of poverty. Accusations of corruption began to embroil Chiluba and several others with, among other matters, an aborted arms deal, a copper and cobalt marketing scam, and the

---

[1] Accounts differ concerning Chiluba's place of birth, which sometimes is suggested to be the town of Kitwe on the Copperbelt.

disappearance of 763 petrol tankers that were destined for the Zambia National Oil Corporation.

The Money Matrix

In 2002, Levy Mwanawasa, a lawyer and former vice president, succeeded Chiluba as president. Soon after his accession to office, President Mwanawasa asked parliament to lift the immunity from prosecution that Chiluba enjoyed for cases that arose while he had been the head of state. The Members of Parliament met his request with massive support: 140 votes to 0. In his address to parliament, Mwanawasa referred to embezzlement and theft, including, according to political scientist Jan Kees van Donghe, a payment of US$1.1 million to Chiluba's tailor, Boutique Basile, an exclusive gentlemen's outfitters in Geneva, and one of US$90,000 to his daughter, Helen Chiluba, who was attending school in Europe. Other payments were later revealed, including payments made between 1995 and 2001 to, for example, his second wife Regina to the amount of US$352,000, payments to Fine Jewelers in Washington of US$30,000, donations of US$70,000 to American fundamentalist churches, and many others. The payments were funnelled through an account, ZAMTROP (Zambia Trans Overseas for the Office of the President), set up in London by the Office of the President during the Kaunda era. In addition, there were alleged payments of US$20.5 million to a Congolese businessman for arms that were never delivered. In his speech to parliament, President Mwanawasa also mentioned the petrol tankers that had vanished (van Donge 2008: 75–76). There were additional allegations.

A special task force, established by presidential decree and financed by the international donor community, handled Chiluba's prosecution. The case involved several other accomplices, including the director general of the intelligence service, a former minister of finance, the director of loans and investments at the ministry of finance, the secretary to the treasury, the chief justice, the auditor general, the Zambian protocol officer at the High Commission in London, and the CEO and executive director of a company called Access Financial Services (AFS). The chief accused were former president Chiluba, intelligence director Xavier Chungu, and the CEO of AFS, Faustin Kabwe.

In spite of the extent of publicity in Zambia about the accusations of corruption, few, in fact, including Chiluba's, resulted in prosecution. Procrastination in the courts hampered the repossession of properties, especially in Europe (van Donge 2008: 76). The cases dragged on, because of legal technicalities and due to Chiluba's health problems.

For medical reasons, he flew to South Africa for treatment several times. In 2007, the Zambian state launched a civil case at the High Court in London. In the Court's judgment, the owner of Boutique Basile in Geneva was requested to return to the task force more than US$1.2 million (plus costs) that he had received from the ZAMTROP account for Chiluba's bespoke suits, handmade shoes, and accessories (*Times of Zambia* 2008, 25 December). The owner, Antonio Basile, wept on several occasions when the extent of his wrongful dealings with Zambian government money was revealed in court.[2] The London Court also found sufficient evidence linking the former president and some of his senior associates to a conspiracy to rob their country's government and the Zambian people of US$41 million and ordered them to pay 85 per cent of what they had allegedly misappropriated. The money had been transferred to London bank accounts, ostensibly to repay government debts, but was siphoned off for other purposes such as expensive clothes, school fees, motorbikes, and a beauty therapy course (*News from Zambia* 2007, 19 April–18 May). Chiluba refused to recognise the British High Court's judgment, which was not registered by the Zambian courts.

That was the London case. The trial in Zambia dragged on for six years until after Mwanawasa's death in 2008. The Zambian judgment of ex-president Chiluba and his co-accused, the two leading businessmen from AFS, CEO Justin Kabwe and director Aaron Chungu, took place in January 2009 in the Magistrates Court of Zambia in Lusaka. The three accused originally faced 169 charges with theft of public funds of more than US$40 million. The state dropped several charges because of lack of evidence, with the result that the trio was charged with theft of US $500,000. The case alleged that money was diverted from the ministry of finance into an account held by the London branch of the Zambia National Commercial Bank, and that a UK-based investment banking firm, with the help of two UK law firms, moved money into a variety of offshore accounts, trust funds, and investment portfolios (Anon 2009: 5). Ever creative with colloquialisms, people in Zambia referred to the financial resources Chiluba and his associates paid out to both local and foreign individuals and institutions as the 'Money Matrix'.

Chiluba and his co-accused denied all charges. When questioned in court about the sources of money, Chiluba consistently argued that he

---

[2] Basile informed the London Court that Chiluba's clothes were made by Italian fashion designers. Describing the former president as a man of small stature for whom clothes had to be specially made, Basile took Chiluba's measurements at the Hotel Intercontinental in Geneva and forwarded them to Italy. Boutique Basile reports visits by travellers from Zambia who pass through Geneva, wanting to take a look at the famous/infamous store.

had received funds from private well-wishers and supporters in Zambia and elsewhere (Anon. 2009). In mid-August 2009, the final judgment was delivered. Dr Chiluba was acquitted. The prosecution found no record of his alleged thefts but sentenced his co-accused Faustin Kabwe and Aaron Chungu to three years each for being in possession of suspected stolen money.[3] When the chairperson of the task force, Maxwell Nkole, decided to appeal the case, Rupiah Banda, who had become president upon the death of Levy Mwanawasa in 2008, relieved Nkole of his duties, arguing that his contract had expired. At the end of October 2009, the task force on corruption was disbanded and merged with the anti-corruption commission. Meanwhile, a number of cases of alleged embezzlement of public funds involving former president Chiluba and several others remain unresolved.

The Dressed Body of the President

Consider Chiluba's dressed body. Frederick Chiluba was a man of diminutive stature, less than five feet tall, shoe size six, with a light complexion, speculated to reflect his Congolese background. When he assumed the presidency in 1991, his sharp double-breasted suits achieved overnight popularity. Judging from photographs, the suits in the trunks were in fairly neutral colours, not the yellows and creams that the former president favoured while being in office. Chiluba accessorised his suits with multi-patterned silk ties and matching pocket-handkerchiefs (see Figure 6.1). His shirts were hand-embroidered with his monogram, while his custom-made Italian shoes had platform heels ('elevator heels') that added two inches to his stature. Some shoes were made of 'exotics', a trade term for reptile skin; others of ostrich; and still others of satin. The trunks also contained monogrammed silk pyjamas.

The body is 'never simply a neutral clothes horse' (Parkins 2002: 5). The effects the dressed body provokes for its wearers and its viewers are always and everywhere situated, and therefore they are bound up with the local body politic in complicated ways (Entwistle 2000: 80). In Zambia, the details of the former president and the first lady's dress were observed with excruciating detail and commented on widely (Hansen 2000a: 93).

In his dress style, Chiluba, who presented himself as the embodiment of a new era, provided instant relief from the drabness and austerity of

---

[3] Several other persons were sentenced, among them, Regina Chiluba, Dr Chiluba's second wife, for accepting stolen property during the years of her husband's administration. Zambia's supreme court acquitted her in 2010. For reasons of space, I cannot provide details on all the individuals involved in the Chiluba cases.

Figure 6.1 Frederick Chiluba in double-breasted suit with wife Regina
Chiluba in the background. Thomas Nsama/AFP via Getty Images.

Kaunda's dress regimen. Throughout most of Kaunda's presidency, the
plain-looking safari suit had been de rigueur for men in power. Over the
years, Kaunda's safari suit had evolved from a colonial-inspired bush suit
to a Nehru or Mao-influenced jacket with a small collar. Kaunda usually

carried a large white handkerchief (into which he frequently wept). Chiluba exchanged this for silk ties and matching pocket-handkerchiefs. Dubbed 'New Culture', Chiluba's distinct dress style was initially copied by civil servants and office workers alike, the latter often sourcing their garments from *salaula* (imported secondhand clothing) markets and calling on tailors to alter large single-breasted suits into double-breasted suits without vents on the back (Hansen 2000a: 92). President Chiluba occasionally varied his sartorial presentation, dressing 'like Cuban President Dr Fidel Castro when he was in a militant mood' (*Post* 2005, 15 March, 4 and 5). He was also seen occasionally sporting Mao-styled single-breasted jackets that were rumoured to be gifts from his Congolese friends. The evolution of Chiluba's double-breasted suit hints at inspirations ranging from zoot suits, through preppy, to retro.

When they moved from Ndola on the Copperbelt to Lusaka in 1991, Chiluba's first wife, Vera, joined him at Plot-Number-One, as the presidential residence, State House, is colloquially referred to in Zambia. A short, full-figured, light-skinned woman, Vera liked to dress in *chitenge* outfits in bold colours accessorised with big head-ties or hats. Some observers questioned the qualifications of her fashion advisor. From an even more humble background than Chiluba, Vera and her flamboyant attire drew the nation's attention as she travelled across the country, promoting the Vera Chiluba charitable initiative, called the Hope Foundation, donating maize grinding mills, *salaula*, and blankets to peasant women and the urban poor. Her initiatives, and mannerisms, attracted considerable negative scrutiny in the media (Hansen 2000a: 95). In 2001 towards the end of Chiluba's second term as president and after 33 years of marriage, he divorced her. Long before the divorce, he had spent large amounts of money on his secretary, Regina, at least according to the court case against him. After leaving office, he married Regina, a more stylish and elegant woman than Vera.

At the outset of a new democratic era in Zambia, New Culture was available to anyone. In addition to referring to a dress style, the term 'New Culture' was also used to describe the shift of political and economic orientation after the change from a one-party state to a multi-party regime and the opening-up of markets. But New Culture soon lost its political lustre and its fashion appeal became threadbare. The initial enthusiasm about the president, his dress style, and the new regime barely lasted into Chiluba's second term. The privatisation of major assets, including the mines, was slow, and did not get under way until the late 1990s. Around that time, accusations began to be made by members of the opposition and from within the ranks of the governing party that Chiluba and his friends had committed a variety of fraudulent acts (van Donge 2008: 75).

Chiluba's Trunks

In March 2005, task force investigators came across 21 trunks and 11 suitcases containing personal effects that had been placed in storage when Dr Chiluba moved out of State House. They were stored in a warehouse owned by his friend, CEO Faustin Kabwe of AFS, the company at the centre of the plunder of state funds. The Bank of Zambia had liquidated AFS. When efforts were made to repossess the warehouse, task force investigators discovered some of Chiluba's excesses. An inventory revealed the trunks' contents of more than 150 bespoke suits, 300 shirts in their original cellophane wrappers, more than 100 pairs of custom-made shoes, and lots of neckties. There were brown envelopes containing cash as well as cheques. The task force investigators also found Chiluba's academic degree certificates, some photographs, and books.

The exposure of the contents of Chiluba's stored trunks made front-page newspaper headlines in Zambia and was picked up by the international news wires. The trunks and their contents were the subject of a biting editorial in the *Post*, at that time the chief opposition newspaper in Zambia: 'It is saddening to see [the former] president having hundreds of pairs of shoes stashed away in a warehouse. And we are not talking about cheap shoes but tailor-made ones of all colours – that make the rainbow look inadequate – with high heels made from the most expensive of all sorts of skins in the world' (*Post* 2005, 14 March).

What was at issue, the *Post* editorial observed, was not that Chiluba had so many clothes but that they would have cost much more than he could afford, given his official income. As the paper argued:

Chiluba by his known earnings and declared assets was neither a millionaire nor a billionaire. We say this because we know how many suits, shirts and shoes he went with into State House in November 1991. He couldn't afford it. Chiluba only started buying and wearing these expensive things, including gold watches and chains, when he had direct control of the Zambian taxpayers' money. (*Post* 2005, 14 March)

Reactions such as these convey deep-seated public scepticism about the political leadership. Chiluba and his associates were not common burglars and thieves operating from the townships; rather, they were the powers-that-be who felt entitled to a lifestyle far beyond the imagination of ordinary Zambian citizens.

A Threshold of the Body Politic

It was the storing of Chiluba's wardrobe of stupendous proportion, especially his Italian fashion designer suits and high-heeled shoes in the trunks in the AFS warehouse, that caught both local and international attention. Because clothing always sends mixed messages, Chiluba's dress practice no longer provoked imitation. In the view of the Zambian citizenry, a threshold was reached and the ex-president's dressed body had become the flashpoint. It is not surprising that the revelation of the contents of the trunks and suitcases did not sit well with Chiluba (*Post* 2005, 15 March, 4). 'The government has exposed my underpants to embarrass me', he complained. But he laughed, he said, 'when he read in the *Post* editorial that he did not have many suits when he went to State House in 1991'. Holding forth on a matter he knew well, he asserted that he had always dressed in smart double-breasted suits with matching shoes:

During the first strike I quenched in 1968 in Ndola, I wore a nice yellow double-breasted suit with matching shoes.... Zambians know that I have numerous clothes and shoes of all colours and from way back. I love colours and I am not allergic to them. I am proud to wear that which I find pleasing in my eyes.... Old pictures are there, so you can see how I used to dress. (*Post* 2005, 15 March, 4)

Chiluba's self-aggrandisement depended on lavish consumption and the transfer of gifts to relatives and friends. The legal charges made against him started and ended with money (*Post* 2006, 22 September). One observer suggested that the former president's most immediate use of money served to gratify his vanity. 'Chiluba's political style towards the end of his rule', claims van Donge (2008: 84), 'was fuelled by money, but much more as a display of vanity than as a means of building support.' But there is much more to it than that. There are several issues to consider: first, the president; second, the citizenry and the nation; and third, the president's allies. Chiluba's comments clearly indicate that he took great delight in the demonstration effect brought about by being well dressed; in short, he loved the dramaturgy of power. This observation pertains to the individual issue concerned with what a person can do with clothing: in this case, show off.

But the sumptuous attire, diamond-studded gold watch, signet ring, and gold chains that Chiluba liked to wear do not in and of themselves confer power. For this, we turn to the president's dressed body, his entire gestalt (Eicher and Roach-Higgins 1992: 13) that was at the heart of the body politic when New Culture suits had quite clearly lost their sheen. The politics alluded to by the term 'New Culture' had failed to improve the welfare of the citizenry. The evidence in the trunks was just 'too much'. It was over the top. The trunks' revelations crossed the threshold of two otherwise incommensurable value registers between Chiluba's individual dress endeavours, on the one hand, and his role as head of state, leading the nation, on the other (Barber 2007; Guyer 2004: 42).

Dress and Power

Historically in this part of Africa and elsewhere, people paid intense attention to their dressed bodies and the effects that dressed body presentations made on the people who surround them. They still do. Leaders everywhere make an impression by the manner and style of their dress, which are commented on widely. Dressing up, in all the colours of the rainbow, the diminutive Chiluba might have played the political types of both chief and big man (Sahlins 1963), pooling as a chief, and redistributing as a big man, with the wads of cash and cheques in brown envelopes representing payments for special favours.

But how do we reckon with the garments and accessories in Chiluba's stored trunks? Long ago, before the money economy had thoroughly penetrated this region, clothing and apparel served as a store of value (Hansen 2000a: 35, 42; 2015: 209) to be used, redistributed, and exchanged over time. But in today's global world of mass-produced goods and constantly changing styles, clothing and apparel no longer serve as common resources for accumulation and redistribution.[4]

Chiluba's stored wardrobe displays desire and vanity as well as need. In addition, there is an aspect of greed, which according to anthropologist A. F. Robertson is a matter scholars have a hard time coming to terms with because we fail to view people as embodied meaning makers (2001: 5). 'Greed', he says, 'is doubly interesting because it is both an aspect of our own growth (I can feel greedy) and one of the ways we come to terms with growth socially – measuring, criticizing, commenting on one another.' He goes on to note that 'when greed is evoked in political contexts it has the leveling effect of reducing comparison to the human body'. 'Kleptocrats from around the world', Robertson continues, 'have profited hugely from this deception, scaling-up their needs to fit their own estimation of their political status' (2001: 28). In Robertson's analysis, asking whether Chiluba deserved numerous bespoke suits and hand-made shoes, and asking whether he really needed all those things are two different questions, but only because we have learned to keep the former

---

[4] Serving as investment objects and valuable assets, haute couture dress, high-end branded designer clothes, and luxury accessories might be an exception to this generalisation.

party president and his body in two distinct conceptual compartments.[5] The deception forged by both the kleptocrats and Chiluba hinges on the merging of two otherwise incommensurable value registers.

On the first day of the court hearing in Lusaka, Chiluba upscaled his needs to fit his own estimation of his status as leader of the nation when the defence lawyer asked him for disclosures of private sponsorships. Private donors, Chiluba explained, insist on 'the golden rule of anonymity … they don't prescribe how their money will be used … for they are made aware that the party president has personal needs as distinct from general party activities' (Anon. 2009: 13–14). Evidently Chiluba's dressed body was entangled with the body politic in complicated ways. The complications involve greed, which as Robertson argues, is a 'gut feeling that has a bodily frame of reference' (Robertson 2001: 31). As I noted at the outset, the dramatic comments Chiluba made in 2005 when the contents of the trunks were first revealed to the public invite repetition for their bold recognition of this body reference in both visual and visceral terms: 'I was one of the sweetest guys in the street, an entertainer, a politician, a unionist, a man of God. Amen' (*Post* 2005, 15 March, 4).

Laughing all the way to court and throughout the hearings, Chiluba most certainly put on a good show. The former president definitely knew how to wear clothes. Perhaps his best creation was himself. Still, it takes a good deal of courage to go to the extent that Chiluba did. Looking like a clothes-horse, he was in fact a consummate politician. He had both enough money and wit to outsmart the system to ensure that he was not implicated directly in any wrongdoing, despite compelling evidence to the contrary.

What Chiluba had achieved was to surround himself with people he knew would be amenable, because of their other involvements, and who would not go after him. The acronym of the ruling party from which he and the country's next two presidents were drawn, the MMD, was by then popularly known in Zambia as meaning 'Make Money Disappear'. This widespread understanding of politics signals an elaborate system of corruption involving Chiluba and several others, politicians, civil servants, and businesspeople, both in the past and at the present. When Chiluba complained that he felt disgraced by the public display of his underwear, he in fact invoked a widely shared sentiment in Zambia that no one should hang their dirty laundry to dry in public. Troublesome

---

[5] Sophie Chevalier suggested that this might resonate with political historian Ernst Kantorowicz's observations about the king's two bodies (1958). The idea of the king's two bodies, the body natural and the body politic, was founded on the distinction between the mortal and personal body and the perpetual and corporate crown.

matters must be resolved privately (Hansen 1996). Yet he showed no shame, no contrition. Instead, he laughed. In the Lusaka court case, the former president continually argued that he had not used government money, that the ZAMTROP account held private money, and that it was his money, money that was given to him by friends and supporters (Anon 2009: 40). This widely shared understanding of how politics works – as private, interpersonal negotiations and exchanges of resources – helps to explain some of the passive response, the lack of public demonstrations, with which Zambians met former president Chiluba's acquittal. The case had dragged on for too long. And what was new about corruption anyway?

The closest we come in this case to Veblen's notion of conspicuous consumption in a society characterised by enormously unequal distribution of income and wealth is in the news commentaries in response to the disclosure of the contents of Chiluba's trunks. One of these, for example, queried how the former president could boast hundreds of pairs of shoes when millions of Zambians could not even afford *pata-patas* (plastic flip-flops) (Pan African News Agency Daily Newswire 2005). But conspicuous consumption is a drab characterisation of Chiluba's huge warehoused wardrobe. With the focus on his hoarding of clothing, popular reactions had shifted from Chiluba's acquisitive individualism to his failure to distribute and circulate the wealth of the nation to the citizenry.

Emblem of Greed

Some of Chiluba's abundant wardrobe was placed in storage when he left the State House in 2002. Perhaps the trunks were meant to be moved into his new home in a high-income residential area in Lusaka at a later stage but somehow remained at AFS's warehouse. The surprising revelation of the contents of the trunks in 2005 might never have been anticipated, and the sensationalism the revelation provoked might never have been foreseen. Still, the revelations proved to be a turning point on which Chiluba's fondness for spectacular dress morphed into his stored wardrobe and in turn became emblematic of corruption.

In 2011, former second republican president, Dr Frederick Chiluba, died. He was given a state funeral in Lusaka and laid to rest at Embassy Park, a newly designated presidential burial site, featuring monstrously large houses for the dead: Mwanawasa's, Chiluba's, and the dead body of president Michael Sata, who passed away while in office in October 2014. Finally, and returning to the trunks with which I began, for a long time the whereabouts of Chiluba's trunks and their contents were uncertain. They were rumoured to be with the special task force on corruption while the cases against him were heard in court. When the task force was disbanded, it was said that they might have been placed with the anti-corruption commission. Finally, after more than a decade in court, the Supreme Court revealed that the Bank of Zambia held some of the seized property, including the trunks, due to various oversights and weak controls (*Zambia Weekly* 2015, 5 June; 2016, 4 November). Chiluba's family was offered the property, but declined, demanding an explanation of how the bank came into possession of the property and why it was not returned to the former president after his acquittal in 2009 (*Daily Nation* 2015, 15 July). To give Chiluba his due, some of the contents of the trunks would undoubtedly enliven an exhibit about a consummate politician and sharp dresser in the political section of the National Museum in Lusaka for future generations to see the material conflation of distinction and corruption.

In July 2016, a memorial service was held to observe the fifth anniversary of Frederick Chiluba's passing, during which the former president was praised for bringing democracy to Zambia and introducing a free market economy. As he was never convicted, his deeds and public persona are subject to historical revision. In an article about the slow pace in the fight against corruption across Africa, journalist Celia W. Dugger (2009, A1) used the caption 'emblem of greed' for a photo of ten pairs of former president Chiluba's handmade high-heeled Italian shoes. Such media depictions are at odds with the expectations of the population at large, who most certainly expected their president to dress to impress. If this is conspicuous consumption, it is so without Veblen's animus, the invidious element (Mills 1953: xv). While his case no doubt will remain open to contending evaluations,[6] we may continue to puzzle the political persona of former president Chiluba of Zambia and his skill at articulating power on his dressed body. Indeed, as I have demonstrated here, clothing and accessories invite more than sensationalist attention; in fact, they demand serious work by scholars.

Snapshot 3: Accessories

It is the accessories that interest me here and how specific personal effects become powerful markers of identity (Miller 2010). Completing our outfits, the accessories we choose contribute to enhance the way we look. In effect, they make the style of dressing our own. Consider the famous

---

[6] Richard Sakala, the late president's former assistant, today owner of the *Daily Nation* newspapers, has already published his effort to 'set the record straight': *A President Betrayed: Serial Murder by Slander* (2016).

white handkerchiefs of Kaunda, a publicly outspoken and also very emotional man with a penchant for crying. Signalling his power, this humble accessory is of course much more than a handkerchief.

In Zambia, as elsewhere, the dressed body presentation of people in the public eye are watched closely and commented on in detail. Politicians are a frequent target for popular commentary – positive, negative, or changing from one to the other, depending on the situation and the issues at hand. We saw earlier how in the 1960s first president Kenneth Kaunda created the image as father of the nation with his plain-looking safari suit, holding a large white handkerchief in his left hand as if to wipe off problems (see Figure 6.2). In the 1990s, Frederick Chiluba's presidential wardrobe lifted his 'New Culture' regime of neoliberal democracy with the business uniform of double-breasted Italian bespoke suits, adorned by colourful silk ties and matching handkerchiefs while wearing handsewn shoes with stacked heels. Presidential image

Figure 6.2 President Kenneth Kaunda (left) in a safari suit and white handkerchief with President Daniel Arap Moi (right) of Kenya in a Western suit during Kaunda's Nairobi visit in 2012. Keystone Press/ Alamy Stock Photo.

management by means of dress sometimes works creatively by incorporating cultural elements from scratch, as for example when the first indigenous president of Bolivia, Evo Morales, was seen in public wearing an Andeanised suit, a sweater, or even a football T-shirt (Salazar-Sutil 2009). Afghanistan's president Hamid Karzai accessorised with his signature striped coat by a *karakul* (astrakhan) hat, a sample of which he is reported to have donated to the British Museum (*Telegraph* (UK) 2015, 21 April).[7] As I suggested in Chapter 6, one of the bespoke suits from the controversially stored wardrobe of President Chiluba would serve well in an exhibit in the political section of the National Museum in Lusaka to demonstrate excessive consumption as a screen for corruption and deceit by a consummate politician and sharp dresser.

Zambian women politicians are watched particularly closely and commented on in intimate detail, as we saw in Chapter 5 in the case of women members of parliament like professor Nkandu Luo, whose wearing of short skirts during parliamentary debates in the 1990s provoked incendiary commentary by her male colleagues. This was just one of several incidents. More recently, the Member of Parliament from the Chongwe constituency, a placeholder of ministerial positions in several governments, Sylvia Masebo, made front-page news on account of her huge fanciful hats to which a male parliamentarian took exception. 'It has been one hat after another since the house resumed its sitting', he lamented. 'Today, there is even a feather of a peacock in her hat' (*Post* 2014, 19 July). The speaker of the house dismissed the laughter-provoking matter and relegated it to a discussion after the session outside the house of parliament (www.parliament.gov.zm). Ms Masebo, often seen in public wearing *chitenge* outfits with matching headwraps, was used to being showcased in the news on account of her dressed body presentation, as I describe in more detail in Chapter 9.

Museum donations and auctions of clothing apparel are a trendy way of keeping oneself in the limelight for not only the rich and famous, dead or alive, but also past and present presidents. In 2004, former president Kaunda is reported to have consented to popular requests for his handkerchief to be auctioned at an event during the country's 40th independence celebration. Prior to and after independence, Kaunda, a skilled guitarist and accordion player, had recorded several freedom songs, some of them together with popular Zambian musician Rikki Ililonga, with whom an album was launched at the auction event (*Post* 2004,

---

[7] I discuss the Indonesian-inspired 'Mandela shirt' favoured by South Africa's first African president (Hansen 2023). See also Klopper (2000: 227–28).

7 October; *China Economic Net* 2004, 7 October).[8] And Edgar Lungu, Zambia's president between 2015 and 2021, a lawyer by profession whose fondness for sharp suits once propelled him into the news headlines as a pimp for wearing white tuxedos, liked eye-catching hats that became money-making auction inventory on several occasions. President Lungu accessorised his frequently worn single-breasted blue suits, popularly known as Chagwa suits after his middle name, with a red tie and pocket handkerchief. Some of Lungu's personal effects, especially but not only his hats, have been auctioned at several party (Patriotic Front, PF) fundraisers. His auction accessories include a wristwatch, bow ties, portraits, and paintings of himself and the first lady at a 'Meet the President Dinner' in Lusaka in 2017, organised by the youth wing of the ruling PF party. A hat worn by the president during the 2015 and 2016 election campaigns and one of his favourite ties were also auctioned during the event that raised pledges and cash donations (*Zambia Weekly* 2017, 5 May; *Zambia Daily Mail* 2017, 1 May).

The news media have tended to describe Lungu's preferred headwear as Panama hats, which according to my style book is incorrect; most of the hats I have seen in photos are fedoras. The reference I made above to Lungu's white tuxedos as pimp suits had no cachet but was laughed off, perhaps because the person who made the suggestion held no public respect.[9] In short, public evaluations of the dressed bodies of people in power are always subject to change, depending on the issue at hand and the circumstances. What remains is the important role accessories play in making our style of dress into our own unique presentation with none other quite like it.

---

[8] Other than identifying the listed sources, I have not been able to verify this auction or its outcome. Famous in the 1970s, Rikki Ililonga and his Musi-O-Tunya zamrock band had an on and off recording collaboration with Kaunda. Ililonga's politically critical songs were banned several times. According to the *China Economic Net* news item listed above, Ililonga was based in Denmark, which he himself described as his second country (*Times of Zambia* 2015, 29 May).

[9] The suggestion was made by Andrew Banda, a son of former president Rupiah Banda. Andrew Banda had a chequered career and his public respect had suffered badly because of a two-year court conviction for corruption while in government office (*Zambian Watchdog* 2014, 27 December). He also criticised the president for wearing expensive suits and not caring for ordinary people. Social media dismissed this petty news with the question of whether Banda would rather that the president wore *salaula* (*Zambian Watchdog* 2015, 18 August).

Part III

Fashionable Transformations

'Watch Lusaka', argued Samuel Ngoma, a feature writer for one of the daily Zambian newspapers. 'All who are gorgeously attired mostly get their clothes abroad.' The capital's so-called boutiques, he went on, 'have become rather like museums ... Neither Lusaka's Cairo Road nor Kamwala shopping area is the place to look. You have a better chance at the secondhand clothes dealer, the flea market or even the city centre market dealer who jaunts between Lusaka and Johannesburg' (Ngoma 1995). As Samuel Ngoma acknowledged in this excerpt from 1995 that showcases international style inspirations from the secondhand clothing market and the cross-border suitcase trade, people in Zambia have shaped their material culture, including their clothing, with commodities and ideas from far away.

The great value placed on clothing during the colonial period persists powerfully into the present and with a multitude of new dress options. Today in Lusaka, influences 'from outside', as Zambians refer to the world away from home, are more present and more visibly evident than they have ever been before. The city has grown enormously: from a population of 123,146 on the eve of independence in 1956 through one million in the early 1990s to more than three million in 2020 (Hansen 1997: 49; World Data Atlas 2020). In 1995 when Samuel Ngoma wrote his feature article, Zambia's capital did not feature a single shopping mall. Since then, financed by a mix of business interests, local and foreign, numerous shopping malls have opened, the first in 1999, the second in 2003, and the tenth in 2021 (Miller, Nel, and Hampwaye 2008; Wragg and Lim 2013). South African retailers were among the first to take advantage of the liberalisation of Zambia's retail sector, as did companies from Britain and China as well as several local businesses. My focus in this chapter is on dress matters prior to this retail transformation, the ramifications of which I turn to specifically in Chapter 9.

Cities like Lusaka are stages for the translation of globalisation into local terms. Increasing interaction across space and the growing consciousness of such processes are due to globalisation understood broadly, in Ida Susser and Jane Schneider's words, as an 'integrated phenomenon bringing all the world's cities into a single interconnected life' (2003: 2). When exploring the consequences, we must bring the local geography of consumption with its spaces, agents, and performances into the global story in which dressed bodies become the point of contact between local knowledge and the broader global context. It is from this angle that in this chapter I approach the discussion of dress practice in Lusaka with specific focus on young people. As in much of the rest of Africa, Zambia is a country of young people. In 2016, youth below 18 years of age comprised more than half of Zambia's total population, and the age group between 15 and 35 as much as 36.7 per cent.[1] Lusaka's rapid postcolonial population increase along with transformations of the retail sector and huge expansion of the informal economy have prompted new developments in clothing practices and changing cultures of consumption, which I explore in this chapter and the following two chapters.

The international secondhand clothing trade is a part of the global circuit of garment production whose tentacles reach deeply into Zambian markets and consumption practices (Brooks 2015). This circuit moves Western-styled clothing, much of it manufactured in developing countries, into markets and stores in the developed world. Since the early 1990s in the West, high-level consumerism facilitated by declining prices of apparel and footwear has ensured the creation of a large volume of clothing we no longer wear and some of which we donate from time to time to charitable organisations. The vast surplus of unsold donated clothing collected by such organisations is part of a commodity chain on the global garment production circuit in its transfer to textile graders and processors, who sort and bale the clothes destined for export. The consequences of this trade are manifold and controversial (Hansen 2004a).

As scholars of material culture, we should not take the Western significance of such clothes for granted. For secondhand garments do not travel with ready-made meanings attached to them; rather, their meanings change at different stages of the process (Kopytoff 1986). In the view of consumers in Zambia, the only Western thing about such clothes is their origin. This is why globalisation does not flatten out clothing consumption to produce uniformity in dress practice even though we all wear many of the same garments and accessories, for example, jeans and sneakers, shirts and dresses, and suits and ties. But the meanings of dress do not inhere in the garments themselves. They are created in the

---

[1] UNFPA, 'Zambia's young people and the road to 2030', 12 August 2016, https://zambia.unfpa.org/en/news/zambia%E2%80%99s-young-people-and-road-2030.

practices through which we put them to use. It is in clothing performance that meanings are lodged, constructed by wearers and viewers, and therefore meanings are a product of distinct dress practices in specific situations. These observations apply perforce to the import of second-hand clothes to Africa in the analysis of which the association of the West is so hegemonic that it is a challenge to argue, as I have done in my work, for creative localisation (Hansen 2000a). Some of the Western observers who have paid passing attention to the flourishing second-hand clothing markets in cities across Africa have viewed the dress practices such markets are giving rise to as faded and worn imitations of the West, constituting the flip side of Western fashion (Haggblade 1990). In such accounts, the special significance of dress – its unique ability to mediate between the self and society – becomes entirely incidental.

Aside from the utilitarian, monetary value, what in fact accounts for the attractions of imported secondhand clothing? In Zambia, dressing, and dressing up, is both an end and a means. In effect, dress is both a resource and a technique. There is a genuine pleasure to be gained from dressing well, which in the view of others is a sign of well-being. While preoccupations with the dressed body are of long standing in Zambia, specifically styled garments have come and gone. This preoccupation constitutes a highly developed sensibility that implicates discerning skills from a variety of sources in creating an overall look that helps bring about experiences of pride, pleasure, and feeling good. In this way, clothing is an important part of the aesthetic of everyday life. Mediating between self and society, the dressed body also construes desires, including global imaginaries. As a cultural and material resource, secondhand clothing does all of these things.

In their dealings with the West's used clothing, consumers in Zambia reconstruct secondhand garments as 'new' or 'fresh,' and transform them by notions of taste and selection to fit the embodied dress norms of their local clothing universe. It is by crafting themselves through dress that Zambian wearers of secondhand clothing achieve the look they fondly call 'the latest', that fluid appearance of change and novelty that we tend to associate with fashion (Finkelstein 1998). But even if the effect of such appearances is rarely precise or explicit but fluid and volatile, appearance itself is not arbitrary. Rather, it is the product of a set of clearly identifiable, interacting practices the effects of which converge in the moment of display. For behind the commanding appearances of 'the latest' lie a series of practices that entail competence in dealing with the quality and care of garment fabrics as well as strategy and rehearsal of the ways in which people dress and groom themselves.

I call the critical skill that is central to their clothing savvy 'clothing competence'.

This chapter discusses how the West's discarded clothing becomes fashion for young people in Zambia's capital, Lusaka, in a process that expresses a vibrant aesthetic sensibility in its cultivation of appearances that makes people take notice. I first provide a brief overview of the secondhand clothing markets I examined in Zambia during the 1990s. Then I explore how fashion works out in some specific cases. I begin with examples of young men's dress preferences and turn next to young mid- to upper-income women's engagements with their dressed self-presentation in public settings. I argue that the meanings of 'new' or 'fresh' and 'the latest' do not inhere in the garments themselves but are constructed anew in each context. While the crafting of 'the latest' hinges both on the material properties of garments and on identifiable 'techniques of the body' (Mauss [1935] 1973), the process also has an affecting hold that makes heads turn. When this occurs, the problematic reference to the Western origin of these clothes has long vanished.

Secondhand Clothing Markets in Zambia

Zambia's economy has been on a downward slide since the mid-1970s with a period of upturn during the early 2000s. Between 1980 and 1994, the country received numerous structural adjustment loans from the World Bank and its sister agency, the International Monetary Fund. Today Zambians are poorer, on a per capita basis, than they were at independence from British colonial rule in 1964. Yet the enormous cross-over appeal of secondhand clothing cannot be explained merely in terms of its affordability to poor people but above all is explained by reference to the importance people attribute to dress and appearance.

Dressing in secondhand clothes has been part of this active engagement with clothing for a long time. We saw in Chapter 2 how in the 1940s and 1950s such clothes were brought across the border from the Belgian Congo into Northern Rhodesia where they were resold by local traders. Since the mid- to late 1980s, secondhand clothing has been imported directly from the United States and Europe into Zambia. Because the country is land-locked, imported container loads of second-hand clothes are trucked overland all the way from ports in South Africa, Mozambique, and Tanzania to Zambia's capital, Lusaka. The contents of the wholesale bales in turn are retailed in local markets and distributed across the country. Some towns on the Copperbelt also receive second-hand clothing imports trucked across the border with Tanzania as does the provincial headquarters of the Eastern Province, Chipata, from

Figure 7.1 Secondhand clothing vendors in Lusaka, 1992. Author's photo.

Mozambique. After a period of rapid growth during the first half of the 1990s, imported secondhand clothes appear to have become an established part of the Zambian clothing scene, no longer causing much debate in public. With the increasing import of new garments from China after the turn of the last millennium, secondhand clothing's share of total imports has actually declined.

Since the mid-1980s, imported secondhand clothing in Zambia has been referred to as *salaula*, which in the Chibemba language means approximately 'selecting from a pile by rummaging'. The term describes vividly the process that takes place once a bale of imported secondhand clothing has been opened in the market and consumers select garments to satisfy both their clothing needs and their clothing desires (see Figure 7.1). The shop window of Zambia's secondhand clothing trade, the big public markets, create an atmosphere much like shopping malls where consumers pursue almost unlimited desires with an abandon not possible in formal bricks-and-mortar stores, where employees often deal with them offhandedly or pressure them into making purchases.

On first sight, the *salaula* markets meet the non-local observer's eye as a chaotic mass of secondhand clothing hung up on flimsy wood contraptions, displayed on tables, or dumped in piles on the ground. But that

Figure 7.2 Young men selling secondhand draperies in Lusaka, 1992.
Author's photo.

view is deceptive. A variety of informal rules in fact organise the vending space and structure sales practices. And both vendors and customers know these practices. A prospective customer looking for a specific garment will go to a particular part of the market. The vendors of men's suits, for example, one of the most expensive items, tend to be located in a part of the outdoor market that is near major thoroughfares such as a main road passable by automobiles. So are vendors of other high-demand garments, such as women's skirts and blouses, and the best-selling item of all, at least in Zambia, baby clothes. Zambia's high birth rate, combined with the desire to dress babies in good-looking clothes, helps explain this popularity. There are spatial clusters of vendors selling shoes and, during the winter in the southern hemisphere, cold weather clothing such as sweaters, jackets, and overcoats. I have seen fur jackets for sale as well (see Figure 7.2). Because vendors sometimes change inventory, the spatial demarcations are not static. An entire section of Kamwala market is dedicated to recycling where items that do not sell easily are turned into new garments. Here, trousers and dresses made from crimplene (polyester knit) are cut into pieces and sewn together in contrastive patterns or colours, for example, as girls' dresses and boys' shorts. Colourful curtain fabric is made into women's dresses and two-piece outfits, and draperies with metallic sheen become men's trousers. One workshop with young male tailors specialises in sewing such trousers, adding cut-off labels from other garments as a decorative feature.

The display on most secondhand clothing stands is carefully designed. High-quality items are hung on clothes hangers on makeshift walls. A clothesline or a wood stand may display a row of cotton dresses. Everything that meets the eye has been carefully selected with a view to both presentation and sales strategy. Lively discussions and price negotiations accompany sales. The piles on the ground include damaged items and garments that have been around for a while. Such items are sold 'on order', that is, several pieces at a discount, and they are often purchased by rural customers who take them to the villages to resell.

Near the high end of the secondhand clothing display, and close to the major roads of the market section, cluster the 'boutiques'. Boutiques in these markets sell specially preselected items, coordinated to form matched outfits that are stylish. They tend to be operated by young vendors who 'pick', in the language of the market. Once other traders open secondhand clothing bales, the pickers descend on them, selecting garments they buy on the spot. Then they put together, for instance, women's two-piece ensembles, men's suits, and leisure wear. Most of the boutique operators I met were young men who were very skilled at choosing quality stock and had a fine eye for what might sell, a great sense of style, and a flair for making stunning combinations. I also met boutique operators who were women. Some of them had tailoring skills, and some also sewed clothing to order from their own homes.

Consumers in Zambia go to secondhand clothing markets for many reasons. White-collar workers in Lusaka's city centre often spend their lunch hour going through the secondhand clothing stalls, sometimes making purchases at whim. Others go in order to find just the right item to match a particular garment or to find something unique to wear for an upcoming event. Some women who tailor in their homes search the markets for interesting buttons, belts, and trim to accent garments. And some go to purchase garments with the intention to resell. But the vast majority shop from *salaula* for clothing for themselves and their families. Secondhand clothing not only serves people with few financial means. Consumers come into the city centre from residential areas like those in which I examined clothing consumption and where roughly two-thirds of all households supplied most of their members' clothing from secondhand clothing markets (Hansen 2000a: 184–92). Only the very tiny high-income group in Zambia has an effective choice in the clothing market. This group, called *apamwamba* from a term in the Chinyanja language that means approximately 'those on the top', purchases clothing everywhere, including from secondhand clothing markets. People from these better-off households spend more money on second-hand clothing than those who are less well off. As I discuss in more detail in Chapter 9, recent years have witnessed the emergence of entrepreneurs who have launched themselves as designers and are beginning to make a mark with 'African designs', some of them with *chitenge* fabrics, which is adding new value to the local fashion scene.

Clothing Competence

Clothing consumption is hard work. A vital dimension of the demand side concerns issues about cultural taste and style that come together in the creation of a 'total look'. Concerns with fabric quality, texture, and construction precede that creation, which in turn revolves around the anticipated dress needs of the specific situation. When shopping at secondhand clothing markets, consumers' desire to create attractive appearances is inspired by styles and trends from across the world. Through this exposure, *salaula* fashions bring consumers into a bigger world: the world of awareness, of now.

Consumers draw on these influences in ways that are informed by local norms about bodies and dress. The desired clothing silhouette for both adult women and men is neat and tidy. It is a product of immaculate garment care and of wearing clothes in ways that are not considered to be too revealing. Even then, women's and men's garments are understood differently. The cultural norms about how to dress weigh down on women much more heavily than on men, with the result that many women feel restrained in their freedom to dress so as not to provoke men. For example, women should not expose their shoulders; above all, as noted in Chapter 5, they must cover their 'private parts', which in this region of Africa includes their thighs and buttocks. This means that dress length, tightness, and fabric transparency become issues when women interact with men and elders both at home and in public. With such dress norms as background, it is perhaps not surprising that controversies that date back to the 1960s over women's wearing of miniskirts continue to occur.

The desire for uniqueness, to stand out, while dressing the body on Zambian terms entails considerable skill in garment selection from the abundance of *salaula*, in making discriminating decisions concerning quality, style, and value for money, in garment co-ordination to fit specific occasions and contexts, and in the overall presentation and comportment of the dressed body to produce a 'total look'. Many consumers are extraordinarily savvy when it comes to clothing purchases aimed to produce particular effects. In fact, shopping from *salaula* does not mean that anything goes but depends critically for its success on the skilled 'clothing competence' of consumers. In this creative process, consumers are active in putting together an attractive and unique look for themselves. The underlying sensibility of their clothing competence is a visual aesthetic that on first sight cultivates endless variation yet on closer analysis also is in the service of continuity.

Young Men's Dress Dilemmas

Unlike young women who carefully monitor the way they dress in public, young men like to draw attention to themselves, in different ways to be sure, depending on their socioeconomic circumstances and regional location in Zambia's declining economy. They actively seek to present a smart appearance that is both fashionable and neat. Young men's self-conscious preoccupations with suits and jeans illustrate different constructions of these attributes of dress.

Suits are worn widely across the civil service ranks and other white-collar jobs in Zambia and are often referred to as corporate wear. Formal suits index young urban men's desire to become adults, hold jobs, and head households. Consider George Chulamanda, in 2005 the youngest ever minister of sport, youth and child development, whom fashion pundits characterised as a very trendy and fashionable guy. Wanting to be an inspiration to young people, he told a reporter that his favourite clothing was dark pinstriped suits, the dress of today's leaders: 'We are leaders of today and tomorrow and should lead by example' (*Post* 2005, 2 December) (see Figure 7.3). To be sure, cutting a fine figure in a sharp suit conveys something important about personal background, respectability, and responsibility. In this view, suits are identified with authority and patriarchal social power, which is widespread throughout Zambia.

Most of the young men in their late teens or early twenties in a secondary school in Lusaka who in 1995 described for me where they bought their clothes and how they liked to dress aspired to this dress practice and the ideal it conveys.[2] Some of their essays were written with an immediacy and directness that draws the reader into the student's household. We can almost see Moses' father, an employee of a parastatal company in Lusaka whom his son described as 'a thin birdlike man pushing forty who always wears rimless glasses'. In his spare time his

---

[2] I discussed the student essay as a research methodology in Chapter 5. The quotes in the next two sections are from Hansen (2000b: 40–49).

Figure 7.3 Young man in his first store-bought suit on a visit to the secondhand clothing market in Kabwe, 1993. Author's photo.

father liked to sew clothes and was, according to Moses, 'one of the best tailors in town'. He commented: 'Usually on weekends he would sew from morning till evenings; his face placid at the sewing machine with a thin whistling from his lips. In the backyard at lunchtime, he would sit behind the desk attending to his clients on a bench.'

Suits were the preferred wear for male white-collar workers in 1995, as they continue to be today. 'Suits are the clothes I like most', explained Simon, 'because they make me look decent and soon I will be joining the society of workers.' The word 'workers', in the Zambian context, does not mean working class but office employment. Morgan, his classmate, described a pair of trousers and a jacket he recently had received: 'I was full of joy ... I like these clothes because a lot of people say that I look like a general manager and not only that, they also say that I look like a rich man.' And Moses' delight in a double-breasted jacket his father had given him is evident: 'After wearing it I surveyed myself in the mirror. I looked like a film actor ... it was really a nice jacket. I like jackets because they suit me like a second skin. I have plenty of beef and muscles around my shoulders which forms a good round shape if [I] wear one [a jacket].' The reverse applied to Norman, who felt physically awkward. As he explained: 'Whenever I am wearing a suit, I am always thinking that everybody is looking at me.... My physical structure does not earn me the prestige of wearing suits. I am slightly short and very thin. So whenever I put on a suit, it does not accord me the beauty of appearing best in clothes.'

Other classmates liked jeans, particularly because of their durability but also because 'they are in style now'. But wearing jeans had a flip side that too readily called forth the image of scruffy youths and street vendors, who in the popular view readily are associated with illegal activities. According to Moses, 'I hate wearing jeans because people may fail to distinguish between cigarette sellers and myself.' Lusaka's downtown streets are full of young men who are selling all kinds of goods. They put much effort into being seen, and many of them dress in a striking manner.

If suits and jeans framed young urban men's desires for a better life, young men in rural areas had similar desires but were more circum-scribed by the conditions in which they lived. Secondary school stu-dents in Mansa, a provincial town in Luapula Province, expressed this clearly. As Joshua explained: 'Of all the clothes, I like strong ones which can serve me longer such as jeans. I like them because it is not easy for me to buy soap, and most of the time I do manual work in order to earn my living.' The suit figures in the desires of these young rural men mostly by its absence. Describing why the suit combination did not fit his situation, Nicholas explained: 'Such clothes can easily be torn and I think they are for office working people, so they don't suit me.' Yet he added as an afterthought, 'If I had a choice, I would really like to wear suits.'

Jeans were a must in the evolving street vendor style. In addition to the style explanations I describe below, the preference of street vendors for denim has an obvious practical reason. Jeans, one of them explained, 'are durable; they are nice and easy to keep especially for bachelors like me who have no one to look after our clothes'. What the young vendors my assistant interviewed in 1997 did for their own pleasure was to dress up in public in variations on the baggy-jeans look, influenced by the spread of

American hip-hop music and its fashions.[3] The layered look was in vogue that year, as were knitted caps, referred to as head-socks, and shoes with thick rubber soles, often worn without socks.

The secondary school students and the young street vendors purchased their clothes from several sources. Some bought imported clothing from suitcase traders who bring in garments from abroad; some went to the tailor for specific wear; and they all scoured the *salaula* markets for just the right items. As one of the street vendors explained, 'In *salaula* you will find things you can't believe how good they are.' When shopping for clothes, the young vendors look for garments that will contribute to the overall creation of a particular style, which in the late 1990s was 'the big look' rather than for brand-name items. 'I wear the big look because it is fashion', one of them said, while another explained how he liked to 'move with time'. I don't like 'common clothes and imitations', said yet another.

Making associations between specific articles of clothing and behaviour, young people construct an understanding of their world and how they inhabit it. Young male secondary school students with high economic aspirations for themselves do not want to be mistaken for school dropouts turned street vendors. They desire suits. The vendors for their part wear clothes they equate with the influence and success achieved by popular performers from Africa and beyond. Putting themselves together with clothing, a major part of which is from *salaula*, both groups of young people are dressing to explore who they are and who they would like to become.[4]

Dress Codes and Choices: *Apamwamba* Women's Dress Practices

If suits are the garments to wear for young men who wish to be upwardly mobile, 'decent dress' that does not reveal too much is the style for young women to wear, including young women of better means who have real options in the clothing market because of their economic background. The *apamwamba* are trendsetters in many lifestyle matters, including clothing consumption, and as such they loom larger in debates about clothing and dress practice than do other groups.

---

[3] Oscar Hamangaba assisted me with this work.
[4] Eileen Moyer offers comparable insights about young men working and living on the streets of Dar es Salaam, Tanzania (2003). While influenced by American hip-hop culture and Jamaican Rastafari ideals, they dress to achieve a look that is suitable to their local living environment and reflects their own desires.

The dress presentation by women and men announcers of the daily evening news on national television in Zambia, the government-controlled Zambia National Broadcasting Corporation (ZNBC), illustrates the almost iconic status of the suit and decent dress in Zambia. I tracked these dress presentations over the course of my two-month stay in Lusaka during the southern hemisphere's cold months of July and August both in 2003 and 2004. Back in 1995, I had interviewed then popular television announcer Mary Phiri about dress protocol for the news announcers. There was none, she said, other than 'decent'. Unlike on South African television where clothing firms sometimes dress announcers and have their names appearing in the credit line, clothing firms do not to my knowledge dress the news announcers on Zambian television.[5] The announcers themselves purchase what to wear, including garments from *salaula*. Without exception, male announcers always wore a suit and tie. While the severity of their suits varied from striped and check to single colours of very dark, grey, and beige, ties and handkerchiefs offered variation. By contrast, the women announcers' clothes were more diverse. Some female announcers were more likely than others to wear *chitenge* suits or dresses, that is, the very ornamented outfits, tailored with much elaboration and attention to detail of colourful printed fabric. This dress presentation sometimes included complicated head-ties constructed in what women referred to as the 'West African fashion'. A pan-African fashion fusion is evident here, as Zambian women refer to such headdresses as *dukus*, a term that I perhaps mistakenly thought derived from the Afrikaans language word *doek* for scarf, but I have also seen *duku* used for a headdress from Ghana (Dogbe 2003: 387). More women news announcers wore *chitenge* dresses in 2003 than in 2004 for reasons that may have to do with the absence of some very popular announcers. The rest of the women news announcers wore world or global dress, most frequently jackets with contrasting shirt or blouse with a variety of decorative trim. In Zambia, the combination of skirt and jacket is usually referred to as office wear.

In male-dominated Zambian society, the considerable scrutiny women's dressed bodies receive in public extends into the television production studio. In Chapter 5, I mentioned in passing a highly profiled 1997 event involving popular television announcer, Dora Siliya, who was suspended by the ZNBC for 'insubordination arising from her wearing miniskirts' (*Post* 1997, 22 May). Storming out of the office, Ms Siliya claimed that 'dressing is personal and has nothing to do with my work'.

---

[5] I have seen names of hairdressers acknowledged on Zambian television.

Letters to the editor by women ridiculed the management's decision. In the words of three such women letter writers from Lusaka: 'This is the 20th century for God's sake and not the Elizabethan era! Young women have to move with times and keep up with fashion. Besides, women should not have their right to dress as they please stifled by old hags' (*Post* 1997, 26 May).[6]

Some segments of Zambian society continue to attribute highly charged sexual meanings to women's dressed bodies. Controversies over miniskirts keep recurring, not in a déjà vu sense but in accentuated versions in the time of HIV and AIDS, as for example in February 2006 in a series of letters to the editor of a major paper, prompted by a ban on miniskirts and tight trousers issued in Tanzania (*Weekend Post* 2006, 19 February). Young women are well aware of the sexual implications of their use of miniskirts, and they reckon with them in situational terms. In fact women, both young and adult, claim that men have a much easier time dressing than they do because men have far fewer issues to be concerned with in terms of body shape, covering specific parts of the body, and coordinating garments and accessories. When young women from middle-income and *apamwamba* backgrounds move about in public settings away from home, they are intensely aware of male society's problematic attitude to their dressed bodies. Some of them seek to avert the male gaze through their dress, while others hope to catch it.

Interacting with young people of mid- to upper-income background in 2002 and 2003, an assistant and I sought to learn where they hang out in their free time, with whom, and how they dress.[7] Here the focus is on the women. Such women constitute a small segment of Lusaka's huge youth population. Pursuing further education at colleges, training institutions, and universities, including some abroad in Australia and the United States, most of these young women have the means, usually because of well-placed parents, to socialise and meet with friends at Lusaka's new shopping malls, other shopping venues, popular pool halls, bars, and parks. There is a nightclub and disco scene as well, which some of them also frequent. In their daytime interactions, aside from sharing news about friends and talking about their futures, relationships, sex, and the entertainment scene, these young women spend considerable time

---

[6] Keeping up with fashion, Dora Siliya has moved with the times, obtaining a BA degree in mass communication from the University of Zambia and an MA degree in development economics from the University of Cambridge. In 2006 she was elected Member of Parliament representing Petauke Central district. She has held several ministerial appointments, first as deputy minister of commerce and industry and in 2020 as minister of information and broadcasting.

[7] Tamara Nkhoma assisted me with this work.

discussing 'looks', exchanging information about the availability of particularly desired garments, and who has been seen wearing what and where. Most of them love clothes. Unlike some parts of the world, in Zambia their interest in dress is valued in positive terms by the friends with whom they move about. They all spend considerable time and effort discussing the latest. 'It is the combination of clothing', explained a 22-year-old psychology student, 'that demonstrates your sense of style.'

'Clothes', said a 24-year-old marketing student, 'place me in my class.' Like many others, she did not like baggy jeans, 'no boring loose slacks', as one of the young women expressed it, 'because they are tomboyish, and gangsta', a comparison that we also heard some young men make. During the daytime interactions when we interviewed the young women, they dressed decently but casually, meaning controlling for body size, in tight jeans, or knee-length denim skirts resting on the hips with waistlines accentuated by cropped short tops. Young women who were heavy-set wore long, fitted skirts with slits. A 22-year-old university student explained that her outfit, combining jeans, matching top, and smart shoes, 'makes me look mature and outlines my model[-shaped] body'. Altogether, by Zambian norms, there was nothing too revealing in the way these young women presented their dressed bodies when moving about in public space. Their hair was either elaborately braided or cut short, the most popular women's hairstyles at the time. They accessorised their overall look with cell phones, handbags, shoes, and jewellery. I made these observations years before the availability of smartphones with cameras, which in Zambia as elsewhere are offering their users new means of self-styling (Gilbert 2019).

These young women sourced most of their clothing from stores and boutiques, including from abroad. They also, as we saw earlier, shopped from *salaula* as a pastime, not a need. Some had never been to a tailor. Some of them were not keen to wear *chitenge* dresses, and they did not all own one. Young women's attitude to wearing *chitenge* outfits revolves around body size and age. Looking best on full-figured women, these elaborately styled dresses evoke a level of maturity that some young women consider to be 'old', something that they associate with what their mothers and grandmothers wear. With such an outlook, no wonder that casual is the way to dress.

'Everything I wear', said a 21-year-old woman, 'should make people look and say "wow, she is nice …".' In their concern to create their own fashion statements and demonstrate an individual sense of style, these young women from middle- to upper-class backgrounds make sure that they show off their *apamwamba* status. While their self-styling has something in common with the hip, cutting-edge, middle-class lifestyles that

Sarah Nuttall has described for the Y generation of Rosebank in Johannesburg (2004), it does not come close to the sartorial, visual, and sonic dimensions of youth culture in Rosebank. The reasons may have to do with Zambia's status as one of the world's least developed countries. In their self-styling through dress, *apamwamba* women in Lusaka seek to avoid 'sliding down' in local socioeconomic terms. While they wear world or global fashions, the presentation of their dressed bodies becomes meaningful on Zambian terms, that is, in the local context of economic decline, urban poverty, and other processes set into motion by Zambia's unequal place in the global economy.

Dress Performativity

Because young people are everywhere in African urban public space, conspicuously present and highly visible, the creativity of their dress practices drew attention in scholarship long before the flourishing of research on youth, beginning around the late 1990s. I briefly note one such practice dating back several decades, the fashions of which have 'baffled scholars with their panoply of paradoxes and ambiguities' (Gondola 2010: 172). This is the flamboyant fashions of the *sapeurs* in Brazzaville and Kinshasa in the two Congos, who celebrated well-dressed appearances by wearing expensive high-end clothing obtained from Paris, proudly displaying *la griffe* (the label) (Gandoulou 1989: 12–13). This work invites attention for two reasons, one for its spectacular findings, and the second for situating dress practice in the social and cultural histories of the local contexts in which they occur. With experiences from the diaspora, including some political dissidence, the *sapeurs* were a product of an environment different, for example, from that of the *Swenkas* in South Africa and their dapper dress style in high-street brands with a jazz-age inspired look. Their transition from segregated life in a colonial town to a global city like Johannesburg entailed another context. A documentary suggests that migrant workers dressed in this style during the 1950s on visits to their rural homes during the Christmas holidays. Their striking suits showed their families that they had reached a measure of success working in the city (Rønde 2005).

Rather than viewing the wearing of elegant Western-styled suits of the *sapeurs* and *swenkas* as copying, the works I just referred to describe their dress performances as combining African and Western dress elements, creating cosmopolitan masculine identities. Sharing an obsession with high-end brands and grooming, embedded in socioeconomic and cultural inequality, the *sapeurs* and *swenkas* are very much the outcomes of their distinct local circumstances. Probably one of the most cited studies of spectacular dress practice in Africa, the *sapeur* style is not directly comparable to those presented in other local contexts where young men's dressed appearances also are both conspicuous and spectacular (Masquelier 2013; Newell 2012; Scheld 2007).

Moving with the Times

Cities like Lusaka are the prime stages for the translation of globalisation into local understandings and experiences. Monitoring how they dress in public, clothing-conscious Zambians pay considerable attention to the possibilities of their garments when dressing in world or global styles, seeking to anticipate their desired effects. Across class, the dress of young Zambians invokes aspirations, desires, and imaginaries. When describing in her clothing essay how everyone in her family liked to dress, secondary school student Rachel from Lusaka explained that her sister 'is the one who lives in dreamland, because she always wants to look the best, that's why we all at home call her Alexis [the lead role in the TV series *Dynasty*, played by actress Joan Collins]. She likes looking expensive, by which I mean she doesn't like cheap clothes. She is 14 years old now.' Rachel, whose father was a businessman, explained that she liked all sorts of clothes as long as they fitted her nicely and her 'African figure' felt comfortable in them. When she was uncertain about how to dress, she sought advice from her grandmother.

Young men eager to become adults desire suits because they convey notions of authority and independence, which their everyday life in school and at home denies them. Young male street vendors dress in oversized jeans not only because they are durable and easy to care for, but also because such garments are part of a global dress style turned fashionable by popular international performers. Young *apamwamba* women reckon with their body size and shape, making careful choices to present their dressed bodies in public, decently, in what is 'in fashion now' but with their local sense of class distinction.

Will they pull off wearing it? The meaning and value of Zambian preoccupations with clothing do not inhere in garments themselves and therefore do not have much to do with whether clothes are secondhand or new. This chapter's descriptions demonstrate that clothes are not worn passively but require active collaboration by their wearers. This means that experiences of dress, the evaluations viewers make of it, are not given or fixed but created anew in each context. In their daily rehearsal for dressing and dressing up, young people try to anticipate the situations and contexts in which they will be finding themselves. Seeking to negotiate the specific moment of such situations, they may experience the thrill of enjoyment, or disapproval. In this affecting experience, the distinction between used clothing and new fashions becomes irrelevant, as does the problematic differentiation between Western and non-Western dress styles. The attraction of secondhand clothing to consumers in Zambia about which I inquired earlier is now evident. Masked in accounts of global inequities, imported secondhand clothes are not incidental accessories but active participants in transforming the lives of their new wearers. In spite of the aggressive forces that structure the global circuit of garment production and, along with it, the international secondhand clothing trade, there do exist spaces where locally authored dress distinctions may take over.

Snapshot 4: *Salaula*

When we name the objects that enter our daily lives in our own language, we take ownership of them (see Figure 7.4). We appropriate them and domesticate them to become part of our social relations and make them into active agents in our everyday lives and histories. Imported second-hand clothes are given many names in different African countries. In some parts of Ghana and Nigeria their local names mean 'dead white

Figure 7.4 Sign on gate to secondhand wholesaler, Lusaka, 1997. Author's photo.

people's clothes'. The expression *obroni w'awu* in the Akan language in Ghana, for example, invokes the idea that imported secondhand clothes must have been the property of foreigners. The Wolof term *fěggy jaay*, meaning 'shake and sell', names the marketing process of secondhand clothing in Senegal (Scheld 2007: 240). In East Africa they are referred to in the Swahili language as *mitumba*, which refers to the bales in which they are transported. In some regions of the Democratic Republic of Congo they are called *sola*, meaning to choose, while in Mozambique they continue to be referred to as *calamidades*, a term that references the Civil War calamities in the wake of independence in 1975, when relief agencies began bringing in used clothing for distribution.

Sometime in the mid-1980s in Zambia, the term *salaula* developed as a common name for imported secondhand clothing. It means, in the Chibemba language, 'to select from a pile in the manner of rummaging', or in short, 'to pick'. The term names, graphically, the selection process that takes place once a bale of imported secondhand clothing has been opened in the market and consumers select garments to satisfy both their clothing needs and clothing desires. What is remarkable about the name *salaula* is that it makes no reference whatsoever to the origin of the clothes as used garments from the West. In effect, when used clothing has been sorted and pressed into bales in Europe and North America for export and has arrived in Zambia, it has been stripped of its former social life.

During the colonial period in Zambia imported secondhand clothing was often spoken of as *kombo*, according to some alluding to the border crossing point Mokambo between Northern Rhodesia and the Belgian Congo. There, as we saw in Chapter 2, during the post–World War II years, traders from Northern Rhodesia purchased used clothing from Europe, as its import into the colony was prohibited.[8] Several years later in the late 1980s, the availability of imported secondhand clothing in Lusaka began to grow markedly. Before that, township markets used to include but a few secondhand clothing traders, who sourced used garments at the door of expatriate households or had connections to people

---

[8] I have attempted to trace the origin or etymology of the term *kombo*. The specialists in the Chibemba language I consulted have not offered any suggestions. Swahili experts suggest that *kombo* might be a word from the version of the Swahili language that is spoken in Katanga/Shaba. The term stems from Katanga, according to Mwelwa Musambachime (personal communication, 28 April 1999). He remembered from his childhood in Mansa in the Luapula Province in the early 1950s that the term applied to 'used clothes' from abroad. It was used 'only for imported secondhand clothes which came in bales', and not for used clothing bought in shops.

who brought used clothing to the capital from Zaire (today the Democratic Republic of Congo).

During Zambia's socialist-inspired second republic (1972–91), severe import restrictions applied to so-called nonessential commodities including secondhand clothing, yet import licences were occasionally granted to persons who, judging from popular commentary, were closely linked by kinship, marriage, and connections to the powers-that-be. Then in the late 1980s, Zairean traders began to bring bales of secondhand clothing into local markets for resale, and the first direct importers appeared on the scene. This took place against the backdrop of growing popular criticism of the politico-economic regime of the one-party state, when the economy gradually began opening in the late 1980s. The import grew rapidly in the early 1990s when all township and city markets included expanding sections of secondhand clothing, which increased hugely after the turn to multi-party politics and economic liberalisation in 1991. By then, the secondhand clothing sections of local markets in urban and rural areas far surpassed the produce sections in both size and activity.

The name for *salaula* in Chibemba, selecting from a pile by rummaging, captures the enormous choice and the ability to select from an abundant supply of garments. Everyone wants to cut a good figure, and purchasing their clothes from *salaula* markets is a means to that end. Adult Zambian women prefer to wear dresses with a variety of decorative accents that display their mature bodies without exposing them, and adult Zambian men like to dress in formal suits that present a tidy body silhouette. And many young adults of both sexes who dress within the prevailing cultural norms for gender-appropriate clothing also like to experiment with style. What matters in their clothing selections is not the Western origin of suits and dresses but that these garments have been incorporated into local dress repertoires so long ago that today they are considered as standard Zambian wear (see Figure 7.5). In short, as I suggested at the outset of this 'Snapshot', the West's used clothes have become appropriated and domesticated, and naming them *salaula* is a part of this process.

The value of clothes no longer wanted in the West is then redefined in a process through which secondhand clothes come to be considered as 'new'. The process unfolds through contacts and communications between exporters and importers, and in on-site visits. It continues in warehouses when local traders purchase the imported bales and in the big markets where people talk about clothing. And it manifests itself in how people in Zambia dress in secondhand clothes. Taken together, it is a process through which the meaning of clothes shifts. When we dress,

Figure 7.5 Woman wearing *chitenge* outfit examining a skirt in the *salaula* market, Lusaka, 1992. Author's photo.

something happens to our entire expression. The distinction is in the wearing, which involves the body. It is during social interaction that secondhand clothes become new outfits. In turn we notice the results in everyday life, on the street, and during social occasions through how people dress and in their commentaries on other people's clothes.

8   Fashioning Demonstrative Displays

It is people who move things. In this chapter I demonstrate the fleeting qualities of dress by focusing on different contextual evaluations of the involvement of clothes with their wearers' changing lives. The 'social life of things' perspective opened up the way for many important insights by drawing our attention to the constructed nature of things whose value and meanings change as they move through time and across space (Appadurai 1986). Yet this approach to exploring material culture and value falls somewhat short by 'squeezing out' considerations of the social death of things (Colloredo-Mansfeld 2003: 246). When it comes to dress, that death, release, or ephemerality may be captured by changing the focus from things to social relations and interactions. With this change, the point of departure is not the things themselves but rather the strategies within which they are embedded. Jonathan Friedman, whose suggestion I am following here, argues that 'things do not have social lives. Rather social life has things' (Friedman 1991: 161).

I begin by describing an episode that highlights the fleeting qualities of dress in social interaction and turn next to the aesthetic sensibilities that are at play in clothes-shopping from the *salaula* market. Women's cultivation of appearance is perhaps most dramatically evident in their efforts at demonstrative displays of dressed bodies exemplified in specific performance situations such as kitchen parties (bridal showers) with which I begin and end this chapter.

When my friend Lily attended her sister-in-law's kitchen party in one of Lusaka's high-income residential areas in August 2006, she wore a two-piece 'Indian' inspired outfit in blue-toned colours.[1] Kitchen parties are all-female events where relatives and friends, including expatriates like myself, come together with presents to help the bride-to-be with utensils for 'the kitchen'. They are modelled on a loose version, a fusion, of local initiation ceremonies and Western bridal showers. There are

---

[1] This is a fictive name.

drums, played by women brought in from the townships; dance, food, and drink; and above all, bodies dressed to be viewed. At this event, Lily, who otherwise was well known as a very stylish dresser, had worn her outfit on a previous occasion. It was obvious to those of us 'in the know' that some guests at the party took note of her low-key dress presentation. For Lily was in the process of divorcing her husband for whose younger sister the kitchen party was held; as a matter of fact, she did not even want to be there. Unlike Lily, the bride-to-be's mother and some of the other women guests experienced the thrill that arises from demonstrative display of clothes and accessories, which the wearer has never before put together in this particular manner. This is the sensation of the dressed body, beautiful in that one glorious instant that will never be experienced in that way again. For that single moment we love, or as Lily, hate what we wear.

Clothes have many lives but this is not my chief concern here. Some clothes outlive us while we exile others from our wardrobes for a variety of reasons, among them changes in fashion and weight loss or gain. Regardless of reason, many of the no longer wanted clothes that we in the West donate to charitable organizations end up in the commercial secondhand clothing market from where a large portion is exported. Zambia is one of the many countries in Africa in which imported second-hand clothing from North America and Europe is extraordinarily popular. Beginning new lives, imported secondhand clothes fulfil both a need and a desire. My concern here is desire and its relationship to dress practice, especially to the pleasure of demonstrative display that I just described.

My specific question is this: How can I possibly consider dress as fleeting and evanescent when in previous chapters I have argued strongly that preoccupations with the dressed body are of long standing in Zambia, constituting a constant, so to speak, a continuity in a fashion world of rapid change? A wearer's experience of dress is hard to pin down because it is a product of the moment, and it vanishes almost as soon as it has been experienced. Because the experience is context dependent, the combination of clothes that prompted it cannot be easily reconstructed, which is why the demonstrative display when an outfit is first seen can never be recuperated subsequently. The outfit remains, as Lily's, an already displayed outfit, now demoted, and soon to be pressed into service as everyday wear for work. On the pages that follow I briefly describe some processes that are at the heart of Zambian preoccupations with clothing and then go on to illustrate some of the material processes that are at play in producing the ephemerality and fleeting experience of dress.

But first a caveat or two. First, the way that I try to work through my question is commodity specific in the sense that it hinges on the very special power of clothing, both old and new, for of course they implicate one another, and therefore it may not apply to explanations of how the materialisation of evanescence and constancy plays out for the case of other commodities. As I noted in Chapter 1, this special power of clothing derives from the ability of the dressed body to mediate both individual and collective identities and desires. And second, my approach to the question I posed above is culturally specific in the sense that what I have to say about Zambia and secondhand clothing consumption may not apply to other countries where this commodity, after its entangled journey, is also in great demand.

Crafting oneself through dress provides that space between the performed and the desired that we may term 'fashion' even for the case of secondhand dress. Joanne Finkelstein, whom I am paraphrasing for this constructive insight, acknowledges that our first inclination is to think of fashion as instantaneous and volatile, that is, really fleeting, and evanescent. Yet she argues that 'the constancy of circulation, whether in ideas or material goods, indicates that the actual function of fashion is to give the appearance of change and novelty without precipitating any rupture in the status quo' (Finkelstein 1998: 5–6). Like Finkelstein, Gilles Lipovetsky also sees permanence as one of fashion's most significant features through 'its logic of inconsistency, its great organisational, and aesthetic mutations' (Lipovetsky 1994: 4).

The relationship between ephemerality and continuity poses only an apparent dilemma when it comes to secondhand clothing consumption in Zambia. While the significance of the dressed body is of long standing, specific garments come and go. The preoccupation with the dressed body is an aesthetic sensibility that involves discerning skills from a variety of sources in creating an overall look that results in pride, pleasure, and experiences of feeling good.

Crafting Dress Uniqueness

Shopping from *salaula* does not mean that anything goes. The underlying sensibility is a visual aesthetic that on first sight cultivates endless variation yet on closer analysis is also in the service of continuity. The two dimensions, as I discuss below, do not cancel each other out. In fact, their simultaneity keeps the options open and it is also, as I noted earlier, at the core of what fashion is about.

To flesh out these suggestions I describe some examples of adult women's dress practice. Distinctions by context are helpful here. We may explore whether a woman is at home or at work, for example, in an office setting, and whether she is moving about in public and for which purpose, for example, shopping in an open-air market in the city centre or a residential area, visiting a supermarket or travelling by means of public transport. There are special occasions as well, among them, church services, funerals, kitchen parties, and weddings. The majority of Zambia's population is nominally Christian. Each denomination dresses adult women members in a distinctive uniform for church service and Bible study and often adds a *chitenge* printed with its name and religious motifs.

Let us consider a 35-year-old schoolteacher whom I called Mrs Miyanda and introduced in a discussion of the hard work of consumption that is invested in a trip to one of Lusaka's largest *salaula* markets to shop for clothing for her children, a shirt for her husband, and 'the latest' for herself (Hansen 2000a: 194–96). As the mother of four school-attending children, Mrs Miyanda keeps track of their clothing needs. With her own earnings she pays for most of their ordinary clothes, except school uniforms, which are paid from the salary of her husband, a road surveyor in a government job. In fact, she does most of the clothes shopping; only the oldest, a youth aged 15, who receives a bit of pocket money for performing chores at home, does some of his own shopping for clothes. Mrs Miyanda tells me that she hardly ever buys clothing 'from the shops' and that although her husband will not admit it, she buys clothes for him from *salaula*, especially shirts and cold-weather garments.

The big open-air markets are *salaula*'s shop window, functioning, as I suggested earlier, much like shopping malls because of the abundance of apparel of all sorts. They also thrive on the significance most Zambians attach to personal interaction and the attention they pay to keeping up pleasant interpersonal terms. In effect, these markets are important sites for both economic and social pursuits.

Walking up and down the *salaula* aisles might appear like casual window shopping, yet it is in fact very strategic. Mrs Miyanda is looking for garments for her children and a top for herself to fit a charcoal grey skirt she likes to wear to school in order to make up a two-piece outfit, like the kind of office wear so popular with urban women in white-collar jobs. When working the *salaula* market, she always looks for shirts of the kind her husband likes to wear. What is more, one never knows what might be available, and she is always on the lookout for something new. On this occasion she had heard that one of the shoe vendors had just opened a 'fresh' bale.

We make many stops. Mrs Miyanda turns garments inside out, carefully scrutinising the neatness of the sewing and the quality of the fabric.

Will the print run when washed? Will the fabric fade after drying in the open air? She pays attention to colour, pattern, and style. And she avoids garments made from fabrics of artificial fibres such as polyester. Wearing them easily provokes perspiration and they do not react well to ironing.[2] When shopping from *salaula*, she seeks the best value for money along with attractiveness and style. She also gathers information both from traders and other customers: 'Where did you purchase that jacket?' and 'Who has good shoes?' she asks, and occasionally she stops passers-by not only to admire their clothes but also to inquire about sourcing: Which tailor can make this outfit? Where did you find gold buttons? Who sells black lace trim?

On this occasion, Mrs Miyanda purchased a pair of trousers and two T-shirts for her 12-year-old son and dresses for her two daughters, aged seven and ten, to wear to church. She bargained over the price of the dresses, which the trader reduced because she bought two. She scanned the men's shirts at several stalls but considered the shirts not to be quite to her husband's taste; they were too colourful; some were checked and others had loud colours; he likes them plain, she explained. In fact, most adult men show the same preference. She spent a long time looking for a top for herself.

In the end, Mrs Miyanda bought a hip-length shocking pink top to go with her charcoal grey skirt. Satisfied with the reduced price she had paid for the dresses for her daughters, she did feel that she had paid too much for the top in spite of arguing with the trader, who was not prepared to yield. Still, she wanted that very top, and so she paid. She took the top, and a pair of shoes she bought on a whim, to the shops on the periphery of the market. A man repairing shoes was asked to build up the heels and soles to give the shoes a platform look, and a tailor was instructed to alter the top. Mrs Miyanda did not care for the effect of the shoulder pads and wanted them removed. The top was slightly longer than she liked; she wanted it shortened; in addition, she asked for two rows of gold buttons to be sewed onto the front, which she considered to be too plain. While at the tailor's, we admired the latest styles of *chitenge* dresses. Mrs Miyanda would like a new *chitenge* outfit, as she had to attend a kitchen party at the end of the month. We also inquired about the tailor's fees and the necessary yardage and received advice about shops selling good-quality and attractive *chitenge* fabric.

---

[2] The putsi fly (*Cordylobia anthropophaga*) lays its eggs in wet laundry. General housekeeping advice about laundry among residents in Zambia is to iron all clothing that has been air dried in order to prevent larvae from entering the skin.

To be sure, *salaula* consumption is hard work. In this brief sketch, we glimpse the household power relations and norms that inform clothing consumption practices and their allocation by gender and age. Having monitored the clothing needs of the members of her household, when setting about the task of purchasing *salaula*, Mrs Miyanda gathers information and screens and sorts through garments. She is careful in negotiating price, if not always successful. Her final decisions not only are need based but also reflect clothing desires as she combines items from *salaula* into the style that is considered the latest in Lusaka. What is perhaps most striking is the extent of clothing competence in matters of quality and style that Mrs Miyanda displays as she skilfully worked her way through the market aisles, examining *salaula* garments. Her clothing competence is only to some extent a product of media exposure to local print and television advertisements, both of which were limited in scope during the mid-1990s when I made these observations, and to foreign television channels, music and film videos, and magazines presenting a range of visual impressions. Above all, her clothing competence is performance-based, inspired by the display of dressed bodies in streets, homes, and at work in everyday interaction and during special events. It is informed as well by normative ideas about dress and gendered bodies, comportment, and presentation, which women are taught from when they are very young.

Mrs Miyanda's dress practice when working around the house is plain, involving almost any worn dress or skirt and blouse combination with a *chitenge* wrapper on top, yet for other occasions she carefully puts items of clothing together, strategically, and with a calculus to produce a particular effect, that 'total look' that makes people take note. Behind this dress practice is a daily rehearsal process that hinges around careful evaluation in which her choice of clothing is influenced by how she wants to be seen, where, when, and by whom. She assesses colours, prints, and fabrics with a critical eye to their match and possible effect. What is more, clothing competence has a practical dimension that enters the rehearsal process. Because the culturally preferred clothing silhouette in Zambia is spic and span, Mrs Miyanda's daily evaluation includes checking if her garments are clean and neatly ironed.

The desire for uniqueness produces considerable variation in how Mrs Miyanda dresses for work. Like most other women whose dress practice I observed closely, Mrs Miyanda never wears 'the same' dress to work, at least according to her own account. She arranges and rearranges her garments. One ensemble is succeeded by another and so on, leaving the impression of infinite novelty and indeed of ephemerality as one outfit gives space for another. But this process is a strategic gesture, a sleight of hand that showcases rapid turnover while indeed continuity prevails. In fact, Mrs Miyanda rotates her garments and makes new combinations of dresses and skirts. Her rotation might occasionally include dresses in a cut and style that in the West might be considered evening wear. She also wears *chitenge* outfits to work occasionally, something that I rarely saw in the 1980s. And as an active member of the Seventh Day Adventist Church, she wears a church uniform for service on Saturdays: a blue dress with white trim and a white headscarf.

The inclusion of Mrs Miyanda's evening dress and her *chitenge* outfits among the garments she rotates for work testify to the many lives that clothes go through in their involvement with their owner's changing life. Once the demonstrative moment of display has passed, garments continue their utilitarian lives. When she tires of specific garments as dress for school, she decommissions them from public work scenes to work around the house where she might wear them until they stop being useful.

It takes a while for dresses, two-piece suits, and *chitenge* outfits to be demoted to kitchen wear. For the case of *chitenge* wear, the decision hinges on how frequently a particular outfit has been seen. Women like Mrs Miyanda possess quite a number of *chitenge* dresses that were originally commissioned from a tailor for particular occasions and after some time are taken out of wardrobes or boxes to be worn as variations on office wear. Each year *chitenge* fashions change in the detailed construction and trim of neckline, sleeves, waist, and length. *Chitenge* wear is women's special dress asset in Zambia. Wearing *chitenge*, they take safe clothing conventions in their own hands and develop them to the fullest.

Tournaments of Value

Above all, Zambian women dress in *chitenge* outfits on formal visits and special occasions such as weddings and kitchen parties where they are worn proudly by mature women who are full bodied to display them to their advantage. During my years of comings and goings in Lusaka, kitchen parties have become increasingly popular. In the early 1970s I never came across kitchen parties, but by the mid-1980s even women living in low-income areas spoke of organising them, if not in their own residential settings then in the homes of friends or acquaintances in more affluent neighbourhoods. They are all part of networks of relatives and friends that cross townships, occupational groups, and class distinctions. Some parties are elaborate events staged at hotels and park-like suburban venues (see Figure 8.1).

Figure 8.1 Women at kitchen party. The woman on the left covers her exposed legs with a piece of *chitenge* fabric, the second from left wears a stylish *chitenge* outfit with large piece of embroidery around the neck, the two women on the right dressed in tailor-made office wear. Lusaka, 2002. Author's photo.

Modelled on a loose version of initiation ceremonies, kitchen parties feature a party manager or matron, a senior woman marriage instructor who, prior to the party has taught the bride-to-be how to behave towards her husband both sexually and interpersonally. The party gets going in the afternoon after a night-long private instruction session and the bride-to-be's demonstration of her dancing skills, especially of how 'to dance in bed'. The marriage instructor and senior relatives then bring out the bride-to-be covered in a piece of *chitenge* fabric, followed by the women drummers. The young woman and the marriage instructor seat themselves on the ground in front of the guests. After an opening prayer, and in Christian homes sometimes a brief Bible lesson, the young woman is unveiled. She remains seated with downcast eyes for the duration of the party. Subsequent events include individual performances, as each guest who cares to or can be coaxed by the mistress of the ceremonies into dancing then steps into the centre, commenting on the gift she has brought 'for the kitchen' in terms of its importance to the marital relationship.

Regardless of the ethnic background of the bride-to-be, the senior marriage instructor and the female drummers in Lusaka tend to have Eastern Province origins. 'They know about such things', I was told. The drummers are usually recruited from the low-income residential areas. While some of the dances and songs may be regionally specific and derive from another era, kitchen parties are characterised by their ethnic and socioeconomic heterogeneity, and above all by their preoccupation with male–female relations and heterosexual norms. Guests are served individually wrapped portions of food; in *apamwamba* households the parties are sometimes catered by hotels. Except in some Christian homes, such events feature a good deal of drinking, especially of beer but also, in wealthier homes, of wine and alcohol-spiced punches. One of the Zambian friends with whom I attended several kitchen parties in the mid-1990s used to inquire not only what present I was bringing but also if I had remembered to put 'my baby' (a small bottle of rum or brandy to mix with soft drinks) into my handbag.

Such parties offer entertainment and merrymaking, as mature women who can dance shake their hips and bottoms and are sometimes joined by other women who enjoy displaying their dancing skills. Women who are less amply endowed produce some of this effect with the help of a prop, a piece of *chitenge* fabric, wrapped around their hips; the *chitenge* has been thrown at them by the mistress of ceremonies, who opens and comments on the gifts and cajoles the givers into dancing. She herself is a very skilled dancer and improviser. For instance at one party, when showing a present to the audience, a broom, she demonstrated how not to use it: wrapping her loose, black skirt with a long slit around her hips, she danced, bending over with the broom in a posture revealing both her thighs and *masecrets*, the term in Zambian English for women's underwear.[3] The guests screamed. As the afternoon of the party progresses, the sexual gestures of dancing often become very explicit. Any literal interpretation of the sexual enactment in dance and gestures must be tempered with acknowledgement of the subversive atmosphere this entire performance event generates.

Kitchen parties are one of the few occasions that bring adult women together in Zambia to share experiences about their joys, successes, troubles, and tribulations as well as information with which they assist one another. Given the male authoritarian atmosphere that characterises sociability across all class levels in Zambia, it comes as no surprise that some men view kitchen parties as events where married women get drunk

---

[3] Ma is a plural prefix of a noun class in the Chinyanja language.

and indulge in social evils such as exposing unmarried women to 'offensive' songs about sex and gossip about extramarital relationships (*Zambia Daily Mail* 1984, 27 November; *Times of Zambia* 1985, 5 December). But aside from the alcohol, sex, talk, and gossip, what also irks some men about women's attendance at such parties is their own lack of control. While some men may help sponsor kitchen parties by providing money to help cover expenses, they have no input into their organisation and staging. By participating in kitchen parties, women act as independent consumers, spending money on both presents and clothing.

Some young women are ambivalent about kitchen parties but do attend them when the bride-to-be is a special friend or colleague. But if you do not dance or drink, they say, these afternoons can be very long. And some young women are rather reluctant to enter the dance floor. They know that in the cultural terms that inform these events unmarried women ought not to be exposed to the presentation of special dance skills that are considered to be the exclusive domain of married women.

Fewer young women than mature married women follow the predominant dress practice at such parties: the wearing of *chitenge* outfits. At parties where either the bride- or groom-to-be's relatives, or both, are Lozi, some women wear *misisi* dresses, the missionary-inspired dress of the Lozi home region, Zambia's Western Province. In its contemporary version the *misisi* is sewn of floral print fabric and consists of a top with gathered sleeves, a yoke around the neck, and a tiered skirt with a marked bustle and a shawl worn on top, tied around the waist, accentuating the wearer's buttocks. Underneath the skirt are usually several underskirts to support the effect of the bustle. In general, the kitchen party dress scene includes a very large proportion of *chitenge* wear, in wealthy homes constituting a veritable *chitenge* fashion show, including some Western-styled dresses and two-piece suits from the tailor as well as from *salaula*.

I have seen several young women who were wearing stylish jeans with decorative tops receive critical remarks by women of the senior generation, who insist that trousers have no place at a kitchen party. One young woman who turned up at a kitchen party in 1995 in a *chitenge* outfit consisting of a short-sleeved top and loose Bermuda-type shorts got so much flak that she wore a piece of *chitenge* fabric as a wrapper for the rest of the afternoon. And one of the worst commentaries I have heard about dress on such an occasion was directed towards a heavy-set young woman who turned up at a Christian kitchen party in black tights and a T-shirt hugging her waist. But short and tight garments, displaying 'private parts' and 'body structures' for all to see, are definitely not *comme il faut* at this event. According to widespread cultural norms, a husband is the only person allowed to gaze at the 'private parts' of a wife's body.

The kitchen party is probably the principal event for demonstrative display of women's dressed bodies in *chitenge* fashions (Hansen 2000a: 208–14). In fact, an important dimension of owning a *chitenge* outfit is demonstrating it for others to see. As a competitive presentation a kitchen party may be viewed as a social situation set apart from everyday life in terms of place, setting, and props. The most important prop is women's dressed bodies. At kitchen parties, the participants' evaluation of and commentary on heterosexual behaviour extends into preoccupations with stylish appearance and dress. The focus on competitive display in sexually inflected dances, songs, presents, and clothes, and the status politics that take place between women, turn kitchen parties into what Arjun Appadurai has defined as tournaments of value. He coined the concept to refer to

complex periodic events that are removed in some culturally well-defined way from the routine of economic life. Participation in them is … both a privilege … and an instrument of status contests…. The currency of such tournaments is also set apart through well understood cultural diacritics…. What is at issue … is not just status, rank, fame, or reputation of actors, but the disposition of the central tokens of value in the society in question. Finally, though such tournaments of value occur in special times and places, their forms and outcomes are always consequential for the more mundane realities of power and value in ordinary life. (Appadurai 1986: 21)

The currency of the kitchen party's tournament of value is the female body, clothed in dress. At such parties, participants evaluate and judge both behaviour and dress, collect information, trade, and share insights into the sources of clothing design and style. In effect, the group of women participating in such an event constitute specialists who are in the know about clothing competence. Taking note, they work out the meanings that distinct clothing styles convey, just as they did disparagingly of Lily's previously worn outfit at her sister-in-law's kitchen party. As Appadurai advises, such tournaments of value should not be isolated analytically from everyday life. Their articulations with other domains of life are actually rather complicated, as I discuss below.

Taken together, the marriage counselling and the consumption aspect of the kitchen party make this pan-ethnic invented tradition into a contemporary uniquely Zambian ceremony, and as such, it is shaped by some of society's general problems in both the economic and cultural domains. As an occasion for giving presents 'for the kitchen' to help the bride-to-be look after husband and home, the kitchen party articulates with the domain of consumption. As a matter of fact, careful calculations go into the planning of such parties, since the expenses can easily exceed the value of gifts. Calculation takes place concerning those who are invited as well. Women with medium-income earnings like my teacher friends deliberately limited the number of kitchen party invitations they accepted. One of them said that teachers did not receive many invitations since 'everybody knows' that they are paid poorly and have little money to spend. While the party unfolds, guests scrutinise both performance and dress as well as the quality of the presents. They comment not only on the dancers' skills but also on the food and drink they are served. From the participants' point of view, the success of a kitchen party often hinges on those aspects. In short, while kitchen parties offer marriage counsel to brides-to-be, they are a performance production of entertainment and consumption for both organisers and invited guests.

Perhaps the kitchen party's most marked contradiction lies in the celebration of the subordinate wifely role as enacted in the dance performance and dressed bodies of mature married women, many of whom in fact are employed and work in their own right. While young unmarried women who are contemplating proactive agendas for themselves may enjoy some of the merrymaking and socialising that kitchen parties offer, they may not fully agree about their message. One woman journalist pointed out how the traditional marriage counselling provided in connection with these events 'reduces a woman to a house servant'. The problem, she argued, 'is exaggerated respect. Women are taught to regard their husbands as bosses ... respect should certainly be there but not to the extent where a wife becomes a slave' (*Zambia Daily Mail* 1998, 11 January). This interpretation of the kitchen party's celebration of women's subordinate roles should not, as I suggested earlier in the chapter, be read literally, for it ignores the subversive authority structures and sociability that animates it.

Wardrobe Selections

Guests at a kitchen party will have carefully considered what to wear and examined a variety of dress options. Adult women scrutinise their collection of *chitenge* wear, and some young unmarried women contemplate whether to borrow garments for the occasion from a friend. Before dressing, a woman assesses colours, prints, and fabric texture with an eye to their probable effect while she carefully coordinates accessories and make-up. When dress scholars discuss wardrobes, they do so largely with reference to a collection of clothing whereas research focused on clothing consumption explores questions about the acquisition and purchase of the garments and accessories that make up a person's wardrobe.[4] Some of my colleagues have devised a 'wardrobe method' that entails biographical interviews about what people include in their wardrobes; how they decide what to wear, purchase, and discard; as well as what they like and dislike wearing, and why (Fletcher and Klepp 2017; Skjold 2016). Such questions also reveal another dimension of wardrobes: as storage space for the collection of clothes of which only some are in use. Because they contain several garments and accessories, wardrobes easily give rise to questions about wardrobe selections. And questions about what to wear (Woodward 2005) highlight that both cultural norms and idiosyncratic issues shape decisions about how people decide to dress for specific situations.

I bring the term 'wardrobe' into play because of its creative ambiguity. The two meanings of wardrobe, as stock or archive of clothing and as storage space, overlap in some respects, yet dress scholarship has been so focused on the relationship between body and clothing that it has paid little attention to the physical storage of clothes. Important exceptions are the works by Norris (2003), and Banerjee and Miller (2004) on women's dress in India. Trunks, chests, and wardrobes enter most Indian women's lives at marriage. They store saris presented as gifts and dowries, or due to changes in a woman's life across her life cycle. And saris need to be cared for and maintained. In effect, managing the wardrobe becomes 'a technology of the self' (Norris 2003: 70).

In colonial Zambia, as I described in Chapter 2, the function of clothing as a store of wealth folded up in boxes in stores, pushed under beds, placed on top of rafters, put in inexpensive suitcases (travel kits), or tied up in bundles of wrapped cloth gradually gave way to individualisation in the urban context. When during the post–World War II years mine and township authorities began to provide 'married housing' for their workers, wardrobes began to enter the bedrooms of some African urban households, while boxes and suitcases held the garments in households of lesser means, much like today. Even then, in urban low-income areas clothes are not everywhere stored out of sight. Poor families living in one room may divide it by a clothesline on which they hang their garments. Garments hang on nails on walls as well on hooks and hanging rails. In effect, the wardrobe's role to facilitate private contemplation does not hold across class and culture, which do not everywhere set aside or enclose private space for clothing storage (see Figure 8.2).

What extends across class, culture, and the rural-urban divide was in the past, as it still is today, an active preoccupation with cutting

---

[4] The discussion in this subsection draws on Hansen (2008: 80–81, 84).

Figure 8.2 Young woman displaying part of her *chitenge* wardrobe, Lusaka, 1997. Author's photo.

a fine figure in dress. This concern invokes the dimension of the wardrobe as a collection of wearing apparel. No matter how limited, such a collection enables the creative, strategic manipulation of dress for display that is at the heart of dress performance. The selection is an outcome of a woman's social position and her individual desire. It can make or break her, as we saw in Lily's choice of dress for her sister-in-law's kitchen party.

Dress Practice, Uniqueness, and Continuity

Let us return to Lily to round off this discussion of the body surface as a cultural and political battleground on which questions about dress and its acceptability are tested. As a very stylish dresser, Lily had an extensive wardrobe of specially tailored *chitenge* wear in many different designs and casual Western-styled wear. I recall her shoe storage consisting of several shelves of high-heeled shoes and decorated sandals for festive wear as well as more ordinary footwear. Clearly, she had faced a clothing dilemma when considering what to wear for her sister-in-law's kitchen party. Such dilemmas, as described in Emma Tarlo's inspiring work on dress in India, arise when dress norms clash (1996: 200–201). Lily's dilemma revolved around whether to dress as expected of a married wife of a member of the family hosting the party, demonstrating the beauty and attractiveness of her dressed body, or whether to present herself modestly, removed from the central action. The murmur during the party caused by her unremarkable dress presentation reveals some of the tensions of the dilemma. In effect, by not respecting dress conventions, she was not in command of the situation and did not pull off wearing the blue outfit successfully.

As I have noted throughout this book, the meaning and value of Zambian engagements with clothing do not inhere in the garments themselves and do not therefore have much to do with whether clothes are secondhand or new. There is an experiential dimension to dress, in both the wearing and the viewing. How the meaning and value of clothes are experienced has to do with context, whether in everyday dress, as fashion, or as new or second-hand. This is why at her sister-in-law's kitchen party Lily's previously worn two-piece outfit had no demonstration effect to make heads turn admiringly.

Experiences of dress and the evaluations viewers make of it are not given or fixed but created anew in each context. Lily can place her tired outfit in a different regime of value by changing the context of its status, for example, from party dress to work wear or to house dress. In the materialisation of value that informs such decisions about how to dress and where, needs and wants converge as do ephemerality and continuity. This is the space between the desired and the performed where dress practice becomes involved in constructing both individual identity and visions about the future.

In their daily rehearsal for dressing and dressing up, women in Zambia seek to anticipate the situations and contexts in which they will be finding themselves. Negotiating the specific moment of such situations, they squeeze the value out of their garments. Now 'socially dead', the clothes they have worn are released for participation in other events in which their status shifts through recontextualization. Ephemerality here is in the service of social reproduction, which is why the active cultivation of aesthetic sensibility in the desire for uniqueness in Zambian women's dress practices is also about continuity.

Snapshot 5: 'Chinese Clothes'

'I wore a pair of Chinese shoes with heels during my lunch break the other day', my young friend Mutinta told me when I popped in to see her at her job as a receptionist at a Chinese-owned scrap metal firm in Lusaka's light industrial area.[5] 'On my way back to the office', she went on, 'one of the heels broke. I'll never buy Chinese clothes again!' she exclaimed. I had followed Mutinta on her path from school to work. Trained as a skilled auto mechanic, her receptionist job for the Chinese firm included working on English translation. The year was 2005, when the World Trade Organization's Multi-Fibre Arrangement ended and Chinese-produced apparel and textiles no longer required import tariffs. I shall have much more to say about the consequences of this, and specifically about the matter of textiles, in Chapter 9.

'Chinese clothes' refer to something specific in Zambia, namely, cheap imports in bulk directly from China. Throughout the 1990s and well into the new millennium, according to James Springford, 'salaula continued to dominate the clothing scene as the only viable dress option for the majority'. When Zambians confronted the new alternative from China, he explained, salaula offered them the closest possible comparison 'within the realm of affordable clothing'. Drawing on research he conducted in 2008, he described in graphic terms how the new imports entered an economy that had 'already marginalised its own producers and pushed its traders within the margins of informality' (2010: 9).

Mining and infrastructure projects, state-driven and private, loom large in accounts of China's engagements in Africa, including in Zambia, especially following the liberalisation of the economy during the 1990s (Lee 2017). Less visible, but perhaps more prominent in ordinary people's lives, are Chinese retail investments in the low-income trading sector (Dopler 2009; Scheld and Siu 2013). Chinese-owned shops and small-scale vendors in Lusaka operate alongside Zambians, traders of Indian background, and migrants from neighbouring countries, among them the Democratic Republic of Congo and Zimbabwe, as well as many others who are pursuing cross-border and suitcase trade within the region. There are 'China malls' in Lusaka and on the Copperbelt and in recent years websites wholesaling inexpensive clothes manufactured in China.

[5] This is a fictive name.

In 2001 part of Lusaka's oldest market, Kamwala, was extended with a concrete-built shopping complex, Kamwala Shopping World, consisting of small stores operated by the China Henan firm on a 65-year leasehold licence from the Lusaka City Council. Behind the new complex, the long rows of old shops still function, the open space between them filled in with overflowing displays of all manner of goods, mostly Chinese imports ranging from housewares to garments. Kamwala is the place to go to buy clothing, accessories, and textiles for personal use as well as for resale in rural areas and even abroad. As a lively regional trading hub, Kamwala market had obvious attractions to investors.

When people in Zambia speak about 'Chinese clothes', they refer to something quite specific, as I just mentioned. The term applies to formal direct imports from China in bulk or sold from warehouses around town, much like *salaula*, to traders for resale in shops, markets, in the streets, and rural areas. By contrast, Chinese imports from other African countries are referred to, for example, as 'Tanzanian clothes' and 'South African clothes' (Springford 2010: 12; Stien 2013: 43–45). In 2008, Springford consulted the Zambian Bureau of Standards where he learned that formal imports from China entered Zambia without being checked at all. No standard had been agreed upon at least at that point in time. And he suggested that informal clothing imports by mobile traders from South Africa and Tanzania were, in the popular view, considered to be of far better quality than the shipments in bales directly from China (2010: 14).

Much like my young friend Mutinta, many Zambians become annoyed at being misled and cheated for buying poor quality and fake designer clothing when they purchase 'Chinese clothing', as Mutinta did when losing a heel on a pair of brand-new shoes. While carrying out research on Zambian workers employed by Chinese shopkeepers at Kamwala market, Kari Stien asked Esther, a Zambian worker at a Chinese-owned shop, if she would purchase clothing for herself from the shop. Surprised, Esther laughed, saying, 'No, of course not!' She explained that she knew well the difference between poor and better quality Chinese clothes, and that she preferred the latter. Buying better quality was a way for her to demonstrate that she had a job and a stable income rather than buying cheap 'Chinese clothes', which as Esther explained was something only poorer people did (Stien 2013: 45).

9   Dressing Zambian

Across most of Africa, dressing well is a source of pride. For quite a while this widespread passion for clothes and lively cultivation of style have inspired international haute couture designers, beginning perhaps with Paul Poiret in France during the 1920s, Yves Saint Laurent in 1967, Jean Paul Gaultier in 2005, and Junya Watanabe in 2009, among others, to incorporate African style elements in their collections (Rovine 2009; 2015: 70–105). And bold fashions in vivid colours and printed fabric brought African designers to work in the world's fashion capitals in the 1980s in Paris with Chris Sedou and Lamine Kouyaté (founder of the Xuly Bet label), both from Mali, and Alphadi from Niger, who helped create the idea of 'African style' in the European fashion imagination (Loughran 2009). Since the Somali-born woman Iman graced the fashion runway in 1975, supermodels from Africa such as Sudanese Alex Wek, Australian Ajak Deng (born in Sudan), Liya Kebede from Ethiopia, and several others have walked the runway in international fashion shows. For some years African designers, some of whom have made it onto high street locations in London and Paris and now operate in the diaspora, have presented their creative work in the biannual fashion shows in New York and London. Some of these fashion weeks have also included a special segment to showcase up-and-coming designers from several countries in Africa.

The outpouring of creative talent on the fashion scene across most of Africa is attracting growing global attention. Contemporary designers from Senegal to Kenya to South Africa are reinterpreting traditions, creating innovative silhouettes, and combining prints and textiles in new and exciting ways. International fashion observers are actively watching style trends during fashion weeks in African cities with a well-established fashion scene, among them, Dakar in Senegal, Accra in Ghana, Lagos in Nigeria, and Cape Town and Johannesburg in South Africa, where people who are serious about fashion are keen to be part of the latest in both local and global terms. Although they may not attract major international attention, yearly fashion weeks are held in a growing number of African capitals, including in Zambia. Embedded in histories of regional and international trade, colonialism, and globalisation, fashion in Africa today is diverse and multidirectional, responding to and interacting with transglobal inspirations.

But even if today's design and fashion scene within individual African countries and abroad shines brightly, it does so against many odds. Presenting their creations during local fashion weeks, many of these aspiring designers have limited opportunities to venture beyond the cities or regions in which they work.[1] For local design initiatives operate largely from within the continent's informal economies with little professional and technical training and financial support. Irregular electricity supply and poorly developed road infrastructure adversely affect production standards and delivery. Online marketing initiatives are challenged by insufficient and unstable Internet services. And in most countries, the clothing market is sharply divided between a tiny, wealthy elite who does much of its shopping abroad, a growing middle class with lifestyle aspirations and purchasing power, and a huge segment comprising more than 50 per cent of the total population who are very poor and have few means yet many wishes and wants – for almost everyone desires to dress well. Fashion comes to life, in Africa as elsewhere, in people's interaction with dress in the context of their everyday location and changing consumption practices in terms of class, gender, age, race, and ethnicity. Religion plays a role as well, visually marking the clothing scene in many North and West African countries and to some extent in coastal areas of East Africa. Because interactions with clothing are embodied, the materiality of dress and the experience of wearing it on the body are central to how fashion comes to life everywhere (Entwistle 2001: 34; Hansen 2013b: 1–11; Sylvanus 2016).

Along with responding to global inspirations, fashion in most African contexts is also resolutely local and shaped by widely shared dress aesthetics and norms. Accounting for changing fashion engagements across the African continent easily mobilises stereotypical representations that invoke the worn-out dichotomies African/Western and traditional/modern. Resonances with these enduring binaries are not hard to find, as two recent examples of what to consider 'African' will illustrate. The first example is the coffee-table book entitled *Not African Enough?* that

---

[1] In vivid presentations of creative dress entrepreneurs, *Fashion Cities Africa* (Pool 2016) focuses on the breadth, diversity, and challenges of the contemporary fashion scene and its many participants from producers to media bloggers in Nairobi, Casablanca, Lagos, and Johannesburg. The publication accompanied an exhibition at the Brighton Museum Art Gallery in the United Kingdom and subsequent displays in Holland.

features clothes and apparel in minimalistic styles without any use of printed fabrics or other 'traditional' embellishments (Dolat 2017). They were created by a group of designers in Kenya intent on stepping beyond the confines of what the world, and Africans, usually are told it means to dress African. The book's subversive title asserts the design collective's desire to pursue their own aesthetic by pushing the limits of established design categories, if not bypassing them entirely. The second example is garments made from printed fabrics that are worn widely for everyday wear and special occasions across most of the continent and sometimes described as 'not African' due to the origin of their manufacturing process in Europe in the mid- to late 1800s and perhaps also, as John Picton has suggested, because of 'their relative late entry into the subject matter of Africanist art-history research' (Picton 1995: 25). Stretching the boundaries of what might be considered African in terms of textiles, pattern, colour, silhouette, and history, examples like these are challenging the way we look at African fashion from within, across, and beyond the continent (Boateng 2021).

In this chapter, I examine the changing place of African print fabric in fashion design and everyday dress practice in Zambia in order to explore how historical connections, political and economic forces, and ongoing global interconnections are shaping and changing dress practice. Because the popular media frequently confuse types of printed textiles when describing African fabrics, the first section draws brief distinctions between printed textiles that are relevant to the subsequent discussion. Then I turn to issues related to cultural appropriation and authenticity, trying to move the presentation beyond polarising tendencies. The rest of the chapter concerns the interaction between small-scale tailoring and the emerging fashion and design scene in Lusaka. Away from the fashion runway and the attention of the media is an everyday world of dress practices that is no less creative in its construction and significance than the formal fashion scene. Involving millions of Africans in creative endeavours and informal business activities, the dress practices that arise in these processes make up the back story of the formal fashion scene. As my discussion demonstrates, the circulation of dressed bodies, garments in many styles, and inspirations for how to dress in everyday life, on the street, in private homes, and at social gatherings help to trouble the tired boundaries between tradition and modernity and Africa and the West.

Wax Print, *Isisheshwe*, and *Chitenge*

During the 2018 American Black Film Festival Honors Award ceremony, actress Angela Bassett, who played the role as queen of

Wakanda in the blockbuster movie, *Black Panther*, wore a dress made by the Zambian designer Mangishi Doll Co. A description of the vibrantly coloured dress introduced it as 'made of a traditional cloth called *chitenge* celebrating history and culture'. The narration continued: 'A *chitenge* is an East, West, and Central African fabric similar to a *sarong*.'[2] When identifying the fabric, the description contained a common mistake. *Chitenge* is not a general term but a regionally specific name for one of several factory-produced cotton textiles, some of them manufactured in Europe from the mid-1800s and on, that reached a variety of destinations in West, East, and southern Africa. They are often called 'African prints' with a designation that turns history on its head (Picton 1995: 25). The frequent everyday use of these printed fabrics wrapped around the body is their only similarity to the Indonesian *sarong*.

Printed cloth has a centuries-old history in Africa, introduced as a desirable commodity in the maritime trade between Europe, the Far East, and America (Gott, Loughran, Quick, and Rabine 2017; Pickton 1995). Today the best known of these fabrics is probably what is commonly referred to as Dutch wax, often simply called wax, especially those with the brand name Vlisco, initially designed in the 19th century by Dutch textile manufacturers to look like Indonesian batik cloth, using a wax-resist printing technique on both cloth faces. West Africa proved to be a much better market than Indonesia, and the fabric was subsequently designed for export to that region, proving immensely popular among market traders and consumers. The Vlisco archives show that fabrics with different designs also were produced for traders on the East African coast from 1884 onward (Picton 1995: 28). In southern Africa, indigo-dyed printed cotton cloth, Blaudruck, today often referred to by the Zulu name *isisheshwe*, was imported from Europe, mainly Germany. It is now produced in South Africa by Da Gama Textiles in bright colours and styles that are popular across the region, including in Lesotho, Eswatini (Swaziland), Namibia, and Botswana (Leeb-du-Toit 2017; Mokwena 2020: 310–11).

As we know from previous chapters, in Zambia elaborately styled dresses made from colourful printed fabrics are referred to as *chitenge* (in the Chinyanja language) or *vitenge* (in the Chibemba language). *Chitenge* (*kitenge* in East Africa and the Congo) is a factory-produced textile, printed with a roller on one face. During the 1930s, some *kitenge* from Japan reached Zambia via the Congo, while Europe, India, and America served as other sources for printed textiles. Soon after

---

[2] Kallon 2018.

independence in 1964, two government-supported textile and clothing manufacturing factories were opened. Privately owned weaving and spinning plants appeared as well, and small-scale garment production grew. The two textile factories initially produced both *chitenge* fabrics and ordinary clothing. Over subsequent decades, production rose and fell in response to import restrictions during most of the 1970s and 1980s and their removal in the early 1990s, when the market was opened up to imports (Guille 1995).

Uncompetitive on global markets, Zambia's two textile and clothing manufacturing factories faced closure by the turn of, and soon after, the millennium when market liberalisation allowed an increase in the importation of textiles and clothing. Above all, from 2005 unfavourable domestic and international trade conditions developed in the wake of the expiration of the World Trade Organization's Multi-Fibre Arrangement on Textiles and Clothing that for about 30 years had restricted exports by textile producers in China and several Far Eastern countries.[3] Many African countries had established textile weaving and printing factories just before or after independence, and most of them had similar experiences as Zambia with their industries (Renne and Maiwada 2020).

Today Chinese manufacturers produce most of the wax and roller-printed textiles that are sold in African markets, and China is the main source of *chitenge* fabrics in Zambia. Chinese-owned firms in several African countries have a long and changing history in this production, including the state-supported Mulungushi Textiles in Zambia. In some countries, Chinese textile and apparel manufacturers operate as well in more recently established tax-free production zones. Innovations in technology, including digital printing, have made printed fabrics widely available in different qualities that appeal to the concerns of discriminating customers as well as to their purses. As the leading producers and exporters of such fabrics, Chinese firms have established offices in several West African countries, among them Senegal, Côte d'Ivoire, Nigeria, and Ghana, while some African wholesalers have set up shop in China (Renne 2015).

Chinese producers of printed fabrics do not merely copy existing brands. They reproduce prints, for example, encouraged by African women clients who bring cloth samples and recommend designs. Women traders from Togo, for example, are actively involved in co-creating a 'new generation of African-print cloth' with Chinese textile

---

[3] The Multi-Fibre Arrangement governed world trade in textiles and garments from 1974 through 1994, imposing quotas on exports from developing countries. Its successor, the Agreement on Textiles and Clothing, expired on 1 January 2005.

engineers, while women tailors in Mozambique collaborate with their Chinese counterparts in the design and manufacturing process to shape 'imports to their own tastes and the fashion of the day' (Sylvanus 2016: 121–25; 2017: 108–11; von Pezold and Driessen 2021: 322–25, 332). Once produced in Europe, these fabrics have become appropriated, domesticated, and Africanised, imbued with meanings whose significance arises from the particularities of time, location, and context. This applies as well to the most recent Chinese-made fabrics, which are being refashioned and localised across the continent.

Cultural Appropriation and Authenticity

The extensive refashioning and localisation of multiple influences on textiles and clothing across most of Africa continue to trigger questions about cultural appropriation and authenticity. This was evident when fashion in the movies went to Africa in the celebratory role clothing played in creating the Afrofuturistic world of the invented nation Wakanda in *Black Panther* (2018).[4] For that movie, costume designer Ruth E. Carter collaborated with designers in several African countries to create a stunning sartorial story by weaving together printed fabrics, colours, and cuts to craft the clothes in a new pan-African vision of the future.[5] The creative combination of elements from clothing styles and fabric designs evident historically and in current dress practice gives rise to vexing questions about the nature and scope of cultural appropriation and meanings of authenticity. Some years ago dress scholars Joanne Eicher and Tonye Erekosima suggested the term 'cultural authentication' for the cut- and pulled-thread textile of the Kalabari in Nigeria that combines imported 'Madras' cloth from India and elements of Western wear. The concept captured the borrowing of elements and their subsequent transformation through local use and meaning (1995). Thoroughly hybrid sartorial styles like these challenge Western dress

---

[4] In addition to the cultural stereotypes that trouble distinctions between what is authentically traditional and African, modern, and Western is a marked class bias. The widely watched web series, *An African City* (2014; www.anafricancity.tv), set in Accra, Ghana, featuring well-educated women returnees from the diaspora, pitches them as 'new African women' preoccupied with Afrocentric fashion and lifestyle issues. By contrast, local African women, less educated, appear as not fashionable, beautiful, or modern (Ogunyankin 2016).

[5] Ruth E. Carter on 24 February 2019, the first African American woman to have done so, won the award for Best Costume Design for her work on *Black Panther* at the 91st annual Academy Awards. The 2021 movie *Coming 2 America* also showcased Carter's African-inspired costumes, sourced from numerous collaborators, including well-known African designers, among them Laduma Maxhosa from South Africa (Cooper 2021).

norms. For example, according to South African art historian Sandra Klopper, South African designers often use large quantities of fabric rather than highlighting the body shape, as is common in much Western dress practice (2000: 223). In Senegal, where fashionable styling has a long history characterised by *métissage*, the mixing and crossover of different materials and inspirations fuse African, Islamic, European, and Asian elements (Kastner 2019: 169).

With its multiple references, sartorial code-mixing is mobile and therefore lends itself easily to reappropriation. It invites reading through the lens Nina Sylvanus applied to wax prints when she argued that 'wax cloth complicates claims about origin, originality, and authenticity' (Sylvanus 2017: 109): 'The cloth's many points of manufacture defy any conception of origin/ality that is not already deeply global. The shifting terrain of African-print reproduction redirects the conversation about authenticity, copy, and culture, suggesting that the question of what is authentic is not really the one we should be asking' (2017: 113). What matters here is less where fabrics and dress inspirations come from but rather the social and cultural contexts in which they are put to use. Daniel Miller expressed this view well in his analysis of consumption and identity in Trinidad when arguing that authenticity is something that is produced rather than preserved. It should be judged, he suggested, according to local consequences and not local origins (1994). History, time, and place matter, which is why there is no universal framing of the way in which textile and clothing engagements play out locally, as we shall see for the case of *chitenge* in Zambia.

Sourcing and Production of *Chitenge*

When women in Zambia tell you that their colourful *chitenge* dresses are traditional, they are talking about an invented tradition that keeps evolving as a result of changing inspirations from across the African continent and beyond. It is 'our wear', they say, and indeed *chitenge* is deeply embedded in an ongoing history of changing cultural representations and global trade. As I just noted, although most *chitenge* fabric today is imported from China, it constitutes the emblem of Zambian women's fashion.

Because *chitenge* identifies both a fabric and a dress practice, the agentive medium of the fabric and dress practice merge when women wear it. As I describe below, the materiality of the fabric and the sensuality of the experience of wearing it are central to how consumers evaluate *chitenge* fabric in terms of quality and how they appraise it for its design and price. When a woman intends to source *chitenge* fabric, she has quite a variety of options, ranging from commissioning *chitenge* manufactured in the Democratic Republic of Congo from a suitcase trader to shopping herself at a market venue that specialises in imported fabrics. Lusaka has several large urban markets with open and covered stalls displaying African print fabrics and outdoor vendors with piles of *chitenge* on the ground. In the areas adjacent to markets like Kamwala are the retail premises of many traders of Indian and Pakistani background. Some of them sell only fabrics, while many offer a mix of fabrics, garments, and shoes as well as household objects and dry goods, mostly made in India and China.

In these shops and in other areas where they are sold, the fabrics are generally displayed on shelves along the walls and hung from lines under the ceiling. In the more exclusive stores, *chitenge* fabrics are sold only in the full length (ca. 5.5 meters or approximately 6 yards), sufficient for a two- or three-piece outfit, while smaller shops may sell cuts of two meters (ca. 2.2 yards), the standard length for a wrapper. When a potential customer wishes to scrutinise a fabric, a shop assistant has either to bring a sample from the shelves or remove it from the line of hanging fabrics with the use of a long pole. As this approach does not readily encourage the customer to touch and rub the fabric to assess its quality, it is not surprising that women are fond of shopping in open-air and market stalls where they can engage actively with both the fabric and the vendor. For touch is an important part of fabric selection. How will the fabric drape? If a fabric contains 'too much' starch, for example, the customer will know that it is of poor quality and that the starch will wash off when laundered, making the fabric difficult to fold and leaving it with a worn and tired look. In effect, fabric quality contributes actively to the sensuous experience of wearing *chitenge* and the embodied materiality of *chitenge* dress practice.

Consumers are attracted to the colourful imagery on *chitenge* fabric, which includes symbolic and geometric motifs, images of human beings, animals, mythical figures, and masks, in many different designs. Some designs copy existing fabrics and graphic art. Diverse aspects of changing everyday life appear on *chitenge* fabrics, among them shoes with stiletto heels, sunglasses, and new forms of technology such as cell phones and laptops. There are also commemorative *chitenge* fabrics with political and religious motifs. Presidents and political parties are depicted on *chitenge*, as was Pope John Paul II during his visit to Zambia in 1989. In Mali, participants in large gatherings wear printed textiles with photographs as evidence of admiration for public personalities or as promotional gifts (Röschenthaler 2015). The naming of specific designs, which is widespread in Central and West Africa, is not very common in Zambia

(Berzock 2017: 71–79; Sylvanus 2016: 91–94). In recent years, the popular practice in Nigeria of groups of friends or family members wearing identical dresses tailored from printed textiles at important events and social gatherings has gained popularity in Zambia (Nwafor 2012).

Chitenge fabrics have many usages. They are worn as wrappers and plain dresses for everyday use as well as tailored ensembles for special occasions. After independence in the 1960s, tailored *chitenge* outfits became popular as national dress. Over time, they incorporated style elements from across Africa, especially the Congo but also Nigeria and Ghana, and spread regionally in southern Africa.[14] When a woman wishes to commission *chitenge* wear, she can call on local and foreign tailors (from the Democratic Republic of Congo, Ghana, and Nigeria), many of them men, and designers, most but not all of them women. The styles undergo frequent change as I have observed since the early 1970s. In addition to storing *chitenge* outfits, today in Zambia most adult women's wardrobes hold Western-styled garments, which they wear on the job in schools, banks, and offices. For festive occasions and special events, women may dress in elaborate *chitenge* outfits, as some do occasionally to work on their free dress day, Friday. If active church members, they have a church uniform and *chitenge* cloths with religious symbols. At home and when they go shopping, they often tie a *chitenge* wrapper around the waist. They carry their infants in a piece of *chitenge* on their back. Because *chitenge* fabric is multi-purpose and worn in both town and country, it is unlikely to be replaced by Western-styled garments.

Going to the Tailor

Until recently, Zambia's fashion scene centred on tailors, small stores, and boutiques, and on entrepreneurs who became known as suitcase traders. Going to a tailor to place an order for a garment is a long-standing dress option in Zambia, especially in the not-so-distant past due to the limited choice in the government-owned department stores during the era of the one-party state (1972–91). Most tailors then were men, as many still are, though more and more women have since joined their ranks.

If small-scale tailoring in markets, alleyways, and storefronts is dominated by men, there is another setting in which many women have taken up the tailor's craft. Home-based production, often with hired tailors, both women and men, is a side-line activity organised by women who work away from home but also by some who pursue design full time. Such operations may take place within the house or in servants' quarters in homes in medium- to high-income residential areas. Some of these women entrepreneurs go to office buildings soliciting orders. In the last half of the 1990s most of their output consisted of women's two-piece office wear and *chitenge* dresses.

When a prospective client wishes to commission a *chitenge* outfit, she can call on local and foreign tailors. Throughout the 1990s, for example, I commissioned my latest *chitenge* outfits from two male tailors, beginning with a small-scale corridor tailor of Malawian background, and then turning to a man from the Democratic Republic of Congo who worked from his downtown alleyway atelier with six women tailors in Lusaka since the 1980s, if not earlier. On the advice of a friend, herself a former clothing vendor, suitcase trader, and apparel entrepreneur, in the present millennium I have called on a woman tailor, again of Democratic Republic of Congo background, with an all-female atelier, where several women tailors work, located in a never-completed downtown office building. I have also bought *chitenge* wear already made directly from displays in arcades, alleyways, and markets in spur-of-the-moment decisions, attracted by the styling of the outfit, its printed pattern, colour combination, and/or design.

How do people attribute meanings to dress in Zambia? Going to the tailor offered rich insights into one phase in the meaning-making of clothing. Participant observation in tailors' workshops enabled me to see how tailors and their clients reached decisions about design and style, to discuss how tailors created and developed style, and to ask clients about their decision to go to the tailor rather than to formal stores, boutiques, or secondhand clothing markets. Some tailors display photo albums of their styles, old pattern books, and European and South African fashion magazines, while others use simple drawings. Many customers bring garments or photos of dresses they want to have copied or they describe what they want the tailor to create. Since the turn of the millennium, Nigerian posters of women's tailored outfits in African print fabrics have been on display in many tailor shops, adding further regional inspirations to a thoroughly Africanised dress practice (Sizaire, dia Mwembu, and Jewsiewicki 2002). Today, the Internet multiplies such inspirations, extending them across the globe.

Tailors have played an important yet somewhat unappreciated role in the making of fashion-conscious consumers in Zambia (Hansen 2013a). Satisfying both needs and desires, tailors' creations help to fabricate dreams. Tailors sew anything from school uniforms to party wear. They also mend and alter *salaula,* as we saw in the previous chapter, and change garments to fit with the fashion of the day. Today some of these practices are referred to as upcycling, while others revolve around giving quality garments a vintage look. Many tailors produce *chitenge* outfits and develop them in new directions. Some tailors produce job lots for established boutiques, and others make *chitenge* dresses 'on order' for suitcase traders who in turn sell them in Zimbabwe and South Africa. Perhaps throughout the entire southern African region, as Leslie Rabine has suggested for Kenya, such 'global African dress signifies not tradition but modernity [that constructs] an elusive and ambiguous ... national identity' (Rabine 1997b: 163).

In addition to tailors, dress shops, and boutiques – some of them in newly developed shopping malls – secondhand clothing markets offer an abundance of clothing choices for all income groups that were unknown in Zambia's controlled economy prior to the turn of the 1980s, as I discussed in Chapter 7. No longer facing currency restrictions, in recent years apparel entrepreneurs fly to London, New York, Dubai, Hong Kong, Bangkok, and other long-haul destinations, including China, to purchase clothing, shoes, and accessories for resale in a grow- ing number of exclusive shops as well as by private arrangements. Suitcase traders, catering to less upscale consumers, travel across the region to South Africa, Botswana, Tanzania, the Democratic Republic of Congo, and West Africa, as well as to Mauritius, India, and China, buying more affordable apparel and textiles, some on commission for established traders and the rest to resell to traders in city markets or from homes and offices to individual clients. *Chitenge* is one of the commod- ities they source in this way.

Designers and New Style Creations

During most of the two first decades after Zambia's independence in 1964, the economy was strictly controlled. When import restrictions were removed in the late 1980s and early 1990s and markets gradually opened up, the clothing scene changed dramatically. Throughout the 1990s, tailors and their clients benefitted from the improved availability of imported fabrics and clothing, a lot of it tailored into *chitenge* outfits. And residents in both urban and rural areas eagerly bought clothes for themselves and their families in rapidly growing markets that sold sec- ondhand clothing imported from the West. Gone were the days of the state-run monopoly stores with their drab clothing.

The design scene is the most recent twist in the ever-changing appre- ciation of stylish dress in Zambia, as it is in many other countries in Africa (Delhave and Woets 2015; Grabski 2009; Rovine 2015). In the mid-1990s, downtown Lusaka had several production units with boutique-style outlets, operated by well-educated women, often married to wealthy men. Such women were able to travel abroad where some attended design and fashion courses. They concentrated on making 'high quality fashion garments for high-income clients who prefer imported clothing from London, Paris, and New York' to what they perceived as cheap local wear (Kasangele 1998: 96–98). But in 2007 when I began to explore the emerging fashion and design scene in Lusaka, the preferences for Western-styled wear were being challenged. Seasonally changing and creatively constructed *chitenge* outfits had begun to take centre stage alongside other dress inspirations in fashionable women's wardrobes.

Between 1999 and today, several upscale shopping malls have opened in Lusaka, as I have already noted. New consumption spaces, clothing stores, and boutiques appeal to urban residents with money to spend. Against this backdrop, two processes have helped fuel the growth of a more vibrant fashion design scene. For one, the production potential of the new designers has been greatly improved by the ready availability in recent years of imported sewing machines, dress fabric, and sewing notions. Second, and above all, their exposure to a global world of fashion and styles has expanded and, along with it, the scope for local dress entrepreneurship. The Internet and social media have made available networks of previously unimaginable interchanges, spanning the globe.

There now is a formal fashion circuit in Zambia, complete with organisers, promoters, models, and photographers. Some dress entrepreneurs view themselves as designers and label their clothing lines. The first organised Zambia Fashion Week unfolded in Lusaka in October 2005. It has been staged subsequently every year except for a brief hiatus between 2009 and 2011.[6] Since then, the event has been part of the annual fashion calendar, spearheaded by a Zambian woman entrepreneur and media personality who heads a media and events company.[7] The show receives endorsements by Zambia's national arts council and ministry of tourism, arts, and culture, and financial sponsorship by a changing line-up of local businesses and Africa-based firms, among them major South African stores and Nigerian banks. Over the years, Zambia's annual fashion week has expanded with established as well as up-and-coming designers, and it also includes designers and models from other African countries. Alongside this, other fashion shows and competitions take place, and new events and venues keep appearing.

---

[6] The woman entrepreneur who launched a woman's magazine, *Beauty Zambia*, and launched the annual fashion week, left the country in 2011.
[7] Zambia Fashion Week was not held during the coronavirus pandemic.

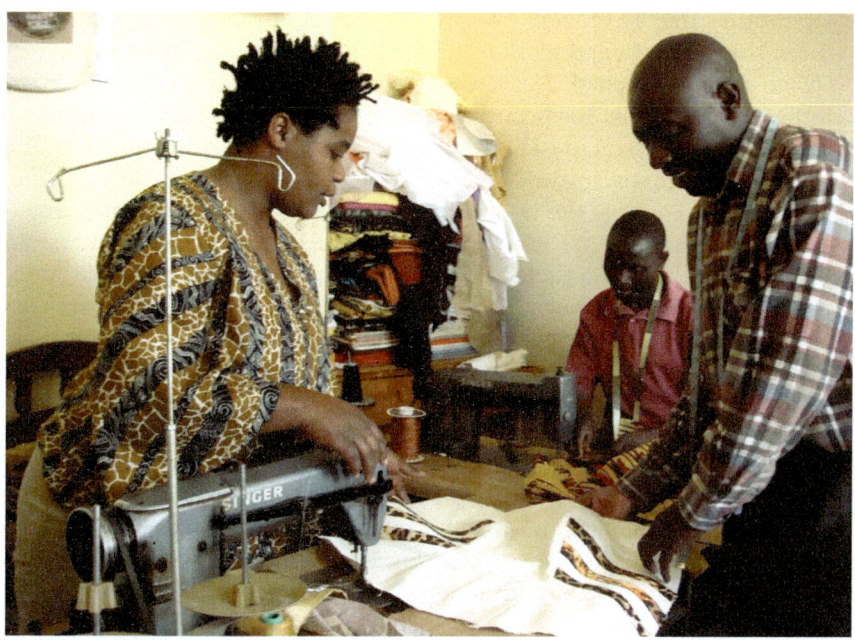

Figure 9.1 Charity Mwakilima Ngoma, who in 2002 established Sefyeni Designers and Florists, instructing her tailors, Lusaka, 2007. Author's photo.

Most of these designers are women, although they include a few men. Among them are people of several national and cultural backgrounds; that is, not all of them are black Zambians. What they all share is a keen sense of style acquired from diverse experiences and exposures that do not always include formal training. Some of these designers, in fact, do not sew themselves but hire tailors, mostly men, to carry out the basic tasks. A few put out their work for completion by tailors (see Figure 9.1). Many operate from their own or their parents' homes or rented premises. They use several types of sewing machines, mostly their own but at times also rented, including chain-stitch sewing machines, lock-stitch machines, and machines for embroidery and knitting. Some had industrial sewing machines as well as old-fashioned treadle machines. Consider Angela Mulenga, for example, whose production of the Queen's Wear label takes place in a tiny workshop in one of downtown Lusaka's oldest shopping venues, the Central Arcade, with four industrial sewing machines and one embroidery machine.

Her mother started Queen's Wear. Angela employs four male tailors, of whom the oldest began working for her mother several years ago.[8]

Who are the clients? A growing crop of style entrepreneurs design clothes, for example, for beauty pageant and *Face of Africa* contestants.[9] In 2009, a group of designers created part of the wardrobe for the Zambian participant in the Miss Universe contest in Brazil. For a while, My Choice, an upscale boutique in Lusaka's oldest shopping mall, Manda Hill, sold some garments produced by the new designers. In 2014, Zambia's first designer boutique featuring locally created fashion, Vala: Local Design House (*vala* meaning wear in the Chinyanja language), opened in a strip mall for commission sales of the clothes by local designers. This new emporium was the brainchild of the Zambia Fashion Council, which aimed to support up-and-coming designers with a passion for fashion with workshops and pop-up exhibits.[10] Designs produced for such events have ripple effects in the form of referrals. Women of means call on these designers to get special dresses made, particularly for kitchen parties and weddings. Some designers have a special clientele of women in high-level jobs and public positions who are well known throughout Zambian society and regarded as trendsetters when it comes to fashion. But more than anything else, it is the production of bridal wear and dresses for bridesmaids that ensures a flow of income for many aspiring designers. And some would not be able to keep operating if they did not have husbands in well-paid positions to support them. To keep their creative design going, some of them pursue additional income-generating avenues, for example, producing uniforms for restaurants and sports teams or designing graphics for special occasion stationary and invitation cards. The designer of the Kutowa label told me that she would not be able to keep her workshop going if she did not also work as a yoga instructor in a small building on the premises.[11]

The new designers operate on a fashion scene where tailors continue to be important. Consider Sylvia Masebo, who in this account from 2005 was Member of Parliament and minister for local government and housing. In her 40s, she used two local designers and a Nigerian tailor. A flamboyant dresser, depending on whether she was visiting her

---

[8] Interview, July 2009, Lusaka.
[9] *Face of Africa* is a yearly modelling competition for which young women are scouted from across the continent.
[10] The Zambia Fashion Council was established in 2014 by a group of fashion professionals to promote locally produced fashion. As many other initiatives, it may have been short-lived. The last online news from the Zambia Fashion Council I have seen was posted in 2016. By June 2019, its website had expired.
[11] Interview with Towani Clarke, designer of the Kutowa label, 25 September 2014, Lusaka. By 1920, she had closed her workshop and, following marriage, relocated to the United States.

local constituency or seated in parliament, she mixed Western-styled and *chitenge* wear, often with impressive hats or folded headdresses. 'I have a lot of *dukus* [headdresses] which I usually do myself', she said in an interview; 'it is just that I am captured [by media photographers] more in Western hats as opposed to African.' Loving jewellery, she carefully selects it to fit with every outfit along with matching shoes and bags. When traveling abroad, Ms Masebo makes sure to dress in 'African outfits' as a representation of who she is and where she comes from. 'Fifty percent of my clothes are western while the others are African.... I do not wear Zambian or Nigerian or Kenyan, I wear African because that's who I am' (*Post* 2005, 2 December).

Cultural Passions for Clothing

Seasonally changing *chitenge* outfits have wide appeal in a dress universe that is strongly inflected by Western-styled wear. Propelled by the aesthetic sensibilities of a new generation of Zambian creative designers, *chitenge* dress has developed in new directions with inspirations from many angles. Mature women continue proudly to display their dressed bodies in *chitenge*, as occasional and special events wear. And young women who used to complain that *chitenge* outfits made them look old are increasingly attracted to the new, creatively styled *chitenge* fashions. Today's young designers work to change the way Zambian women dress by adding a new edge to *chitenge* as everyday wear in the wardrobes of young, upcoming, and professional women with disposable incomes.[12]

The lively fashion scene in Zambia's capital, Lusaka, that I have introduced in this chapter challenges worn-out distinctions between traditional and modern dress as well as between African and Western clothing. Rather than being in opposition to one another, European/Western-style clothing conventions and local/traditional ways of dress play out together on women's dressed bodies, depending on context. Their meanings are very much forged by local circumstances. Developing within changing political, economic, and cultural contexts with its multiple origins and ever-changing styling, *chitenge* wear continues to be considered traditional. The cultural passion for clothing I have described in this book dresses Zambian bodies through trade and interchanges that span the globe. And it does so across class in plain *chitenge* wrappers as well as in elaborately tailored *chitenge* outfits and in upcycled secondhand dress. No doubt in the future, dress practice involving secondhand clothing and emerging new design will unfold

---

[12] Towani Clarke interview.

Figure 9.2 Zambian author Namwali Serpell wearing a *chitenge* dress of
Kutowa design from Lusaka when receiving the Caine Prize for African
writing in Oxford, 2013. Photo by Ranka Primorac, reproduced with
permission.

creatively simultaneously, dressing different bodies but inspired by a
shared cultural passion for fashion.

The story of how tradition and modernity play out together in African
and Western inspirations on women's dressed bodies is at the heart of
much new creative design that incorporates *chitenge* fabric in Zambia (see
Figure 9.2). Though small and mainly, but not exclusively, oriented

towards a local clientele, the emerging fashion scene demonstrates creativity and style with new designs that connect with wearers and viewers who are making sense of their place in the world in both local and global terms. 'The vibrant dress' from Mangishi Doll Co. worn by Angela Bassett during the 2018 American Black Film Festival Honors Award ceremony, 'which was modernised with leather piping and a fringed hem, [was] ethically crafted in Zambia'. To be sure, as the narration about the dress I quoted at the outset of this chapter noted, *chitenge* celebrates history and culture even if the writer who described it as an 'East, West, and Central African fabric' got the specific regional reference wrong.[13] Selling out quickly on the website, the dress, called the MD Marsha Pencil III, was quickly restocked, creating enormous exposure for the four-year-old brand and its Zambian designer, Kapasa Musonda.[14]

Snapshot 6: A Digital Fitting Room

Women dressmakers in Zambia are commonly referred to as tailors rather than seamstresses, as I have done throughout. A Nigerian woman educated in a European design school once tried to set me right when she argued that tailors are not designers. They copy, she explained matter-of-factly. Writing about the clothing scene in Dakar, for a long time the diverse fashion capital of francophone West Africa, anthropologist Kristin Kastner gives voice to some of the mutual stereotypes. 'Tailors laugh', she says, 'at stylish and skilled fashion designers' who might need more time to craft a single garment because of their 'conceptual approach and frequent use of patterns'. Tailors 'never use patterns and are proud of their ability to cut the fabric based only on six different measurements taken from the client'. For their part designers, much like my Nigerian interlocutor, 'dismiss the tailor-made garments mostly as simple copies of models which already exist' (2019: 180).

But a copy might be precisely what the client wants. The power of a copy plays out in the complex work it performs in our everyday lives (Sylvanus 2016: 138–64). Consider the custom-made dress my tailor from the Democratic Republic of the Congo sewed for me in 2019. As I noted in Chapter 9, she had sewn for me several times previously and was recommended by Lily, who appeared in Chapter 8 and who is the eldest daughter of my late research assistant. On a bright summer day Lily and I met with her daughter at a downtown Lusaka lunch venue.

[13] Kallon 2018.   [14] Carpenter 2018.

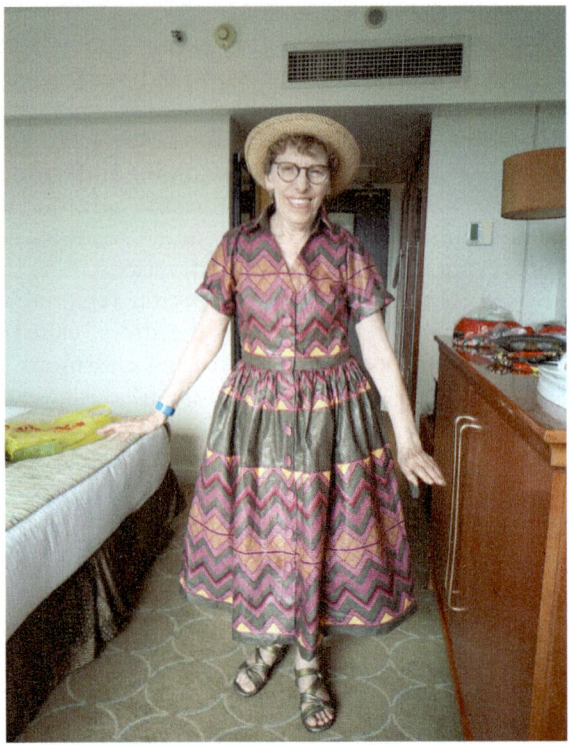

Figure 9.3 The author in a newly tailored dress. Author's collection.

I admired Lily's stunning dress, for both its shiny colourful fabric and its styling. 'Oh', she exclaimed, 'I'll have one made for you, the material is still available.' Since time was an issue because I was about to return to Denmark within a few days, she asked me to send my measurements by phone for her to give to the tailor once she had purchased the fabric. Back from the restaurant, a German friend who herself was skilled at sewing expertly took my measurements, which we then sent by phone to Lily. Only a couple of days passed before Lily delivered the dress in time for me to take it home. The fit was perfect, made by a true dress artisan, testimony to the tailor's skills at cutting (positioning the fabric to avoid misalignment of the printed design and other awkward mistakes) as well as to her excellent body-hugging styling without the use of a fitting room (see Figure 9.3).

An item of clothing is more than a garment. The point about this dress was precisely that it was a replica. Sharing the fabric and styling of Lily's garment, my copied dress had an emotive power that stemmed from my long acquaintance with her family in Lusaka beginning in the early 1970s. The dress triggered memories that helped situate me in the local world. A designer creating a more adventurous dress might not have helped bring about a similar affecting experience.

Since the mid-2000s, adult women in Zambia have begun wearing outfits tailored from identical *chitenge* fabric to show solidarity on occasions such as kitchen parties, *amatebetos* (food presentation by relatives to a son-in-law prior to or soon after marriage), funerals, and memorials. Not witnessing such dress practices prior to that time, I expect that their growing popularity has to do with the ready availability of dress fabric, especially the fresh life breathed into *chitenge* by the huge growth during the first decade of the 2000s in China's African-print trade. Their popularity also reflects improvements in middle-class livelihoods, and last but not least the global abundance of dress options and style influences available to Zambian consumers on the Internet and social media.[15]

Aside from the tailor's work on alterations ranging from adjustments to the fit of a garment to undertaking fashion-oriented changes, the distinction between a tailor and a designer is blurred or even slippery. Perhaps the difference exists mainly in the view of clients rather than of dressmakers and fashion designers themselves, who come and go, as I have observed since around 2007. In fact, across a dressmaker's life course there is considerable sliding between the tasks of tailoring and designing. Economic viability might be affected by the scale of an enterprise and a dressmaker's financial means, including familial support, which as I discussed above often helps keep a workshop together. Many dressmakers have acquired their skills through informal traineeships, learning by doing with senior tailors. In terms of their practical and technical skills they might surpass many of the self-described designers who have no design school education but depend on their creativity and networks. Despite their distinct approaches to fashion, both tailors and designers operate largely from within the informal economy with earnings that rise and fall, influenced by the situation in the overall economy and hinging on their developing reputations with clients. Their success on Zambia's evolving fashion scene also depends on how well in their production they translate the constantly changing global stimuli into what locally is considered to be 'the latest'.

---

[15] Personal communication, Mary Mbewe, 29 August 2021.

Conclusion

Much as in the rest of Africa and elsewhere, dress fashions in Zambia have their own histories and global interconnections. Dress has mattered enormously in Zambia's history and continues to do so today, as I have demonstrated in this book, arguing that dressed bodies are the point of contact between local knowledge and the broader global context. Rich, dynamic, and globally interwoven histories shaped local material culture with commodities and ideas from far away, introducing new textile and clothing practices that people in the region that today is Zambia adapted to their own cultural sensibilities about bodies and dress. In the process, they absorbed diverse and changing styles, creating dress repertoires inspired, for men, by standard formal wear in the West as well as the colonial bush suit and Chinese and Indian elements, and renaming *kente* cloth from Ghana as *kanga* with a term for an East African cloth. Inspirations for women entailed a lively fusion of dress from the West and the rest of Africa with occasional references to India. Zambian women pan-Africanised specific dress elements fusing 'West African' and 'Nigerian *boubou*' while accessorising their *chitenge* outfits with *dukus*, a name for a head-tie from Ghana. They made their own dress, *chitenge*, from African prints produced in Europe with Indonesian inspirations during the colonial era and subsequently developed for export to African markets. Today, most of the African prints sold across the continent are manufactured by Chinese textile firms. And during the 1990s dresses tailored from colourful *chitenge* fabrics sold by suitcase traders in South Africa were called 'Zambia'. With its multiple inspirations and ever-changing styling, dress in Zambia draws on many cultural referents in the creation of a recognisably local touch of elegance.

In this conclusion I briefly return to some of my main observations by highlighting a number of the culturally and politically charged controversies that invoke past contentions yet play out in changed circumstances. Meanwhile, several issues remain for tomorrow's scholars to explore as I discuss next, turning to everyday fashion changes, ongoing designer struggles, and questions about the future.

Dress Desires and Controversies

Dressing well has been at the heart of dress practice in Zambia from the early colonial period through to the present, as it has in several other African countries, especially in West Africa. In fact, because of its coastal location and long history of contacts with the world beyond the continent, Senegal might have received more scholarly attention regarding clothing than many other countries (Brooks 1976; Heath 1992; Kastner 2019; Mustafa 2006; Scheld 2007). This book showcases dress practice in Zambia, where the everyday localisation of Western-styled dress with few exceptions tended to be ignored and barely prompted any recent explorative scholarship. As I discussed in Part I of this book, men from Northern Rhodesia gained access to factory-woven textiles and tailored garments through regional migrant labour they carried out across central and southern Africa, exposing them to new dress conventions and making them keen connoisseurs of style. By the late 1930s when colonial authorities no longer held back their presence in the growing towns, women went for the new fashions with abandon. World War II's restrictions on imports limited the availability of garments, while the tailor's craft attracted customers for everyday dresses and suits as well as for ball gowns.

When away from the condescending view of colonial observers, urban women and men dressed in styles inspired by diverse contacts from across the wider African region and beyond, presenting themselves at leisure in and around their racially segregated residential areas to be viewed with respect and admiration by a world that was undergoing rapid change leading up to independence. Clothing availability during the early postcolonial years improved when local textile manufacturing and garment production were established on a limited scale. In the new nation, President Kaunda proudly turned a modernised bush suit into required office wear as the safari suit, while his wife's elaborately tailored *chitenge* outfits helped invent a new tradition from scratch to become women's national dress. With Western-styled dress as standard wear, *chitenge* occupied a growing place in adult women's diversifying wardrobes.

Postcolonial socioeconomic changes challenged widespread cultural norms that had guided dress and body display, resulting particularly in gender and generational conflicts. Part II of the book examined some dress controversies that have kept appearing in changed forms from the late colonial period through the present. One case involves the changing valuation of women's dressed bodies and shifts in the shame frontier, in short, the accentuated sexualisation of nudity and specific body parts. The second case also concerns women's dress practice, especially the wearing of miniskirts and tight clothing in public, which keeps provoking violent incidents and vocal abuse again and again, some of them reaching into the heart of the Zambian nation, the house of parliament. The third controversial case revolves around the ostentatious dress practice of former president Chiluba, who skilfully articulated power by means of his dressed body. The court case charging him with corruption materially conflated distinction and corruption and made the president's dressed body emblematic of corruption.

The twenty-first century with major changes in global and local economies briefly alluded to in the Prologue is marking many shifts in the cultural dress economy in Zambia, some examples of which I discussed in Part III of the book. While my research focus has turned increasingly towards the creative work of tailors and self-styled designers, secondhand clothing has not fallen away from popular dress practice. As always, used clothes are being repurposed but with new fashionable spins, some of which are turning recycled garments into upcycled outfits. An accepted part of the clothing market that attracts customers from diverse economic and ethnic backgrounds, today select *salaula* has entered a special niche as vintage clothing, while damaged garments are shredded into threads that are creatively recycled into knotted and crocheted toys or woven into baskets, for example. And everyday fashions are changing as young people challenge constraining dress norms by wearing tight and short clothing in public. And young professional women have begun to wear *chitenge* to work while women in public office, including members of parliament, insist on their freedom to dress as they like. Still, cases of violent incidents occur provoked by dress.

Dressed Bodies, Materiality, Agency

The desire to cut a nice figure that privileges men's formal suits and women's carefully coordinated dress presentations in Zambia animate dress performance in everyday life and on special occasions. They produce what I have referred to as the 'wow' effect that makes people turn heads in admiration or with disapproval. Throughout this book I have shown how the effects of such displays are significantly influenced by the agentive power of the dressed body as a social skin that not only reproduces culturally established dress norms but also challenges them. In effect, some garments have made history. We saw this, for example, with regard to miniskirts, the Kaunda-inspired safari suit, *chitenge* outfits, and the conflation of Chiluba's 'new culture' suits and corrupt governance. Unlike these garments that hold particular meaning and value, accessories such as Kaunda's white handkerchiefs, Chiluba's snakeskin shoes with elevated heels, Lungu's 'Panama' hats, and Silvia Masebo's eye-catching headpieces may or may not leave lasting traces in memory and emotion on the constantly shifting sartorial landscape in Zambia.

Dressed bodies and the material texture of clothing play together with the sensual and the aesthetic to produce the 'wow' effect that women with their clothing competence are working so hard to achieve. Materiality is central to this project in women's concerns with the physical properties of fabric and fibre. When shopping, women attend critically to the quality of fabrics and garments as well as to the cut and tidiness of the tailoring. Achieving a pleasant sensuous experience is the chief aim when women shop for fabrics, in addition, of course, to getting a good value for the money. Subsequent stages of this process involve detailed garment care through washing and ironing to ensure attractive dress presentations. For a garment to be successfully displayed, the material texture of dress fabric against the body must feel good to help trigger positive reactions. What is more, the context of display in which viewers perceive and respond ultimately embeds the social success or failure of the dress presentation. This is why, as I have argued throughout, the meaning of dress does not inhere in the garments themselves but is produced through performance.

Creative Potentials

Africa's design promise caught the international fashion headlines, when *Italian Vogue* dedicated the May 2012 issue of men's *Vogue*, *L'Uomo Vogue*, to the theme 'rebranding Africa'. The editor-in-chief of *Italian Vogue* has been appointed a Goodwill Ambassador for *Fashion4Development*, a global campaign using fashion-oriented initiatives to support United Nations' development efforts in Africa. In the special Africa edition, United Nations General Secretary Ban Ki-moon appealed for support of African designers. The magazine featured interviews and photo spreads of several African presidents who recognised the importance of local design and fashion yet had few economic means to back them up. In addition to showing some of today's most famous designers from Africa, such as Nigerian-born, London-based Duro Oluwo, whose bold designs dress clients around the world, among them Michelle Obama and Beyoncé, the issue was packed with photographs of local personalities like first ladies and queens, artists, singers, musicians, writers, and models, who all encouraged support for and investment in the creative professions across the continent (*L'Uomo Vogue* 2012).

The goal to promote the creative work of small-scale African textile entrepreneurs is shared widely by local and foreign non-governmental organizations, brand name producers, and fashion designers such as Vivienne Westwood promoting sustainability initiatives in Kenya, among others.[1] Beginning in 2015 the African Development Bank (and partners) launched an initiative to create jobs and increase market share for small-scale creative enterprises by providing mentorship and networking, digital and financial skills, and access to finance. First directed towards top African fashion markets like South Africa, Nigeria, Côte d'Ivoire, and Ethiopia, during the coronavirus pandemic this initiative, which does not include Zambia, increasingly turned digital with webinars and digital exchanges about sustainability and circular economies. While in Zambia locally and externally supported non-governmental organisations help enable the production capacity of a variety of design initiatives and enterprises by focusing on sustainability and fair labour practices, for example, the creative and economic potential of locally made dress fashion has far from been tapped.

As we saw with the Mangishi Doll Co. dress in Chapter 9, Zambian-made fashion, some including diverse *chitenge* elements as important features, has drawn attention from within the diaspora as well as with Africa-focused fashion presentations in connection with recent bi-annual shows in the fashion capitals of Europe and the United States. The *Black Panther* film (2018) and American singer Beyoncé's music video album, *Black Is King* (2020), showcased designers from Africa for popular audiences internationally. Meanwhile in Zambia, it is small-scale tailors, women and men, along with up-and-coming designers, several of them self-made, who attend to many of the dress needs and fashion desires of Zambian women and men of all classes. Tailors are not designers, as a Nigerian-born designer instructed me a few years ago. While this observation might hold for the production of school and church uniforms that are an economic mainstay of many tailors, it hides the creative potential that Zambian desires for well-dressed bodies unlock in visits to tailor workshops. Local bespoke work draws on influences from many directions, combining the client's and the tailor's inputs in a creative interchange. Some of these tailors have made names for themselves, joining other dress entrepreneurs to draw attention to the local fashion scene by establishing support networks and participating in yearly fashion shows and other venues to display their innovative dress designs. But many designers have come and gone, including some of those I have interviewed over the years. Their work entails an ongoing economic and creative struggle to make a living and professionalise the fashion scene

---

[1] For an overview, see Andrew Brooks (2015), chapter 9, 'Ethical clothing myths and realities' (207–32).

in Zambia, where most of them operate within the country's huge informal economy, lacking substantive state support and enduring sponsorships.

Today in Zambia, small-scale tailors and fashion entrepreneurs operate in a segmented clothing market that is less competitive than it is interactive as they diversify and shift their activities to get by. The secondhand clothing vendor, the retailer of 'Chinese clothing', the upscale boutique operator in the shopping mall, along with the tailor and the up-and-coming designer are serving the different needs of their fashion-conscious customers while they all are contributing to that overall well-dressed presentation for which people from Zambia continue to be so well known in the neighbouring countries. While post-pandemic dress trajectories are difficult to plot with any certainty, there is no doubt that in a dress scene strongly inflected by Western styles, young designers from Zambia will continue to be hard at work with innovative designs, some of them making creative use of *chitenge* as a fabric and a dress style of choice that recognises the Zambian craving for dressing well. Such clothing projects hold significant value for those who pursue them and transformative potentials that are far from trivial. For fashion helps break down cultural boundaries. The rich scholarship about African colonial and postcolonial fashion cultures that I have drawn on in this book demonstrates vividly how local dress influences hold their own in the context of global inspirations.

References

Books and Articles

Akou, Heather M. 2011. *The Politics of Dress in Somali Culture.* Bloomington: Indiana University Press.

Allman, Jean (ed.). 2004. *Fashioning Africa: power and the politics of dress.* Bloomington: Indiana University Press.

Ambler, Charles. 1990. 'Alcohol, racial segregation and popular politics in Northern Rhodesia', *Journal of African History* 31(2): 295–313.

2001. 'Popular films and colonial audiences: the movies in Northern Rhodesia', *American Historical Review* 106(1): 81–105.

Anon. 2009. *Here I Stand: verbatim testimony of second republican president Dr. Frederick Chiluba.* Lusaka: ZDS Press Service.

Ansell, Gwen. 2004. *Soweto Blues: jazz, popular music and politics in South Africa.* London: Continuum.

Appadurai, Arjun (ed.). 1986. 'Introduction: commodities and the politics of value' in Arjun Appadurai (ed.), *The Social Life of Things: commodities in cultural perspective.* Cambridge: Cambridge University Press. 3–63.

Ardener, Shirley G. 1973. 'Sexual insult and female militancy', *Man* 8(3): 422–40.

Banerjee, Mukulita, and Daniel Miller. 2004. *The Sari.* Oxford: Berg.

Barber, Karin. 2007. 'When people cross thresholds', *African Studies Review* 50 (2): 111–24.

Barnard, Malcolm. 2014. *Fashion Theory: an introduction.* London: Bloomsbury.

Barnes, John A. [1951] 1959. 'The Fort Jameson Ngoni', in Elizabeth Colson and Max Gluckman (eds), *Seven Tribes of British Central Africa.* Manchester: Manchester University Press. 194–252.

Barrett, Michael. 2013. '"Walking Home Majestically": consumption and the enactment of social status among labour migrants from Barotseland, 1935–1965' in Robert Ross, Marja Hinfelaar, and Iva Pesa (eds), *The Objects of Life in Central Africa: the history of consumption and social change, 1840–1980.* Leiden: Brill. 93–114.

Barthes, Roland. 1983. *The Fashion System.* Translated by Matthew Ward and Richard Howard. Berkeley: University of California Press.

Bastian, Misty. 2005. 'The naked and the nude: historically multiple meanings of *Oto* (undress) in Southeastern Nigeria' in Adeline Masquelier (ed.), *Dirt,*

Undress, and Difference: critical perspectives on the body's surface. Bloomington: Indiana University Press. 34–60.

Bayart, Jean-Francois. 1993. *The State in Africa: the politics of the belly*. New York: Longman.

Becker, Heike. 2012. 'Anthropology and the study of popular culture: a perspective from the southern tip of the continent', *Research in African Literatures* 43 (4): 17–37.

Berzock, Kathleen Bickford. 2017. 'African prints/African ownership: on naming, value, and classics' in Suzanne Gott, Kristyne Loughran, Betsy D. Quick, and Leslie Rabine (eds), *African-Print Fashion Now! A story of taste, globalization, and style*. Los Angeles, CA: Fowler Museum. 71–79.

Bloom, Leonard. 1972. 'Some values and attitudes of young Zambians, studied through spontaneous autobiographies', *African Social Research* 14: 288–300.

Bloomberg Quicktakes. 'Inside the $130 Billion Second-Hand Fashion Market'. www.bloomberg.com/news/articles/2021-11-26/inside-the-130-billion-second-hand-fashion-market. Accessed 5 December 2021.

Boateng, Boatema. 2021. 'Not African? Contested origins of wax print and its high-fashion appropriation', *Textile Museum Journal* 48: 118–37.

Bordo, Susan. 1993. *Unbearable Weight: feminism, western culture, and the body*. Berkeley: University of California Press.

Brooks, Andrew. 2010. 'Spinning and weaving discontent: labour relations and the production of meaning at Zambia-China Mulungushi Textiles', *Journal of Southern African Studies* 36(1): 113–32.

2015. *Clothing Poverty: the hidden world of fast fashion and second-hand clothes*. London: Zed Books.

Brooks, George, Jr. 1976. 'The Signares of Saint-Louis and Gorée: women entrepreneurs in eighteenth century Senegal' in Nancy Hafkin and Edna Bay (eds), *Women in Africa*. Stanford, CA: Stanford University Press. 19–44.

Brown, Maria Grace. 2017. *Khartoum at Night: fashion and the body politics in imperial Sudan*. Stanford, CA: Stanford University Press.

Brown, Patricia Leigh. 1989. 'Shopper's World: Zambia's social fabric', *New York Times*, 26 November.

Burgess, Thomas. 2002. 'Cinema, bell bottoms, and miniskirts: struggles over youth and citizenship in revolutionary Zanzibar', *International Journal of African Historical Studies* 35(2–3): 287–313.

Burton, Andrew. 2001. 'Urchins, loafers and the cult of the cowboy: urbanization and delinquency in Dar es Salaam, 1919–61', *Journal of African History* 42 (2): 199–216.

Byfield, Judith A. 2002. *The Bluest Hands: a social and economic history of women dyers in Abeokuta (Nigeria), 1890–1940*. Portsmouth, NH: Heinemann.

Cameron, Elisabeth L. 2010. 'Republic of Congo and Democratic Republic of Congo' in Joanne B. Eicher and Doran H. Ross (eds), *Berg Encyclopedia of World Dress and Fashion, vol 1: Africa*. Oxford: Berg. 371–72.

Carpenter, Carrie. 2018. 'Black Panther's Angela Bassett dons $169 Mangishi Doll Co dress to present at American Black Film Festival Honors', *Zambia Daily Mail*. 26 February.

Chauncey, George Jr. 1981. 'The locus of reproduction: women's labour in the Zambian Copperbelt, 1927–1953', *Journal of Southern African Studies* 7 (2):135–64.

Cheang, Sarah, Erica de Greef, and Yoko Takagi (eds). 2021. *Rethinking Fashion Globalization*. London: Bloomsbury.

Chipande, Hikabwa D. 2016. 'Mining for goals: football and social change on the Zambian Copperbelt 1940s–1960s', *Radical History Review* 125: 55–73.

Colloredo-Mansfeld, Rudi. 2003. 'Introduction: matter unbound', *Journal of Material Culture* 8(3): 245–54.

Colson, Elizabeth. 1958. *Marriage and the Family among the Plateau Tonga of Northern Rhodesia*. Manchester: Manchester University Press.

Comaroff, John L., and Jean Comaroff, 1997. 'Fashioning the colonial subject: the empire's old clothes' in John L. Comaroff and Jean Comaroff, *Of Revelation and Revolution, vol. 2: The Dialectics of Modernity on a South African Frontier*. Chicago, IL: University of Chicago Press. 218–73.

Cooper, Leah Faye. 2021. 'Ruth E. Carter dressed the *Coming 2 America* cast in "the Majesty of Contemporary Africa"', *Harper's Bazaar*, 17 March. www .harpersbazaar.com/culture/film-tv/a35855261/ruth-e-carter-coming-2-america-interview/. Accessed 28 October 2021.

Cosgrave, Stuart. 1998. 'The zoot suit and style warfare' in Angela McRobbie (ed.), *Zoot Suits and Second-Hand Dresses: an anthology of fashion and music*. Boston: Unwin Hyman. 23–49

Craik, Jennifer. 1994. *The Face of Fashion: cultural studies in fashion*. London: Routledge.

Daloz, Jean-Pascal. 2003. 'Ostentation in comparative perspective: culture and elite legitimation' in Frederik Engelstad (ed.), Comparative Studies in Culture and Power, *Comparative Social Research* 21: 29–62.

Davis, John Merle. [1933] 1968. *Modern Industry and the African: an enquiry into the effect of the copper mines of Central Africa upon native society and the work of the Christian missions*. 2nd edition. New York: Augustus M. Kelley.

Delhave, Christine, and Rhoda Woets. 2015. 'The commodification of ethnicity: Vlisco fabrics and wax cloth in Ghana', *International Journal of Fashion Studies* 2(1): 77–97.

Diabate, Naminata. 2020. *Naked Agency: genital cursing and biopolitics in Africa*. Durham, NC: Duke University Press.

Dobler, Gregor. 2009. 'Chinese shops and the formation of a Chinese expatriate community in Namibia', *China Quarterly* 199: 707–27.

Dogbe, Esi. 2003. 'Unraveled yarns: dress, consumption, and yarns. Women's bodies in Ghanaian culture', *Fashion Theory* 7(3–4): 377–95.

Dolat, Sunny. 2017. *Not African Enough? A fashion book by the Nest Collective*. Nairobi: Nest Arts Company.

Dugger, Cecilia W. 2009. 'Battle to halt graft in Africa ebbs', *New York Times*, June 10, A1.

Duncan, Tyrell. 1996. *Prospects for sustainable human development in Zambia*. Lusaka: Government of the Republic of Zambia and the United Nations System in Zambia.

DuPlessis, Robert. 2016. *The Material Atlantic: clothing, commerce, and coloniza-tion in the Atlantic World, 1650–1800*. Cambridge: Cambridge University Press.

Eicher, Joanne B., and Mary Ellen Roach-Higgins. 1992. 'Definitions and clas-sifications of dress: implications for analysis of gender roles' in Ruth Barnes and Joanne B. Eicher (eds), *Dress and Gender: making and meaning*. Oxford: Berg. 8–28.

Eicher, Joanne, and Tonye V. Erekosima. 1995. 'Why do they call it Kalabari? Cultural authentication and the demarcation of ethnic identity' in Joanne B. Eicher (ed.), *Dress and Ethnicity*. Oxford: Berg. 139–64.

Eicher, Joanne B. 1995. 'Introduction: dress as expression of ethnic identity' in Joanne B. Eicher (ed.), *Dress and Ethnicity*. Oxford: Berg. 1–5.

Eicher, Joanne B., and Barbara Sumberg. 1995. 'World fashion, ethnic, and national dress' in Joanne B. Eicher (ed.), *Dress and Ethnicity*. Oxford: Berg. 295–306.

Elias, Norbert. [1937] 1978. *The Civilising Process, vol. 1: the History of Manners*. Translated by Edmund Jephcott. Oxford: Basil Blackwell.

Entwistle, Joan. 2000. *The Fashioned Body: fashion, dress, and modern social theory*. Cambridge: Polity Press.

2001. 'The dressed body' in Joanne Entwistle and Elizabeth Wilson (eds), *Body Dressing*. Oxford: Berg. 33–58.

Epstein, Arnold L. 1953. 'The role of African courts in urban communities of the Northern Rhodesia Copperbelt', *Rhodes-Livingstone Journal* 13: 1–17.

1954. 'Juridical techniques and the judicial process', *Rhodes-Livingstone Papers* 23.

1958. *Politics in an Urban African Community*. Manchester: Manchester University Press.

1981. *Urbanization and Kinship: the domestic domain on the Copperbelt of Zambia, 1950–1956*. New York: Academic Press.

1992a. 'Tribal elders to trade unions' in Arnold L. Epstein, *Scenes from African urban life: collected Copperbelt papers*. Edinburgh: Edinburgh University Press. 42–48.

1992b. 'The role of the urban courts' in Arnold L. Epstein, *Scenes from African urban life: collected Copperbelt papers*. Edinburgh: Edinburgh University Press. 22–41.

1992c. 'Linguistic innovation and culture on the Copperbelt' in Arnold L. Epstein, *Scenes from African urban life: collected Copperbelt papers*. Edinburgh: Edinburgh University Press. 99–118.

Fabian, Johannes. 1990. *History from Below: The 'Vocabulary of Elisabethville' by Andre Yav. Text, translation, and interpretive essays*. Philadelphia, PA: John Benjamins.

Fair, Laura. 2001. *Pastimes and Politics: culture, community, and identity in post-abolition urban Zanzibar, 1890–1945*. Athens: Ohio University Press.

2004. 'Remaking fashion in the Paris of the Indian Ocean: dress, performance, and the cultural construction of a cosmopolitan Zanzibari identity' in Jean Allman (ed.), *Fashioning Africa: power and the politics of dress*. Bloomington: Indiana University Press. 13–30.

Farmer, Ben. 2015. 'Harmid Karzai's signature striped coat bound for the British Museum', *Telegraph*, 21 April. www.telegraph.co.uk/news/worldnews/asia/afghanistan/11552496/Hamid-Karzai's-signature-striped-coat-bound-for-British-Museum. Accessed 5 October 2020.

Fee, Sarah, and Pedro Machado. 2017. 'Entangled histories: translocal textile trades in Eastern Africa, c. 800 CE to the early twentieth century', *Textile History* 48(1): 4–14.

Ferguson, James. 1999. *Expectations of Modernity: myths and meanings of urban life on the Zambian Copperbelt*. Berkeley: University of California Press.

Finkelstein, Joanne. 1998. *Fashion: an introduction*. New York: New York University Press.

Fletcher, Kate, and Ingun Grimstad Klepp (eds). 2017. *Opening up the Wardrobe: a methods book*. Oslo: Novus Press.

Fraenkel, Peter. 1959. *Wayaleshi*. London: Weidenfeld and Nicolson.

Fretwell, Elizabeth Ann. 2018. 'Tailoring Benin: Material Culture and Artisan Production in Urban West Africa'. PhD thesis, University of Chicago.

Friedman, Jonathan. 1991. 'Consuming desires: strategies of selfhood and appropriation', *Cultural Anthropology* 6(2): 154–63.

Gandoulou, Justin-Daniel. 1989. *Dandies à Bacongo: le culte de l'élégance dans la société congolaise contemporaine*. Paris: L'Harmattan.

Geisler, Gisela. 1987. '"Sisters under the skin": women and the Women's League in Zambia', *Journal of Modern African Studies* 25(1): 43–66.

Gilbert, Juliet. 2019. 'Mobile identities: photography, smartphones and aspirations in urban Nigeria', *Africa* 89(2): 246–65.

Gluckman, Max. 1955. *Custom and Conflict in Africa*. Oxford: Blackwell.

Gondola, Didier Ch. 2010. 'La Sape exposed! High fashion among lower-class Congolese youth: from colonial modernity to global cosmopolitanism' in Suzanne Gott and Kristyne Loughran (eds), *Contemporary African Fashion*. Bloomington: Indiana University Press. 157–73.

2016. *Tropical Cowboys: westerns, violence, and masculinity in Kinshasa*. Bloomington: Indiana University Press.

Gott, Suzanne, and Kristyne Loughran (eds). 2010. *Contemporary African Fashion*. Bloomington: Indiana University Presss.

Gott, Suzanne, Kristyne Loughran, Betsy D. Quick, and Leslie Rabine (eds). 2017. *African-Print Fashion Now! A story of taste, globalization, and style*. Los Angeles, CA: Fowler Museum.

Grabski, Joanna. 2009. 'Making fashion in the city: a case study of tailors and designers in Dakar, Senegal', *Fashion Theory* 13(2): 215–42.

Guille, Jackie. 1995. 'Southern African textiles today: design, industry and collective Enterprise' in John Picton (ed.), *Technology, Tradition and Lurex: the art of textiles in Africa*. London: Lund Humphries. 51–54.

Guyer, Jane. 2004. *Marginal Gains: monetary transactions in Atlantic Africa*. Chicago, IL: University of Chicago Press.

Haggblade, Steven. 1990. 'The flip side of fashion: used clothing exports to the Third World', *Journal of Development Studies* 26(3): 505–21.

Hansen, Karen Tranberg. 1975. 'Married women and work: explorations from an urban case study', *African Social Research* 20: 777–99.

1980. 'When sex becomes a critical variable: married women and extra-domestic work in Lusaka, Zambia', *African Social Research* 30: 831–49.

1989. *Distant Companions: servants and employers in Zambia, 1900–1985*. Ithaca, NY: Cornell University Press.

Hansen, Karen Tranberg. (ed.) 1992. *African Encounters with Domesticity*. Brunswick, NJ: Rutgers University Press.

1996. 'Washing dirty laundry in public: local court, custom, and gender relations in post-colonial Zambia' in Kathleen Sheldon (ed.), *Courtyards, Markets, and City Streets: urban women in Africa*, Boulder, CO: Westview Press. 105–27.

1997. *Keeping House in Lusaka*. New York: Columbia University Press.

1999. 'Transnational biographies and local meanings: used clothing practices in Lusaka', *Journal of Southern African Studies* 21(1):131–45.

2000a. *Salaula: the world of secondhand clothing and Zambia*. Chicago, IL: University of Chicago Press.

2000b. 'Gender and difference: youth, bodies and clothing in Zambia' in Victoria Ana Goddard (ed.), *Gender, Agency and Change: anthropological perspectives*. London: Routledge. 32–55.

2003. 'Fashioning: Zambian moments', *Journal of Material Culture* 8(3): 301–10.

2004a. 'Helping or hindering? Controversies around the international second-hand clothing trade', *Anthropology Today* 20(4): 3–9.

2004b. 'The world in dress: anthropological perspectives on clothing, fashion, and culture', *Annual Reviews of Anthropology* 33: 369–92.

2004c. 'Dressing dangerously: miniskirts, gender relations, and sexuality in Zambia' in Jean Alman (ed.), *Fashioning Africa: power and the politics of dress*. Bloomington: Indiana University Press. 166–85.

2008. 'Filling up the wardrobe: decision making, clothing purchase, and dress valuation in Lusaka, Zambia' in Hans Peter Hahn (ed.), *Consumption in Africa: anthropological approaches*. Berlin: LIT Verlag. 79–96.

2013a. 'Fabricating dreams: sewing machines, tailors, and urban entrepreneurship in Zambia' in Robert Ross, Marja Hinfelaar, and Iva Pesa (eds), *The Objects of Life in Central Africa: the history of consumption and social change, 1840–1980*. Leiden: Brill. 167–85.

2013b. 'Introduction' in Karen Tranberg Hansen and Soyini D. Madison (eds), *African Dress: fashion, agency, performance*. London: Bloomsbury. 1–11.

2015. 'Urban research in a hostile setting: Godfrey Wilson in Broken Hill, Northern Rhodesia, 1938–1940'. *Kronos* 47: 193–214.

2017. 'From grandmother's dress to the fashion runway: *chitenge* styles in Zambia' in Suzanne Gott, Kristyne Loughran, Betsy D. Quick, and Leslie Rabine (eds), *African-Print Fashion Now! A story of taste, globalization, and style*. Los Angeles, CA: Fowler Museum. 160–61.

2019a. 'Chiluba's trunks: consumption, excess and the body politic in Zambia' in Deborah Posel and Ilana Van Wyk (eds), *Conspicuous Consumption in Africa*. Johannesburg: Wits University Press. 96–111.

2019b. '"Not African enough?" Global dynamics and local contestations over dress practice and fashion design in Zambia', *ZoneModa Journal* 9(2): 1–15.

2020. '"Our Dress": *chitenge* as Zambia's national fabric' in Heike Jenss and Viola Hofmann (eds), *Fashion and materiality: cultural practices and global contexts*. London: Bloomsbury. 140–56.

2023. 'Colonial fashion histories' in Christopher Breward, Beverly Lemire, and Giorgio Riello (eds), *Cambridge Global History of Fashion, vol. 2*. Cambridge: Cambridge University Press.

Hansen, Karen Tranberg, and Soyini D. Madison (eds). 2013. *African Dress: fashion, agency, performance*. London: Bloomsbury.

Haynes, Naomi. 2019. 'The benefit of the doubt: on the relationship between doubt and power', *Anthropological Quarterly* 92(1): 35–57.

Heath, Deborah. 1992. 'Fashion, anti-fashion, and heteroglossia in urban Senegal'. *American Ethnologist* 19(1): 19–33.

Henderson, Ian. 1975. 'Early African leadership: the Copperbelt disturbances of 1935 and 1940', *Journal of Southern African Studies* 2(1): 83–97.

Hendrickson, Hildi. 1996. 'Introduction' in Hildi Hendrickson (ed.), *Clothing and Difference: embodied identities in colonial and postcolonial Africa*. Durham, NC: Duke University Press. 1–16.

Higginson, John. 1989. *A Working Class in the Making: Belgian colonial labor policy and the African mine worker, 1907–1951*. Madison: University of Wisconsin Press.

Hobsbawm, Eric, and Terence Ranger (eds). 1983. *The Invention of Tradition*. Cambridge: Cambridge University Press.

Ifeka-Moller, Caroline. 1973. '"Sitting on a man": colonialism and the lost political institutions of Igbo women: a reply to Judith van Allen', *Canadian Journal of African Studies* 7(2): 317–18.

Innovation Fund Denmark. 2021. 'Appendix 6, 1112-00007A Circular economy with a focus on plastics and textiles: A 2030 and 2050 roadmap'. https:// innovationsfonden.dk/sites/default/files/2021-08/Appendix%206%20_% 201112-00007A%20-%20Circular%20economy%20with%20a%20focus %20on%20plastics%20and%20textiles%20A%202030%20%26% 202050%20Roadmap.pdf. Accessed 14 December 2021.

Ivaska, Andrew. 2011. *Cultured States: youth, gender, and modern style in 1960s Dar es Salaam*. Durham, NC: Duke University Press.

Jansen, M. Angela, and Jennifer Craik (eds). 2016. *Modern Fashion Traditions: negotiating tradition and modernity through fashion*. London: Bloomsbury.

Jennings, Helen. 2010. *New African Fashion*. New York: Prestel.

Kallon, Catherine. 2018. 'Angela Bassett in Mangishi Doll Co. – 2018 American Black Film Festival Honors Awards', Red Carpet Fashion Awards, 26 February. www.redcarpet-fashionawards.com/2018/02/26/angela-bassett-man gishi-doll-co-2018-american-black-film-festival-honors-awards/. Accessed 19 June 2019.

Kalusa, Walima T. 2013. 'Consuming manufactured goods and contracting colonial hegemony on the Zambian Copperbelt, 1845–1964' in Robert Ross, Marja Hinfelaar, and Iva Pesa (eds), *The Objects of Life in Central Africa: the history of consumption and social change, 1840–1980*. Leiden: Brill. 143–66.

2022. 'Educated girls, clothes and Christianity: subverting Mabel Shaw's sartorial agenda on the colonial Zambian Copperbelt', *Journal of Southern African Studies* 48(1): 61–80.

Kantorowicz, Ernst H. 1958. *The King's Two Bodies: a study in medieval political theology*. Princeton, NJ: Princeton University Press.

Kasangele, Mwango. 1998. 'Differentiation among small-scale enterprises: the Zambian clothing industry in Lusaka' in Anita Spring and Barbara E. McDade (eds), *African Entrepreneurship: theory and reality*. Gainesville: University of Florida Press. 93–106.

Kastner, Kristin. 2019. 'Fashioning Dakar's urban society: sartorial code-mixing in Senegal', *Sociologus* 69(2): 167–88.

Kaunda, Kenneth. 1962. *Zambia Shall be Free: an autobiography*. London: Heinemann.

Kitagawa, Katsuhiko. 2006. 'Japanese competition in the Congo Basin in the 1930s' in A. J. H. Lantham, Heita Kawakatsa, and Katsuhiko Kitagawa (eds), *Intra-Asian Trade and the World Market*. New York: Routledge. 155–67.

Klopper, Sandra. 2000. 'Re-dressing the past: Africanisation of sartorial style in contemporary South Africa' in Avtar Brah and Annie E. Coombes (eds), *Hybridity and Its Discontents: politics, science, culture*. London: Routledge. 216–31.

Konaté, Dior. 2009. 'Women, clothing, and politics in Senegal in the 1940s–1950s' in Maureen Daly Goggin and Beth Fowkes Tobin (eds), *Material Women, 1750–1950: consuming desires and collecting practices*. Farnham: Ashgate. 224–43.

Kopytoff, Igor. 1986. 'The cultural biography of things: commoditization as process' in Arjun Appadurai (ed.), *The Social Life of Things: commodities in cultural perspective*. Cambridge: Cambridge University Press. 64–92.

Kriger, Colleen E. 2006. *Cloth in West African History*. Lanham, MD: Altamira.

Küchler, Susanne, and Daniel Miller (eds). 2005. *Clothing as Material Culture*. London: Berg.

Larmer, Miles. 2021. *Living for the City: social change and knowledge production in the central African Copperbelt*. Cambridge: Cambridge University Press.

Laws, Christopher. n.d. 'Behind the song: Charles Mingus: "Goodbye Pork Pie Hat"', CulturedArm. https://culturedarm.com/behind-the-song-charles-min gus-goodbye-pork-pie-hat/. Accessed 30 March 2020.

Lee, Ching Kwan. 2017. *The Specter of Global China: politics, labor, and foreign investment in Africa*. Chicago, IL: University of Chicago Press.

Leeb-du Toit, Juliette. 2017. *Ishishweshwe: a history of the indigenization of blue-print in Southern Africa*. Pietermartizburg: University of KwaZulu-Natal Press.

Lipovetsky, Gilles. 1994. *The Empire of Fashion: dressing modern democracy*. Princeton, NJ: Princeton University Press.

Loughran, Kristyne. 2009. 'The idea of Africa in European high fashion: global dialogues', *Fashion Theory* 13(2): 243–71.

Lutz, Catherine L., and Jane L. Collins. 1993. *Reading National Geographic*. Chicago, IL: University of Chicago Press.

Luvaas, Brent, and Joanne B. Eicher (eds). 2019. *The Anthropology of Dress and Fashion: a reader*. London: Bloomsbury.

Ma, Boyang. 2020. 'Becoming mitumba: transnational secondhand clothing trade between China and Kenya' in Chapurukha M. Kusimba, Tiequan Zhu, and Purity Wakabasi Kiura, *China and East Africa: ancient ties, contemporary flows*. Lanham, MD: Lexington Books. 215–34.

Machado, Pedro. 2009. 'Awash in a sea of cloth: Gujarat, Africa, and the Western Indian Ocean, 1300–1800' in Giorgio Riello and Prasannan Parthasarathi (eds), *The Spinning World: a global history of cotton textiles, 1200–1850*. Oxford: Oxford University Press. 161–79.

Machado, Pedro, Sarah Fee, and Gwynn Campbell (eds). 2018. *Textile Trade, Consumer Cultures, and the Material Worlds of the Indian Ocean: an ocean of cloth*. Cham: Palgrave Macmillan.

Magubane, Bernhard. 1971. 'A critical look at indices used in the study of social change in colonial Africa,' *Current Anthropology* 12(4–5): 419–31.

Martin, Phyllis. 1994. 'Contesting clothes in colonial Brazzaville', *Journal of African History* 35(3): 401–26.

1995. *Leisure and Society in Colonial Brazzaville*. Cambridge: Cambridge University Press.

2004. 'Afterword' in Jean Allman (ed.), *Fashioning Africa: power and the politics of dress*. Bloomington: Indiana University Press. 227–30.

Marwick, Max. G. 1974. 'Some labour histories', appendix B in Helmuth Heisler, *Urbanisation and the Government of Migration: the interrelation of urban and rural life in Zambia*. New York: St. Martin's Press. 144–50.

Masquelier, Adeline (ed.). 2005. *Dirt, Undress, and Difference: critical perspectives on the body's surface*. Bloomington: Indiana University Press.

2013. 'Forging connections, performing distinctions: youth, dress, and consumption in Niger' in Karen Tranberg Hansen and D. Soyini Madison (eds), *African Dress: fashion, agency, performance*. London: Bloomsbury. 138–52.

Matongo, Albert B. K. 1992. 'Popular culture in a colonial society: another look at Beni and Kalela dances on the Copperbelt, 1930–64' in Samuel N. Chipungu (ed.), *Guardians of Their Time: experiences of Zambians under colonial rule, 1890–1964*. London: Macmillan. 180–212.

Mauss, Marcel. 1973. 'Techniques of the body', *Economy and Society* 2(1): 70–87. First published 1935 as 'Les techniques du corps', *Journal de Psychologie* 32(3–4): 271–93.

Maynard, Margaret. 2004. *Dress and Globalisation*. Manchester: Manchester University Press.

Mazrui, Ali A. 1968. 'Miniskirts and political puritanism', *Africa Report*. October 9–12.

1969. 'On revolution and nakedness' in *Violence and Thought: essays on social tensions in Africa*. London: Longmans. 281–305.

Mbembe, Achille. 2001. *On the Postcolony*. Berkeley: University of California Press.

McClintock, Anne. 1995. *Imperial Leather: race, gender, and sexuality in the colonial context*. New York: Routledge.

Miller, Daniel. 1987. *Material Culture and Mass Consumption*. Oxford: Blackwell.

    1994. *Modernity – An Ethnographic Approach: dualism and mass consumption in Trinidad*. Oxford: Berg.

    (ed.). 1998. *Material Cultures: why some things matter*. Chicago, IL: University of Chicago Press.

    2005. 'Introduction' in Susanne Küchler and Daniel Miller (eds), *Clothing as Material Culture*. Oxford: Berg. 1–20.

    2010. 'Clothing: why material culture is not superficial' in Daniel Miller, *Stuff*. Cambridge: Polity. 12–41.

Miller, Dorothy, Etienne Nel, and Godfrey Hampwaye. 2008. 'Malls in Zambia: racialised retail expansion and South African foreign investors in Zambia', *African Sociological Reiew* 12(1): 35–54.

Mills, C. Wright. 1953. 'Introduction' to the Mentor edition, in Thorstein Veblen, *The Theory of the Leisure Class: an economic study of institutions*. New York: A Mentor Book, published by the New American Library. i–xix.

Minter, Adam. 2019. *Secondhand: travels in the new global garage sale*. London: Bloomsbury.

Mitchell, J. Clyde. 1956. 'The Kalela Dance', *Rhodes-Livingstone Papers*, no. 27.

Mokwena, Lebogang. 2020. 'Along the museological grain: an exploration of the (geo)political inheritance in *Isishweshwe Story: Material Women*', *African Studies* 79(3): 305–22.

Money, Duncan. 2021. 'Rebalancing the historical narrative or perpetuating bias? Digitizing the archives of the Mineworkers' Union of Zambia', *History in Africa*. First view, 3 May: 1–22.

Moore, Henrietta L. 1994. *A Passion for Difference: essays in anthropology and gender*. Bloomington: Indiana University Press.

Moore, R. J. B. 1948. *These African Copper Miners: a study of the industrial revolution in Northern Rhodesia, with principal reference to the copper mining industry*. Revised, with appendices by A. Sandilans. London: Livingstone Press.

Moorman, Marissa. 2004. 'Putting on a *pano* and dancing like our grandparents: nation and dress in late colonial Luanda' in Jean Allman (ed.), *Fashioning Africa: power and the politics of dress*. Bloomington: Indiana University Press. 84–103.

Morrow, Sean. 1989. '"On the side of the Robbed": R. J. B. Moore, missionary on the Copperbelt, 1933–1941', *Journal of Religion in Africa* 19(3): 244–63.

Moyer, Eileen. 2003. 'Keeping up appearances: fashion and function among Dar es Salaam street youth', *Etnofoor* 16(2): 88–105.

Musambachime, Mwelva C. (ed.). 1996. *The Oral History of Mansa, Zambia*. Lusaka: University of Zambia Printer.

Mustafa, Hudita N. 2006. 'La mode dakaroise: elegance, transnationalism and an African fashion capital' in Christopher Breward and David Gilbert (eds), *Fashion's World Cities*. Oxford: Berg. 177–99.

Mwanga, Vernon J. 1982. *An Extraordinary Life*. Lusaka: Multimedia Publications.

National Assembly of Zambia. 2014. Daily Parliamentary Debates, 1 July. www.parliament.gov.zm/node/550. Accessed 6 October 2020.

Ndlovu, Nosimilo. 2008. 'Bum deal for Zulu maidens', *Mail & Guardian* (South Africa), 29 August–4 September, p. 13.

Newell, Sasha. 2012. *The Modernity Bluff: crime, consumption, and citizenship in Cote d'Ivoire*. Chicago, IL: University of Chicago Press.

Ngolet, Francois. 2000. 'Ideological manipulation and political longevity: the power of Omar Bongo in Gabon since 1967', *African Studies Review* 43(2): 55–71.

Ngoma, Samuel. 1995. 'Wanted: quality clothing in Zambia', *Times of Zambia*, 26 August, p. 4.

Norris, Lucy. 2003. 'The Life-Cycle of Clothing: Recycling and the Efficacy of Materiality in Contemporary Urban India'. PhD thesis, University College London.

  2010. *Recycling Indian Clothing: global contexts of use and value*. Bloomington: Indiana University Press.

Nuttall, Sarah. 2004. 'Stylizing the self: the Y generation in Rosebank, Johannesburg', *Public Culture* 16(3): 430–52.

Nwafor, Okechukwu C. 2012. 'Of *mutuality* and *copying*: fashioning *Aso Ebi* through fashion magazines in Lagos', *Fashion Theory* 16(4): 493–520.

  2021. *Aso Ebi: dress, fashion, visual culture, and urban cosmopolitanism in West Africa*. Ann Arbor: University of Michigan Press.

Nyaywa, Rosemary Mpuku. 1998. 'Mama "UNIP" Julia "Chikamoneka": the fearless "Mad African Girl"' in Mbuyu Nalumango and Monde Sifuniso (eds), *Woman Power in Politics*. Lusaka: Zambia National Women's Lobby Group and Zambian Women Writers Association. 18–37.

Ogunyankin, Grace Adeniyi. 2016. '"These girls' fashion is sick!": *An African City* and the geography of sartorial worldliness', *Feminist Africa* 21: 37–51.

Olivier de Sardan, J. E. 1999. 'A moral economy of corruption in Africa?', *Journal of Modern African Studies* 37(1): 25–52.

Osiebe, Garhe. 2020 'Fashion in parliament: performances from Nigeria to South Africa', *Leeds African Studies Bulletin* 81: 1–52.

Osseo-Asare, Abena Dove. 2021. 'Kwame Nkrumah's suits: sartorial politics in Ghana at Independence', *Fashion Theory* 25(5): 597–632.

Parkins, Wendy. 2002. 'Introduction: (ad)dressing citizens' in *Fashioning the Body Politic: dress, gender, citizenship*. New York: Berg. 1–17.

  (ed.). 2002. *Fashioning the Body Politic: dress, gender, citizenship*. New York: Berg.

Parpart, Jane I. 1994. '"Where is your mother"? Gender, urban marriage, and colonial discourse on the Zambian Copperbelt, 1924–1945', *International Journal of African Historical Studies* 27(2): 241–71.

Perani, Judith, and Norma H. Wolff. 1999. *Cloth, Dress and Art Patronage in Africa*. Oxford: Berg.

Pesa, Iva. 2019. *Roads through Mwinilunga: a history of social change in northwest Zambia*. Leiden: Brill.

Petrusich, Anne. 2017. 'The magnificent cross-cultural recordings of Kenya's Kipsigis tribe', *New Yorker*, February 16. www.newyorker.com/culture/cultural-comment/the-magnificent-cross-cultural-recordings-of-kenyas-kipsigis-tribe.

Picton, John. 1995. 'Introduction. Technology, tradition and lurex: the art of textiles in Africa' in John Picton (ed.), *Technology, Tradition and Lurex: the Art of Textiles in Africa*. Barbican Art Gallery. London: Lund Humphries Publishers. 9–31.

Picton, John, and John Mack. 1989. *African Textiles*. 2nd edition. London: British Museum Publications.

Pool, Hannah Azieb (ed.). 2016. *Fashion Cities Africa*. Bristol: Intellect.

Posel, Deborah. 2010. 'Races to consume: revisiting South Africa's history of race, consumption and the struggle for freedom', *Ethnic and Racial Studies* 33(2): 157–75.

Powdermaker, Hortense. 1956. 'Social change through imagery and values of teen-age Africans in Northern Rhodesia', *American Anthropologist* 58(5): 783–813.

1962. *Copper Town: changing Africa. The human condition on the Rhodesian Copperbelt*. New York: Harper and Row.

Preminger, Evan. 2009. 'Judge dismisses charges in Zambian article controversy', *Cornell Daily Sun*, 29 September.

Presholdt, Jeremy. 2008. *Domesticating the World: African consumerism and the genealogies of globalization*. Berkeley: University of California Press.

Rabine, Leslie W. 1997a. 'Dressing up in Dakar', *L'Esprit Créateur* 37(1): 84–108.

1997b. 'Not a mere ornament: tradition, modernity, and colonialism in Kenyan and Western clothing', *Fashion Theory* 1(2): 145–68.

2002. *The Global Circulation of African Fashion*. Oxford: Berg.

2010. 'Fashionable photography in mid-twentieth century Senegal', *Fashion Theory* 14 (3): 305–30.

Renne, Elisha P. 1995. *Cloth That Does Not Die: the meaning of cloth in Bunu social life*. Seattle: University of Washington Press.

2015. 'The changing contexts of Chinese-Nigerian textile production and trade, 1990–2015', *Textile* 13(3): 212–33.

Renne, Elisha P., and Salihu Maiwaida (eds). 2020. *Textile Ascendancies: aesthetics, production and trade in northern Nigeria*. Ann Arbor: University of Michigan Press

Republic of Zambia. 1971. *House of Chiefs Debates*. 28–29 September. Lusaka: Government Printer.

Reynolds, Pamela. 2019. *The Uncaring, Intricate World: a field diary, Zambezi Valley, 1984–1985*. Durham, NC: Duke University Press

Richards, Audrey I. [1939] 1969. *Land, Labour, and Diet in Northern Rhodesia*. Oxford: Oxford University Press.

[1956] 2021. *Chisungu: a girls' initiation ceremony among the Bemba of Northern Rhodesia*. London: Routledge.

Richards, Christopher L. 2022. *Cosmopolitanism and Women's Fashion in Ghana: history, artistry and nationalist inspirations*. London: Routledge.

Roberts, Andrew D. 1976. *A History of Zambia*. London: Heinemann.

Robertson, A. F. 2001. *Greed: gut feelings, growth, and history*. Cambridge: Polity Press.

Roces, Mina, and Louise Edwards (eds). 2007. *The Politics of Dress in Asia and the Americas*. Eastbourne: Sussex Academic Press.

Rodgers, Daniel T. 2013. 'Cultures in motion: an introduction' in Daniel T. Rodgers, Bhavani Raman, and Helmuth Reimitz (eds), *Cultures in Motion*. Princeton, NJ: Princeton University Press. 1–19.

Ross, Doran (ed.). 1998. *Wrapped in Pride: Ghanaian kente and African American identity*. Los Angeles, CA: Fowler Museum.

Ross, Robert. 2008. *Clothing: a global history*. Cambridge: Polity Press.

Ross, Robert, Marja Hinfelaar, and Iva Pesa (eds). 2013. *The Objects of Life in Central Africa: the history of consumption and social change, 1840–1980*. Leiden: Brill.

Rønde, Jeppe. 2005. *The Swenkas*. Copenhagen: Danish Film Center. www.dfi .dk/viden-om-film/filmdatabasen/film/swenkas. Accessed 15 December 2021.

Röschenthaler, Ute. 2015. 'Dressed in photographs: between uniformization, self-enhancement and the promotion of stars and leaders in Bamako', *Africa* 85(4): 696–720.

Rovine, Victoria L. 2001. *Bogolan: shaping culture through cloth in contemporary Mali*. Washington, DC: Smithsonian Institution Press.

2009. 'Colonialism's clothing: Africa, France, and the deployment of fashion', *Design Issues* 25(3): 44–61.

2015. *African Fashion, Global Style: histories, innovations, and ideas you can wear*. Bloomington: Indiana University Press.

Sahlins, Marshall D. 1963. 'Poor man, rich man, big-man, chief: political types in Melanesia and Polynesia', *Comparative Studies in Society and History* 5(3): 285–303.

Sakala, Richard. 2016. *A President Betrayed: serial murder by slander*. Lusaka: Sentor Publishers.

Salazar-Sutil, Nicolas. 2009. 'What's in your wardrobe, Mr. president? A study in political dress', *International Journal of Media and Culture* 7(2): 63–78.

Sampa, Annie J. 1996. 'Unequal access to power: policy making and the advancement of women in Zambian development' in Owen Sichone and Bornwell C. Chikula (eds), *Democracy in Zambia: challenges for the Third Republic*. Harare: Sapes Books. 197–221.

Scheld, Suzanne. 2007. 'Youth cosmopolitanism: clothing, the city and globalization in Dakar, Senegal', *City & Society* 19(2): 232–53.

Scheld, Suzanne, and Lydia Siu. 2013. 'Veiled racism in the street economy of Dakar's Chinatown in Senegal' in Karen Tranberg Hansen, Walter E. Little, and B. Lynne Milgram (eds), *Street Economies in the Urban Global South*. Santa Fe, NM: SAR Press. 157–79.

Schumaker, Lyn. 2001. *Africanizing Anthropology: fieldwork, networks, and the making of cultural knowledge in Central Africa*. Durham, NC: Duke University Press.

Schuster, Ilsa G. 1979. *New Women of Lusaka*. Palo Alto, CA: Mayfield.

Seleti, Yona Ngalaba. 1992. 'Entrepreneurship in colonial Zambia' in Samuel N. Chipungu (ed.), *Guardians of Their Time: experiences of Zambians under colonial rule, 1890–1964*. London: Macmillan. 147–79.

Shaw, Jacqueline. [2011] 2014. *Africa Fashion Guide*. London: Jacaranda.

Simbao, Ruth. 2010. 'Dialectics of dance and dress: the performative negotiation of Soli girl initiates (*Moye*) in Zambia', *African Arts* 43(3): 64–85.

Sizaire, Violaine, Dibwe dia Mwembu, and Bogumil Jewsiewicki (eds). 2002. *Femmes – Mode – Musiques: memoires de Lubumbashi*. Paris: L'Harmattan.

Skjold, Else. 2016. 'Biographical wardrobes: a temporal view on dress practice'. *Fashion Practice* 8(1): 135–48.

Smith, Alexander McCall. 1998. *The No. 1 Ladies' Detective Agency*. New York: Random House.

Smith, Daniel Jordan. 2007. *Everyday Deception and Popular Discontent in Nigeria*. Princeton, NJ: Princeton University Press.

Springford, James Bardez. 2010. 'Generating Values: Chinese Clothes in Lusaka'. MA thesis, University of Amsterdam.

Stambach, Amy. 1999. 'Curl up and dye: civil society and the fashion-minded citizen' in John L. Comaroff and Jean Comaroff (eds), *Civil Society and the Political Imagination in Africa*. Chicago, IL: University of Chicago Press. 251–66.

Steiner, Christopher. 1985. 'Another image of Africa: toward an ethnohistory of European cloth marketed in West Africa, 1873–1960', *Ethnohistory* 32(2): 91–110.

Stien, Kari Mjaavatn. 2013. 'Kamwala Shopping World: Competition and Cooperation among Zambian and Chinese Traders in Lusaka'. MA thesis, Norwegian University of Science and Technology.

Susser, Ida, and Jane Schneider. 2003. 'Wounded cities: destruction and reconstruction in a globalized world' in Jane Schneider and Ida Susser (eds), *Wounded Cities: destruction and reconstruction in a globalized world*. Oxford: Berg. 1–23.

Sylvanus, Nina. 2016. *Patterns in Circulation: cloth, gender, and materiality in West Africa*. Chicago, IL: University of Chicago Press.

2017. 'Real fakes: brands, labels and China in West Africa' in Suzanne Gott, Kristyne Loughran, Betsy D. Quick, and Leslie Rabine (eds), *African-Print Fashion Now! A story of taste, globalization, and style*. Los Angeles, CA: Fowler Museum. 107–13.

Tamale, Sylvia. 2016. '"Keep your eyes off my thighs"': a feminist analysis of Uganda's "miniskirt law"', *Feminist Africa* 21: 83–90.

2017. 'Nudity, protest, and the law in Uganda', *Feminist Africa* 22: 52–86.

Tarlo, Emma.1996. *Clothing Matters: dress and identity in India*. Chicago, IL: University of Chicago Press.

Thomas, Lynn M. 2020. *Beneath the Surface: a transnational history of skin lighteners*. Durham, NC: Duke University Press.

Titley, Brian. 2002 [1997]. *Dark Age: the political odyssey of emperor Bokassa*. Montreal: McGill-Queen's University Press.

Turner, Terence. 1993 [1979]. 'The social skin' in C. B. Burroughs and J. Ehrenreich (eds), *Reading the Social Body*. Iowa City: University of Iowa Press. 15-39.

UNFPA. 2016. 'Zambia's young people and the road to 2030', 12 August. https://zambia.unfpa.org/en/news/zambia%E2%80%99s-young-people-and-road-2030. Accessed 30 November 2021.

van Allen, Judith. 1972. '"Sitting on a man": colonialism and the lost political institutions of Igbo women', *Canadian Journal of African Studies* 6(2): 168–81.

van Donge, Jan Kees. 2008. 'The plundering of Zambian resources by Frederick Chiluba and his friends: a case study of the interaction between national politics and the international drive towards good governance', *African Affairs* 108(430): 69–90.

van Onselen, Charles. 2019. *The Night Trains: moving Mozambican miners to and from South Africa, circa 1902–1955*. Oxford: Oxford University Press.

Vaughan, Megan. 1994. 'Colonial discourse theory and African history, or has postmodernism passed us by?', *Social Dynamics* 20(2): 1–23.

Veblen, Thorstein. [1899] 1953. *The Theory of the Leisure Class: an economic study of institutions*. New York: A Mentor Book, published by the New American Library.

Velasco, Matthew. 2021. 'Yves Saint Laurent's signature looks', L'Officiel, 1 August. www.lofficielph.com/fashion/yves-saint-laurent-designer-singature-looks-trapeze-suit-safari-jacket. Accessed 11 November 2021.

Vincent, Louise. 2008. 'Women's rights get a dressing down: mini skirt attacks in South Africa', *International Journal of the Humanities. Annual Review* 6: 11–18.

Vinson, Robert Trent. 2012. *The Americans are coming! Dreams of African American liberation in segregationist South Africa*. Athens: Ohio University Press.

von Pezold, Johanna, and Miriam Driessen. 2021. 'Made in China, fashioned in Africa: ethnic dress in Ethiopia and Mozambique', *Africa* 91(2): 317–36.

Webb, Douglas. 1996. 'The socio-economic impact of HIV/AIDS in Zambia', *SafAIDS News* 4(4): 2–10.

Weiner, Annette B., and Jane Schneider (eds). 1989. *Cloth and Human Experience*. Washington, DC: Smithsonian Institution Press.

Wilson, Elizabeth. 1987. *Adorned in Dreams: fashion and modernity*. Berkeley: University of California Press.

Wilson, Godfrey. 1940. 'Dancing'. 8 February. Longhand notes on dance clubs. University of Cape Town Libraries, Archives and Manuscript Division. Monica and Godfrey Wilson Papers. BC880. E9.9.

1942. 'An essay on the economics of detribalization in Northern Rhodesia'. Vol. 2. *Rhodes-Livingstone Papers* 6.

Wilson, Monica. 1940. 'Dancing'. Typescript notes on frocks. African dance, 2 March. University of Cape Town Libraries, Archives and Manuscript Division. Monica and Godfrey Wilson Papers. BC880. E9.9.

Wipper, Audrey. 1972. 'African women, fashion, and scapegoating', *Canadian Journal of African Studies* 6 (2): 329–49.

Woodward, Sophie. 2005. 'Looking good: feeling right – aesthetics of the self' in Susanne Küchler and Daniel Miller (eds), *Clothing as Material Culture*. Oxford: Berg. 21–40.

World Data Atlas. 2020. 'Zambia'. www.worlddata.info/africa/zambia/index.php.

Wragg, Emma, and Regina Lim. 2013. 'Urban visions of the excluded: experiences of globalisation in Lusaka, Zambia', unpublished paper presented at N-AERUS XIV, Entschede, the Netherlands, 12–14 September.

Wrong, Michela. 2001. *In the Footsteps of Mr Kurtz: living on the brink of disaster in the Congo*. London: Fourth Estate.

Newspapers

United States

New York Times. 2005. 'Zambia. Investigators seize ex-president's shoes', 15 March, A8.

Zambia/Northern Rhodesia

African Listener. 1957a. 'The well-dressed woman', Part 1. 63, p. 12.
1957b. 'The well-dressed woman', Part 2. 64, p. 9.
Central African Post. 1960. 'Monckton commission members greeted with banners', 11 March, pp. 1 and 9.
1960. 'Screaming crowd greeting Macleod in Lusaka: nationalists stone at least 15 cars. Chanting, singing, banner-waving', 28 March, p. 1.
1960. '"Shameful" Action', letter to the editor from K. Mwila, 1 April.
Chronicle. 1996. 'Woman divorced for donning mini-skirt', 5–11 July.
Daily Nation. 2015. 'FJT family rejects clothing', 15 July, p. 15.
News from Zambia. 1991. No. 576. 23 July–6 August.
2001–2. No. 750. 12 December–16 January.
2007. 'Ex-president Chiluba and others stole £23m'. No. 802, 19 April–18 May.
Post. 1997. 'Dora Siliya's minis annoy ZNBC bosses', 22 May, pp. 1 and 5.
1997. 'Dora Siliya's miniskirt defended', letter to the editor, 26 May.
1998. 'The mini-skirt debate; set good examples for girl child', letter to the editor, 8 April.
1998. 'Luo's choice of dress; dignified dress', letter to the editor, 14 April.
2004. 'KK's handkerchief to be auctioned', 7 October.
2005. 'Editorial'. 14 March.
2005. 'I am not allergic to colours … govt has exposed my pants – Chiluba', 15 March, pp. 1 and 4.
2005. 'Trendsetters', 2 December.
2006. 'Cheap demagoguery', 22 September.
2007. 'It's pornography – Longwe', 2 August, pp. 1 and 4.
2007. 'I couldn't have told them to dress up – Magande', 3 August, pp. 1 and 4.
2007. Letters to the editor. 1, 2, 3, 8, and 17 August.
2008. 'Retirees block Kanganja from leaving cabinet office', 2 October.
2009. 'Picture of MMD cadre disgusts ZCEA', 27 July, p. 12.
2009. Letters to the editor, 27, 28, and 30 July.
2009. 'The Chansa Kabwela case: a comedy of errors', by Muna Ndulo, 27 August.
2014. 'Masebo's hat halts business in the House', 19 July, p. 1.
Sunday Post. 2007. 'MMD cadres undressed for love of party', 7 August, pp. 1 and 4.
2008. 'The bare breasts debate', Lifestyle Section, 5 October, p. VII.
2009. Cover photograph, 26 July, p. 1.

Sunday Times of Zambia. 1993. 'Is stage porno to blame for rape?', 12 December.

Times of Zambia. 1971. 14 July.

    1981. 'Modern dresses are tempting', letter to the editor, sometime between June and September.

    1985. 'Kitchen parties turned into beer dens', 5 December.

    1985. 'Dress decently', letter to the editor, 4 February.

    1985. 'Woman in pants', letter to the editor, 18 July.

    1985. 'See-throughs belittle our culture', letter to the editor, 23 August.

    1986. 'How can police in pata-pata nab thieves?' letter to the editor, 26 October.

    1987. 'Poorly dressed teachers', letter to the editor, 28 April.

    1987. 'Dress up newspaper sellers', letter to the editor, 6 June.

    1993. 'Five raped after Koffi rhumba show', 6 December.

    1993. 'Arrests in connection with rampage at Independence Stadium', 7 December.

    1993. 'Show fracas could have been avoided', 10 December.

    1998. 'Professor Luo hounded out of parliament', 4 April.

    1998. 'The mini-skirt debate ... and what about executive trousers?' Feature article, 13 April.

    2008. 'FTJ's Geneva-based tailor ordered to repay govt', 25 December.

    2009. 'Photos disturbed me, witness tells court', 9 September.

    2015. 'Ililonga chronicles his association with Kenneth Kaunda', 29 May.

Weekend Post. 2006. 'Miniskirt debate', 19 February.

Weekly Post. 1994. 'The stripping of women in short skirts is "violation of human rights"', 25 March, p. 4.

Weekly Standard. 1994. 'Fashion conscious ladies in mini-skirts nightmare at Kulima Tower', 21–27 March.

Zambia Daily Mail. 1971. 'Kapwepwe, go home', 30 August, pp. 1 and 7.

    1984. 'Adolescents should not attend kitchen parties', letter to the editor, 27 November.

    1994. 'Vendors blasted for undressing woman', 23 March.

    1994. 'Lusaka ruffians taking law into own hands', 24 March.

    1996. 'Hell descends on Tshala show', 8 November.

    1997. 'Is wearing minis a sin?' Feature article, 21 August, p. 4.

    1998. 'Let not bad rituals hijack noble meaning of kitchen parties', story by Isabel Chimangeni and interviews by Alinedi Ngoma, 11 January, p. 5.

    1998. 'Mini-skirts is food for your eyes', 11 April.

    1998. 'Speaker shouldn't have sent Nawakwi home'; 'Gender focus: is parliament dress code exclusively for female MPs?', letter to the editor, 24 September.

    2017. 'Lungu tie, hat fetch K500,000', 1 May.

Zambia Watchdog. 2014. 'Pimp or president', 27 December.

    2015. 'Photo of the day: Lungu's pot belly and $3000 suits', 18 August.

Zambia Weekly. 2015. 'Bank of Zambia accused of looting', 5 June, 235(6): 4.

    2016. 'Lawyer reprimanded for misadvising the BoZ', 4 November, 296(7): 6.

    2017. 'Lungu's tie sells for K320,000', 5 May, 318(8): 1.

Other Newspapers and News Services

China Economic Net. 2004. 'Zambian 1st president's handkerchief to be auctioned', 5 October.

Pan African News Agency Daily Newswire. 2005. 'Chiluba claims investigators are bias [*sic*] against him', 14 March.

Saturday Argus (South Africa). 2006. 'Reed dance attracts unwanted voyeurs', 9 September, p. 12.

L'Uomo Vogue (Italy), 2012. Rebranding Africa (special issue), no. 431.

Index

Note: Page numbers in italic indicate illustrations and those with the suffix 'n' indicate a note.

Titles in the Series

Printed by Printforce, United Kingdom